THE GAINS OF LISTENING

Perspectives on counselling
at work

Edited by
COLIN FELTHAM

OPEN UNIVERSITY PRESS
Buckingham · Philadelphia

Open University Press
Celtic Court
22 Ballmoor
Buckingham
MK18 1XW

and
1900 Frost Road, Suite 101
Bristol, PA 19007, USA

First Published 1997

A catalogue record of this book is available from the British Library

ISBN 0 335 19280 7 (pbk) 0 335 19281 5 (hbk)

Library of Congress Cataloging-in-Publication Data
Feltham, Colin, 1950–
    The gains of listening : perspectives on counselling at work / by
Colin Feltham.
        p.   cm.
    Includes bibliographical references and index.
    ISBN 0–335–19281–5 (hb). — ISBN 0–335–19280–7 (pb)
    1. Employees — Counseling of.   I.   Title.
HF5549.5.C8F45   1996
658.3'85–dc20   96–24018
                                                                CIP

Typeset by Dorwyn Ltd, Rowlands Castle, Hants
Printed in Great Britain by St Edmundsbury Press Ltd, Bury St Edmunds, Suffolk

In appreciation of the work of
Andrea Adams and Mike Megranahan

Business is definitely business, but just listen for a minute.

Arthur Miller, *Death of a Salesman*

One of the reasons that short-term treatment in general, and especially in EAP settings, is so effective may be because of the healing and restorative effects of being listened to fully for once, being understood, and being valued by the counselor.

Gloria Cunningham, *Effective Employee Assistance Programs: A guide for EAP counselors and managers*

First and foremost we must be prepared to talk about mental health . . . We must gain the confidence to talk about pressure, stress and strain . . . The best thing we can do . . . is to go out and listen to those around us – and indeed hope that they will listen to us.

Sir David Plastow, Chairman and Chief Executive, Vickers plc, 'Foreword' to R. Jenkins and N. Coney (eds) *Prevention of Mental Ill-health at Work: A conference*

Contents

Notes on contributors

Laidon Alexander is a career consultant with a background in management consultancy. He has been with Mentors Counselling Consultants since 1990. This is a professional services group within Midland Bank, staffed and managed autonomously, providing employee, post-trauma, career and retirement counselling services to the Bank and its associated companies and also to organizations not connected with Midland. His work with Mentors Counselling Consultants has involved counselling and coaching career clients, writing and editing training, administrative, promotional and sales material, advising and supporting the head of Mentors. He helped her design and launch Mentors Open Line employee counselling service and the Crisis Mentors post-trauma counselling service. His early career was with ICI, after which he spent 20 years with PA Management Consultants, working with corporate clients in a wide variety of disciplines and sectors, and five years in outplacement consultancy with Sanders & Sidney. Since March 1996 he has been managing Mentors.

Andrew Bull MSc (Counselling Psychology) was formerly a lecturer in counselling at the University of Birmingham. He has worked in the NHS and in industry where he set up an EAP for Lucas Industries. He has published on the subject of counselling in the workplace including the Association for Counselling at Work's *Counselling Skills and Counselling at Work: An introduction for purchasers and providers*. Andrew has a private counselling and supervision practice.

Elizabeth J. Dodgson is Personnel Director for William Hill Organization Limited, a major player in the leisure industry. She graduated with a BSc Hons in Psychology at the University of York in 1982 and subsequently achieved an MSc in HR Management at Sheffield Hallam University. She began her career working as Assistant Personnel Officer for Sheffield City Council. From there she moved to the private sector working in manufacturing and service industries and latterly as Personnel Controller for BBC News and Current Affairs. As an active Member of the Institute of Personnel and Development, Elizabeth is currently a member of the National Recruitment Forum Steering Committee and is a speaker at conferences on a variety of subjects.

Jane Fawcett trained as a counsellor and person-centred art therapist after being a senior manager in the personnel field. She is an accredited member of the Counselling Division of the British Register of Complementary Practitioners. She has been an employee counsellor in both the private and public sector, where redundancy and change have been a major part of the work. Jane has found a co-operative approach with mental health units successful when working with clients with severe mental health problems. She currently works part-time with Mentors Counselling Consultants as a post-trauma and employee counsellor, as well as having a small private practice and continuing to provide training in adjustment to change.

Colin Feltham is Senior Lecturer in Counselling at Sheffield Hallam University. He is a BAC accredited counsellor and Fellow of the British Association for Counselling who has worked in private practice, mental health, probation, alcohol treatment, student and workplace counselling settings. He was formerly a Regional Consultant with Mentors Counselling Consultants. A trainer and supervisor, he created the Thameslink/University of East London Diploma in Counselling. He has in the past worked in various administrative and manual jobs. His publications include *Psychotherapy and its Discontents* (Open University Press, 1992), *Brief Counselling* (Open University Press, 1992), *Dictionary of Counselling* (Whurr, 1993), all with Windy Dryden; and *What Is Counselling? The promise and problem of the talking therapies* (Sage, 1995).

Liz Friedrich works with Mentors Counselling Consultants as a crisis counsellor and a trainer on their pre-retirement courses. She also runs a staff counselling and stress management service in a large NHS Trust in London. She began her career as an information officer at The Industrial Society and has since trained in counselling and family therapy. She has experience in conciliation work, bereavement counselling and telephone counselling with the NSPCC. She runs training courses in stress management and on bereavement and loss. Her publications include books for teenagers on marriage and divorce and *The Twins Handbook* (Robson books, 1983).

Catherine Green originally trained as an SRN at Westminster Hospital, London and went on to specialize in cardiac surgery, working in the Intensive Care Unit at the Groote Schuur Hospital in Cape Town. Returning to

England she became a desk top computer specialist and subsequently set up her own training company which she later sold. She then trained in Personnel Management and as a Systemic Psychotherapist which enabled her to practise as a career development consultant. In 1995 she attained her MA in the Psychology of Therapy and Counselling and from 1989–1996 she set up and was director of Mentors Counselling Consultants, a wholly owned subsidiary of Midland Bank providing career counselling, an EAP, pre-retirement counselling and post trauma counselling to employees and their families.

Andrew Guppy is a chartered psychologist and Reader in Applied Psychology at Liverpool John Moores University with research interests in the alcohol and drug misuse field as well as occupational psychology. He has been a member of the Parliamentary Advisory Council for Transport Safety since 1985 and has been an adviser to the United Nations Drug Control Programme concerning alcohol and drug misuse in the workplace. Andrew was involved in the management of local advisory and counselling services in Buckinghamshire for over ten years, and was Chairman of the Buckinghamshire Council for Alcohol and Drugs between 1989 and 1993. His publications list includes over 60 journal articles, book chapters, conference papers and reports, primarily in the substance misuse and stress fields.

John Marsden is a chartered psychologist and is Project Co-ordinator of the National Treatment Outcome Research Study based at the National Addiction Research Centre in London. Previously Research Manager within Turning Point, John completed major projects related to Community Care and residential services, alcohol and drug problems in the workplace (for the CEC) and was commissioned by the Department of Health to review outcome criteria in the alcohol and drug rehabilitation field.

Gary Mayhew is a trained psychiatric nurse, family therapist and individual counsellor, currently working for Mentors Counselling Consultants as well as for a national drug and alcohol charity and in private practice. He has worked for some years as a senior counsellor in private, public and voluntary organizational settings, with clients exhibiting the full range of emotional, relationship and psychiatric problems. He has published several articles relating to the use of Solution-Focused Brief Therapy, and presented a paper at the International Conference on Alcoholism and Addiction in Berlin in 1990.

Daphne Mullins has a background of working for social services, the Probation Service and as organizer of a mental health day centre. She currently works as a counsellor with Mentors Counselling Consultants, and in a GP practice. She also has a private practice in counselling and homeopathy and is a trainer.

Denise Nelson is accredited by BAC and the British Association of Sexual and Marital Therapists (BASMT); she is also registered with the UKCP. She is a psychotherapist and psychosexual counsellor with long- and short-term clients, both individuals and couples. She works part-time with Mentors Counselling Consultants and counsels and supervises in private practice. Her main areas of interest are in relationship difficulties, sexual problems, sexual orientation, and survivors of childhood sexual trauma. Denise also has experience in the field of health, HIV/AIDS and disability-related issues.

Jan Symes has been Head of Counselling for the Employee Assistance Programme for British Airways since 1992. She is an Accredited Member of the British Association for Counselling and the British Association of Sexual and Marital Therapy and is United Kingdom Council of Psychotherapy registered. She also has experience working as a counsellor in the National Health Service and in education and is a qualified nurse.

Roger Thistle worked in banking and credit marketing before training as a counsellor at the Westminster Pastoral Foundation, obtaining Diploma Membership of the Institute of Psychotherapy in 1986. He has considerable experience of debt counselling, and offers a general counselling service from private practice in Sutton, Surrey. He is a consultant to Crisis Mentors, where he manages a country-wide post-trauma debriefing and counselling service for the victims of bank raids and other violent incidents. He is currently writing a book on private practice for counsellors.

Clare Townsend is a BAC accredited counsellor working in private practice and, since 1991, with Mentors Counselling Consultants. She counsels individuals and couples and teaches counselling skills to managers. She has worked for MIND, the NHS, and was an honorary psychotherapist at Guy's Hospital, London. She currently supervises for two counselling organizations and for a diploma course in counselling. She recently undertook further training in couple counselling at the Tavistock Marital Studies Institute. She specializes in counselling couples with a co-therapist.

Acknowledgements

The editor wishes to thank Blackwell Scientific Publications for permission to reproduce Table 2.6 from Ivy-Marie Blackburn and Kate Davidson, *Cognitive Therapy for Depression and Anxiety*, 1990. Thanks are also due to Mark Scoggins of Davies Arnold Cooper Solicitors, to Terry Mullins and to numerous colleagues who have indicated areas of relevant concern, and to Angela Tann for her timely help in wordprocessing some of the material.

Introduction

○ **COLIN FELTHAM**

The title of this book is intended to emphasize the relationship between listening, counselling and interpersonal sensitivity at the levels of the individual and the organization. In its professional sense, the term 'counselling at work' refers to specific services, provided by employers for employees, which offer usually short-term, psychotherapeutic assistance, and also advice, guidance and information. Often known as employee assistance programmes (EAPs), such services address mainly individual concerns, or problems in living. In a broader sense, the gains of listening and the ethos of counselling are about promoting the values of respect for others, of understanding the aspirations and limitations of unique individuals and of genuineness, caring and humanitarian concern generally. Thus, as Pearce (1989) among others has noted, counselling at work is also potentially a powerful tool for organizational change and development.

Listening may be considered partly a skilled *technical* enterprise. Counsellors in training learn to appreciate and use active listening skills, which include a concern for non-judgemental, objective listening, free from distortion and preoccupation; understanding at various levels (the emotional, intellectual and practical, the conscious and unconscious); and disclosing what has been heard in order to check on its accuracy and helpfulness.

Listening may also be considered to be part of the *commercial* enterprise. The 'business of listening' permeates (or should preferably permeate) good human relations, employee and customer relations throughout corporations (Bone 1988). Failure to listen, to attend to, results in poor communication, unaddressed workplace problems, employees' frustrations being driven underground and ultimately customers complaining and changing loyalties. Bone estimates that we commonly listen at work at only 25 per cent of our capacity to listen. Millar *et al.* (1992) remind us that skilled listening is one of the most crucial aspects of the process whereby people enter any organization – the job interview.

Listening can also be considered a *philosophical* enterprise with profound social implications (Levin 1989). If we were really to heed deeply what is going on around us socially, ecologically, commercially and in every other sphere, we would be more likely to understand and meet challenges appropriately than to delay our response until a crisis occurs which forces us to listen and act belatedly.

When people are preoccupied, their minds are busy with thoughts about certain problems, memories, daydreams or fears. There are degrees of preoccupation, from fleeting hopes and regrets to chronic, morbid ruminations. But whatever the degree of preoccupation involved, it implies that full attention is not available for the task in hand. Many routine jobs lend themselves to absent-minded performance, but obviously absent-mindedness always incurs risks of errors, sloppiness and accidents. Staff who are frequently preoccupied or preoccupied at unfortunate times (when attention and precision are crucial) may incur serious accidents. Staff who are preoccupied when dealing with customers and clients are unlikely to give high quality service. Indeed, we may observe that staff who deal with customers simply do not listen fully or accurately when they are preoccupied with their own concerns.

A major implicit argument of this book is that when people learn to identify and express their preoccupations in an appropriate context – when they are respectfully listened to – they may subsequently become freer to attend to their immediate tasks. When employers acknowledge the significance of this, and listen to their staff, they are likely to initiate and reinforce a virtuous circle of listening and attentiveness which may have valuable knock-on effects. As Tysoe (1988) reminds us, it is all too easy to mis-attribute instances of employees' poor performance to incompetence or unsuitability when in fact these may often stem from domestic and other sources of stress, such as trying to care for chronically sick family members.

Counselling is not a panacea, but an instrument for dislodging preoccupations and helping to solve personal problems that has an important part to play in occupational efficiency and conviviality. Counselling is, of course, more than listening and is aligned by some with problem-solving or as Egan (1990, 1994) argues, with 'problem-management', 'change agent skills' and 'opportunity development'. Reddy (1987) has shown the particular relevance of Egan's counselling model to the workplace. Counselling is implicitly about helping people to discover better ways of dealing with personal problems both at home and at work and it is widely recognized that no final distinction can be made between a person's work-based and home-based concerns, since they are inevitably likely to feed into each other. In terms of problematic overspill, commuting, unpaid overtime and 'bringing work home' may be weighed against absenteeism or using the company's telephone for personal business, for example. It is necessary to point out that counselling cannot claim invariably to produce happy and willing workers, since its focus is usually the person, his or her own values and choices, and this can sometimes lead to a choice for oneself that might not be approved of by one's employers (Einzig and Evans 1990).

The work alluded to in the title of this book is primarily mainstream employment. Unfortunately it is outside the scope of the present volume to discuss the relationships between unpaid work such as housework; self-employment and unemployment; the newly emerging phenomenon of short-term contracts; and the mental health issues surrounding them. It is now well documented and largely accepted that housework and other 'shadow work' is enormously important, that it remains economically unacknowledged in spite of evidence that it props up national economies (Stromberg and Harkness 1978) and that housewives and others who work in the home are susceptible to mental health problems due to isolation, lack of stimulation and lack of social recognition. The impact of working hours on family life is a large subject which is touched upon here but has been receiving far more detailed attention elsewhere (Hewitt 1993). The self-employed frequently experience stress related to long working hours, insufficient rest, and anxiety about income. The unemployed are known to suffer stigma, poverty and demoralization (Warr 1987). All these groups may be said to need and deserve counselling as well as other appropriate assistance and recognition.

Studs Terkel interviewed a large number of American workers and recorded their views on their everyday experience of work. A spot-welder says: 'I don't understand how come more guys don't flip. Because you're nothing more than a machine . . . They give better care to that machine than they will to you' (1975: 152). A bus driver freely admits that

> You have your tension. Sometimes you come close to having an accident, that upsets you . . . So you take the tension home with you . . . Most of the drivers, they'll suffer from hemorrhoids, kidney trouble, and such as that. I had a case of ulcers.
>
> (1975: 182)

An ex-president of a conglomerate who acts as a business consultant observes about the typical high-flying manager that

> As he struggles in this jungle, every position he's in, he's terribly lonely. He can't confide and talk with the guy working under him. He can't confide and talk to the man he's working for. To give vent to his feelings, his fears, and his insecurities, he'd expose himself . . . The president *really* doesn't have anybody to talk to, because the vice presidents are waiting for him to die or make a mistake and get knocked off so they can get his job.
>
> (1975: 337)

Terkel claims that his book is a fair reflection of people's true feelings about work and hence is about 'ulcers as well as accidents, about shouting matches as well as fistfights, about nervous breakdowns as well as kicking the dog around'. Readers of the present book may or may not recognize these rather grim pictures as their own or their friends' experiences of work, but it cannot be denied that for those millions who spend the larger part of their adult, waking lives at work, there are many stories, voiced and unvoiced, that would resonate with those collected by Terkel. One of the closest British equivalents to Terkel's project is an anthology of writings about office life which depicts some of the typical stresses endured by many office workers, including environmental unfriendliness, commuting, office politics, fear of the boss, tedium and redundancy (Lewis 1992).

This book is not primarily about occupational psychology, occupational health, industrial relations, the social psychology of industry or ergonomics, although its concerns often touch on these areas. It is not a comprehensive guide to every conceivable area of mental distress or problem in living and its remedy. Nor is it a textbook on the history and nature of employee assistance programmes. Space does not allow extensive treatment of certain subjects (for example, women's issues and ethnic minority considerations), which are, however, covered in other, more specific texts. The decision has also been taken not to devote a specific chapter to individual stress, for two main reasons. First, stress, its definition and its management, is a complex subject, with stress manifesting itself in many areas of people's lives: it therefore appears within the chapters on organizational issues, health and health-related concerns, and mental health concerns. Indeed, Wheatley (1993) suggests that there are *nine* main areas of human functioning in which stress can be quantified. Second, the subject of stress has received enormous coverage from other writers, and the reader is advised to consult, for example, Cooper *et al.* (1988), Cox (1993), Cartwright and Cooper (1994), Ross and Altmaier (1994) and Palmer and Dryden (1995).

This book is largely a counsellor's eye-view of some of the typical problems and concerns brought to EAPs. It is to some extent an attempt to help in the building of a partnership of understanding between the worlds of the caring professions and the business sector. It is hoped that personnel managers, general managers, welfare officers, occupational health professionals, union officials and counsellors and psychotherapists interested in knowing more about the subject of counselling at work will benefit from reading or referring to this text. To date, British businesses have been rather slower than their American counterparts to institute EAPs and, accordingly, the literature on counselling at work in Britain has been sparse. Martin (1967) presented an account of the work of welfare officers, part of which certainly anticipated the challenges now faced by employee counsellors. One or two journals and a small stream of useful booklets, plus the notable contributions of Watts (1977), Reddy (1987), Megranahan (1989) and Carroll

(1996) still characterize the field. (For examples of American literature on EAPs, see Shain *et al.* [1986], Feit and Holosko [1988], Masi [1992] and Cunningham [1994].) A great deal of relevant research, however, has issued from British academic departments of occupational and organizational psychology. Hopefully, along with these, the present volume may have some modest impact on policy makers responsible for matters concerning health and employment.

Many chapter writers are linked professionally with Mentors Counselling Consultants, the careers consultancy and employee assistance programme that has grown from the Midland Bank's pioneering work in this field. The views expressed in this book are, however, those of individual writers and do not represent the policies of Mentors Counselling Consultants, the Midland Bank or any other organization, unless explicitly stated. All case material has been composed from many cases and presented in a fictionalized manner, so that no possibility exists that any of it will identify any individual.

The book opens with an account of the historical rise, social context and key issues of counselling at work. Chapter 2 raises some unsettling issues regarding organizations and how their decision makers may construe the stress within them. Early chapters look at obviously work-related concerns (conflict, careers and health). Common problems of debt and relationship difficulties are then focused on. Chapters on mental health and illness, Post-Traumatic Stress and substance-related problems follow, and various residual and polemical questions are addressed in the final chapter. The subjects of the chapters in themselves reflect interesting historical shifts in knowledge of problematic workplace issues; for example, employee alcohol abuse and counselling have a history of some decades, while bullying at work has only recently emerged as a significant subject. In order to give a flavour of organizations' variable and internal provisions for the psychological welfare of employees, two very pertinent appendices have been provided. Appendix 3 offers interested readers information on some organizations involved in counselling at work or which may prove helpful to anyone seeking specific assistance with the subjects represented in the various chapters.

References

Bone, D. (1988) *A Practical Guide to Effective Listening*. London: Kogan Page.
Carroll, M. (1996) *Workplace Counselling*. London: Sage.
Cartwright, S. and Cooper, C.L. (1994) *No Hassle! Taking the stress out of work*. London: Century.
Cooper, C.L., Cooper, R.D. and Eaker, L.H. (1988) *Living with Stress*. Harmondsworth: Penguin.
Cox, T. (1993) *Stress Research and Stress Management: Putting theory to work*. HSE contract report no. 61. Nottingham: Department of Psychology, University of Nottingham.

Cunningham, G. (1994) *Effective Employee Assistance Programs*. Thousand Oaks, CA: Sage.

Egan, G. (1990) *The Skilled Helper* (4th edn). Pacific Grove, CA: Brooks/Cole.

Egan, G. (1994) *The Skilled Helper* (5th edn). Pacific Grove, CA: Brooks/Cole.

Einzig, H. and Evans, R. (1990) *Personal Problems at Work: Counselling as a resource for the manager*. Rugby: British Association for Counselling.

Feit, M.D. and Holosko, M.J. (eds) (1988) *Evaluation of Employee Assistance Programs*. New York: Haworth.

Hewitt, P. (1993) *About Time: The revolution in work and family life*. London: Rivers Oram.

Levin, D. (1989) *The Listening Self*. London: Routledge.

Lewis, J. (1992) *The Chatto Book of Office Life*. London: Chatto & Windus.

Martin, A. (1967) *Welfare at Work*. London: Batsford.

Masi, D.A. (ed.) (1992) *The AMA Handbook for Developing Employee Assistance Programs*. New York: American Management Association.

Megranahan, M. (1989) *Counselling: A practical guide for managers*. London: Institute of Personnel Managers.

Millar, R., Crute, V. and Hargie, O. (1992) *Professional Interviewing*. London: Routledge.

Palmer, S. and Dryden, W. (1995) *Counselling for Stress Problems*. London: Sage.

Pearce, B. (1989) Counselling skills in the context of professional and organizational growth, in W. Dryden, D. Charles-Edwards and R. Woolfe (eds) *Handbook of Counselling in Britain*. London: Routledge.

Reddy, M. (1987) *The Manager's Guide to Counselling at Work*. London: Methuen/British Psychological Society.

Ross, R.R. and Altmaier, E.M. (1994) *Intervention in Occupational Stress*. London: Sage.

Shain, M., Suurvali, H. and Boutilier, M. (1986) *Healthier Workers: Health promotion and Employee Assistance Programs*. Lexington, MA: Lexington Books.

Stromberg, A.H. and Harkness, S. (eds) (1978) *Women Working: Theories and facts in perspective*. Palo Alto, CA: Mayfield.

Terkel, S. (1975) *Working: People talk about what they do all day and how they feel about what they do*. London: Wildwood House.

Tysoe, M. (1988) *All This and Work Too: The psychology of office life*. London: Fontana.

Warr, P. (1987) *Work, Unemployment and Mental Health*. Oxford: Clarendon.

Watts, A. (ed.) (1977) *Counselling at Work*. London: Bedford Square Press.

Wheatley, D. (1993) The Wheatley Stress Profile. *Stress Medicine,* 9(1): 5–9.

Employee counselling: historical developments and key issues

○ CATHERINE GREEN

This chapter will give a brief overview of industrial relations and personnel management in the UK and examine some of the history and developments of employee assistance programmes (EAPs) in the USA and the UK. It will begin by identifying changes that have taken place in society which have reduced family and social support given to individuals. Partly as a result of these changes employers have rationalized their need to provide EAPs in the workplace. I will put forward a definition of EAPs including a description of counselling and the different levels of counselling and services available from EAPs. The chapter will describe the characteristics of EAPs and outline the key issues and benefits for providers and consumers. It will also discuss some of the problems that may be faced by EAP programmes and assess these against the benefits and possible future direction for EAPs.

Industrial relations and personnel management

Industrial relations in Britain has been mainly structured and established on a voluntary basis. The system is based on the organization of employees and employers into trade unions and employers' associations, and freely conducted negotiations at all levels. In recent years there have been a number of trends which have affected Britain's industrial relations system. The introduction of new technology has caused organizational changes which have led to enforced redundancies and the continuing shift towards part-time, temporary, and sub-contracting employment together with increased self-employment which has encouraged greater labour market flexibility. In many sectors job demarcation (for example, between manual, technical and clerical skills) has broken down.

There has been a decline in trade union membership, and by the end of 1989 total union membership was about ten million, of whom 81 per cent were in the 23 largest unions. The decline reflects the change in the UK's manufacturing and public services sectors – both of which had a relatively high level of union membership – to a workforce that is increasingly self-employed or a service industry which has a history of low union membership. The number of unions has also fallen, reflecting a number of mergers between the larger and smaller unions and the long-established craft unions. Nearly all occupations have trade union members. The unions provide benefits and services such as educational facilities, financial services, legal advice as well as negotiating pay and other terms and conditions of employment with employers.

In the early stages of the industrial revolution labour administration did not exist and as Crichton (1968) points out, it was only towards the end of the nineteenth century that a few caring entrepreneurs began to develop a genuinely paternalistic concern for their workers. Mary Wood was one of the first industrial welfare workers when she joined Rowntree's in 1896. Her work was supported by Seebohm Rowntree, the Chairman, who believed that welfare workers were representatives for both the directors and the employees. As representatives of the employees, he wrote about them:

> It is the duty of the social helpers to be constantly in touch with them, to gain their confidence, to voice any grievances they may have either individually or collectively, to give effect to any reasonable desire they may show for recreative clubs, educational classes, etc. and to give advice in matters concerning them personally.
>
> (quoted in Niven 1967)

This allowed welfare workers to be seen as intermediaries between employer and employee and not subordinate to either.

As Farnham (1984) points out, World War One gave added impetus to welfare work and in 1915 the government appointed a Health of Munitions Workers' Committee which recommended that welfare supervisors should be appointed to all factories employing women. The supervisors' tasks were to recruit staff, maintain administrative records, investigate absenteeism, low productivity and dismissals, advise on working conditions, visit the sick and organize training.

Personnel management may be said to have begun at the turn of the century, and by 1914 it was estimated that there were between 60 and 70 welfare workers in Britain. During World War Two more labour managers were employed in factories and the report of the Chief Inspector of Factories 1943 suggested that there were nearly three times more 'personnel officers' employed in 1943 than in 1939.

The definition of personnel management during World War One was:

part of the management function which is primarily concerned with human relationships within an organization. Its objective is the maintenance of these relationships on a basis which, by consideration of the well-being of the individual, enables all those engaged in the undertaking to make their maximum personal contribution to the effective working of that undertaking.

(Niven 1967: 107)

By the end of World War Two Moxon (1946) suggests that six areas being managed by personnel officers were employment, wages, joint consultation, health and safety, employee services and welfare, and education and training.

Personnel management as a function continued to grow and the Institute of Personnel Management was established in June 1946 and recently merged with the Institute of Training and Development to become the Institute of Personnel and Development from 1 July 1994. As a managerial function, personnel work is a product of complex cultural and historical forces as is its employee counterpart, contemporary trade unionism. Implementation of personnel policy depends upon several factors including the socio-economic context of the employment market and the cultural and historical context of personnel management in the private and public sectors. Personnel management grew out of changes in society which resulted from two world wars and a changing workforce. The original personnel tasks identified by organizations and carried out by personnel specialists were considerably wider than those tasks carried out by the welfare workers who staffed the first EAPs.

Although EAPs date back to the early 1940s, very few social workers were actively involved in these programmes until the last decade. Googins and Godfrey (1985) note that, as recently as 1978, only 100 social workers in the USA carrying out EAP work could be identified to participate in a conference on the subject.

Changes in society

The underlying causes in the change of lifestyles in Britain in the second half of the twentieth century may have precipitated the increase of stress. These changes include a trend towards later marriage, a lower birth rate, a higher divorce rate, longer life expectancy, wider educational opportunities, technological progress and an expectation of a higher standard of living.

In 1989 there were 392,042 marriages in Britain, of which 36 per cent were remarriages of one or both parties. In the same year there were approximately 12.7 decrees of divorce made absolute for every 1000 married couples in England and Wales; 150,872 divorces were granted, of which 71.6 per cent were granted to wives. The average age of people at the time of divorce in England and Wales in 1994 was approximately 38.3 for men and 35.7 for women. At this age individuals are often building their career and find personal, emotional stress disrupting of their professional performance. A Health and Safety Executive report, *Mental Health at Work* (1988), states that up to 40 per cent of absenteeism at work is through illness that can be attributed to mental or emotional problems such as those stemming from divorce.

Babies that are born to mothers out of wedlock now account for 28 per cent of all births in the UK. There is also evidence, however, of a growing number of stable non-married relationships, but for women having children later in life there are also stressors that can affect their work performance. These include infertility, lack of childcare facilities, returning to work after maternity leave or even discrimination at the recruitment stage.

At birth, life expectancy for a man is 72 years and for a woman 78 years. Although life expectancy has increased due to better nutrition, rising standards of living, the advance of medical science, improved health measures, better working conditions, and education in personal hygiene, the UK is near the top of the world league table of mortality from coronary heart disease. The British Heart Foundation estimates that heart disease costs an organization of 10,000 employees £1.6 million for men and £370,000 for women in lost productivity. Longer lives, however, can also ironically be a stressor to adults who find themselves burdened with dependent parents when they neither have the time nor the money to support them. Few resources are available in the community for care of the elderly. However, there is a long tradition in Britain of voluntary service to the community and the partnership between the voluntary and statutory sectors is encouraged by the government. There are thousands of voluntary organizations concerned with health and social welfare, ranging from national bodies to small local groups. Organizations concerned with personal and family problems include the Family Welfare Association, Family Service Units, and the National Society for the Prevention of Cruelty to Children. They also include Relate (formerly National Marriage Guidance Council), the National Council of Voluntary Child Care Organizations, the National Council for One-Parent Families, and the Child Poverty Action Group. Voluntary service to both the sick and people with disabilities is given by organizations such as the British Red Cross, Royal National Institute for the Blind, Royal National Institute for the Deaf, the National Association for Mental Health (MIND) and the National Society for Mentally Handicapped Children and Adults (MENCAP). National organizations whose work is religiously inspired include the Salvation Army, Toc H, Catholic Marriage Advisory Council, the Jewish Welfare Board and the Churches Urban Fund. There are also 1300 Citizens' Advice Bureaux throughout the country which are staffed by people who advise on individuals' social and legal rights. Many areas have free law centres and housing advisory centres.

However, even with all these voluntary organizations the demand for support and care far outweighs the provisions within society, so it is not surprising that the trend towards in-company counselling or employee assistance programmes is on the increase and organizations are once again following Seebohm Rowntree's example and adopting a caring philosophy for their staff.

As previously described, the UK has a long tradition of welfare help which can be traced from the social welfare era to personnel management. EAPs in the UK started with a broader remit than those in the USA, which were started specifically to address alcohol problems in companies. British EAPs often take a 'broad brush approach' to counselling and are equipped to handle a range of problems. Employee assistance programmes are primarily counselling programmes in organizational settings but there are characteristics of an EAP which make it different from other counselling services. For example, it is important that senior management accept the service as an integral part of organizational culture and one that can contribute to corporate success. Sponsoring organizations must accept that information which may identify individual users will not be fed back to management and that the service should be available free of charge to staff and in some cases to their immediate families.

History and developments of EAPs in the USA and UK

From the end of the nineteenth century, organizations in the USA such as Kemper Insurance and Eastman Kodak offered employees support in these areas: personnel counselling, occupational health and alcoholism. In 1940 occupational alcoholism programmes (OAPs) were initiated and these were developed to support recovering alcoholics. They were based on the premise that the employee with an addiction problem should be confronted while still on the job and the employer should not try to cover up the problem. By doing this the addiction could be treated and the employee would be able to remain in his job.

It is currently estimated that 20 per cent of the employees in the American workforce suffer from problems which affect job performance (Myers 1984). These include chemical dependency, marital and family conflicts, financial problems, legal difficulties and emotional disorders (Costello 1987). The National Household Survey conducted by the National Institute of Drug Abuse found that in 1985 approximately 10,500,000 Americans were alcoholics; approximately 5,750,000 were current users of cocaine; and approximately 4,360,000 were current users of marijuana (Appelbaum and Shapiro 1989). In the USA the growth of EAPs has been staggering in the last 20 years. While there were only about 50 programmes in the 1950s, by 1980 many large employers in the financial sector, industry, hospitals and small companies were becoming aware of alcoholism as a problem in their workforce and, as a result, the Drug Free Workplace Act of 1988 was passed, encouraging companies to implement EAPs. Now there are estimated to be over 5,000 (Myers 1984).

Growth of EAPs in Britain

In a survey carried out by ICAS (Reddy 1993) 1,500 UK organizations with more than 100 employees were systematically chosen from the Personnel Managers' Yearbook and questioned about whether they provided some sort of counselling for their staff. From their response it was ascertained that 85 per cent of organizations provided some kind of stress counselling, 24 per cent redundancy counselling, 30 per cent retirement counselling, 24 per cent skills training, and 4 per cent of UK companies provide an employee assistance programme of which most of the growth took place during 1992. Financial, emotional and work-related problems were most frequently reported and the majority of those organizations offering counselling services believed that the service reduced absenteeism and increased productivity.

In calculating the cost–benefit ratio, Reddy (1987) says that it is generally acknowledged to be extremely difficult to quantify in precise terms the advantages and savings which accrue; however, conservative estimates would put the benefit-to-cost ratio in the region of two-and-a-half to one, whereas the more optimistic would suggest as much as ten to one.

The overwhelming motivation for the implementation of EAPs has been a recognition that employees bring their problems to work (Megranahan 1990). Whether the problem is work-related or personal, if it has become distressing to the individual it may impair their judgement, morale, or performance and therefore ultimately reduce organizational effectiveness.

Not all EAPs are cost-effective and some may lack professional integrity. However, while some EAP providers may engage in practices that border on the unethical, Scanlon (1991) suggests that such practices are probably in the minority. Nevertheless, the profession has a responsibility to ensure that the highest standards are maintained. Both the Employee Assistance Society of North America (EASNA) and the Employee Assistance Professional Association (EAPA) developed programme standards in 1990. EASNA standards for Accreditation of Employee Assistance Programmes are similar to EAPA's, and while EASNA's standards are more clinically focused, EAPA's standards frequently refer to 'work performance' and 'problems of the workforce'. Both sets of standards are important contributions to the 'counselling at work' profession.

Kinds of EAPs

There are several types of EAP models specifically designed to deliver different levels of help to meet the needs of a wide variety of companies. Practitioners distinguish between services that are provided internally and those provided externally and they fall into one or a combination of the following categories (Masi 1992):

- *In-house model* The staff of an EAP that provides an in-house model are employed by the company and a company manager sets the policies and designs the procedures. The programme may be housed in the company or located in offices away from the workplace. Companies such as Boots, Shell UK, W.H. Smith and Johnson & Johnson chose to develop in-house services for many reasons. Senior management may be unfamiliar with mental health treatment and to ensure that the company has expertise in this area it hires clinicians on a part-time or full-time basis to develop and implement the programme. Some companies believe, as paternalistic employers, that this initiative expresses their humanitarian concerns for their staff and other organizations implement such a service because they believe it can be economically more cost-effective than other kinds.
- *External model* In this scenario a company will approach an external provider to deliver the counselling services to meet the employees' needs. Companies like Dupont, Dixons plc, Kleinwort Benson and Mercury Communications have been attracted to external providers to solve the problem of lack of internal experience. Acquiring an external service relieves any one person or department in the company from the responsibility of providing counselling to staff.
- *Affiliate model* A purchaser sub-contracts with a local professional (e.g. clinical psychologist) rather than employing salaried staff. Hong Kong Bank was an example of an organization that used this model before they merged with Midland Bank. Midland Bank has their own in-house service that was set up in 1991. Often smaller-sized companies opt for this affiliate model.

In determining the most suitable approach, each organization must decide on its level of commitment, and the services it wishes to provide to meet the needs of its staff, the managers and the organization.

External EAP providers in the UK

There are still only relatively few providers of EAPs in the UK and the following are some of the major ones:

EAR – Employee Assistance Resource grew out of Control Data with Mike Megranahan running it. It started in 1986 and was one of the first in this country. The head office is in Uxbridge and they have a network of counsellors providing mainly telephone counselling throughout the UK.

FOCUS – Forum for Occupational Counselling and Unemployment Services Ltd was started by Bridget Litchfield in October 1982. Originally Focus specialized in redundancy counselling but they now provide EAP services.

ICAS – Independent Counselling and Advisory Services is based near Milton Keynes and has been established since 1987. Michael Reddy set up a UK network of over 500 affiliated counsellors, which can provide a 24-hour telephone counselling service and also access to face-to-face counselling.

Mentors Counselling Consultants was started by Catherine Green in 1991. It is a wholly owned consultancy of Midland Bank. Mentors is based in London but has satellite offices in other parts of the UK. Their counsellors are self-employed but work as a team in Mentors offices providing advice, information, telephone and face-to-face counselling and a referral service.

PPC – Personal Performance Consultants (UK) Ltd have specialized in EAPs since May 1988. The company is part-owned by an American company, Willis Faber. Alistair Anderson heads up the company, which operates a network of regional offices throughout the UK.

Definition of EAPs

My definition of an EAP is a confidential service operating within a work organization providing various levels of support, ranging from advice, information, counselling and a referral service which is available to employees and their families at no cost, as it is paid for by sponsoring organizations.

The term 'counselling' is best used as suggested by the British Association for Counselling, which is as follows:

> Counselling occurs when a counsellor meets with a client in a private and confidential setting to explore a difficulty the client is having, distress he may be in, or perhaps his vague dissatisfaction with life and loss of a sense of direction or purpose. It is always at the request of the client and no one can properly be 'sent' for counselling.
>
> (BAC 1990)

It is important to mention that the values of counselling act as a foundation upon which the ethical principles and standards of practice are built and these values of integrity, impartiality and respect as outlined by Bond (1993) are not unique to counselling.

Employees who are counselled in an EAP context are usually offered a limited number of sessions ranging from two to 12. If the individual is in need of longer-term counselling they may be referred to counsellors or therapists who do long-term work or other specialist professionals.

Essential characteristics of EAPs

Unions

Most labour-management experts would agree that to ensure support for the EAP, the union should be involved in the formulation of the EAP policy. Union support and involvement can also be increased by including union officials in training sessions that equip managers and supervisors to use counselling skills.

Professional ethics

Counsellors must work to a specific code of ethics and practice which should be on display for all users to read. This code should set out the terms of counselling which include, for example, the number and duration of sessions and the fact that the counsellors must be professionally qualified and 'should not counsel when their functioning is impaired due to personal or emotional difficulties, illness, disability, alcohol, drugs or for any other reason' BAC (1990: B.2.18).

Referrals

In the EAP policy statement it is essential to clarify for the users and managers exactly how members of staff and their families can contact the programme. Most EAP providers suggest that self-referral is the most effective approach as it shows that the individual has taken responsibility for their own concern or problem and has made the decision to explore ways of dealing with it. However, line managers who refer staff to the service can often effect an introduction if the individual lacks confidence or is unable to make the decision to get help for themselves. Some users may prefer to be accompanied by their line manager or a friend but this also impacts upon the confidentiality of the service.

Contract with users

It is essential for users of an EAP to be aware of the extent of counselling support they can receive and the breadth of the problems they can discuss.

The policy statement should clearly outline the number of sessions an individual can attend with a counsellor and the areas of support on offer. Most EAP programmes offer different levels and kinds of assistance, ranging from advice and information-giving, to a counselling service of a stated number of sessions, to other referral services that may include advice from external lawyers, doctors, specialist therapists, pastoral or financial counsellors. If the EAP refers the user to outside specialists it should be clearly stated in the policy statement who is responsible for that payment.

Supervision

All counsellors are obliged to have ongoing supervision by BAC's Code of Ethics and Practice for the Supervision of Counsellors (BAC 1992). Clinical supervision has been described as an interpersonal interaction with the general goal that one person, the supervisor, meets with another, the supervisee, in an effort to make the latter more effective in helping people. Proctor (1987) describes the process of supervision in terms of formative, restorative and normative processes. The formative aspect is about sharing responsibility for the development of the worker in skills, knowledge and understanding. The restorative aspect provides opportunities for discharge and for the 'recharging of batteries', and the normative aspect is about taking responsibility for standards and ethics. It is important to form a clear contract for every supervisory relationship. Both the supervisor and the supervisees have responsibilities within their relationship. The BACs Code of Ethics and Practice for the Supervision of Counsellors suggests that it is 'a breach of the ethical requirement for counsellors to practise without regular counselling supervision/consultative support' (BAC 1992: B.3.1).

Counselling supervision is a formal arrangement which allows counsellors to discuss their work with one or more experienced professionals who have an understanding of counselling. The counselling supervision should be independent and separate from line management supervision, as they have two very different functions. A clinical supervisor has a confidential and enabling relationship with the counsellor, whereas the line manager has a more official and often judgemental relationship with a member of staff which cannot include confidentiality. Both professionals must be aware of the contracts which they may each have with the organization and a key point raised by Feltham and Dryden (1994: 24) is that the supervisor should 'clarify his position with regard to line managers, trainers, colleagues and anyone to whom you are accountable for your supervisory work, and do not underestimate the subtle areas in which boundaries may become dangerously blurred'.

The supervisor's areas of responsibility will be to ensure that there is enough opportunity for the supervisee to set out practice issues and to explore counsellors' clarity of thinking and feeling which underlie their actions. Supervision allows the supervisor and the supervisee to share experiences, client information and their developing counselling skills appropriately and to be able to challenge aspects of practice which may be regarded as unethical, unwise or incompetent.

The supervisee has the responsibility to bring practice issues to individual supervision or if the supervision is given in a group then the supervisee needs to identify the issues with which they need help and to ask for time. This practice ensures that counsellors are able to take any concerns they have to an experienced colleague and that clients are protected against misconduct or abuse. Group supervision is a forum that can enhance learning and the sharing of skills. Most EAP providers recognize that their counsellors need regular supervision to ensure that they are supported and that a high standard of counselling is maintained and the BAC Code of Ethics and Practice for Counsellors suggests: 'the volume of supervision should be in proportion to the volume of counselling work undertaken and the experience of the counsellor' (1992: B.3.4).

Evaluation

It is crucial for the sponsoring organization and the EAP provider to know how well the programme is working and if it is doing what it purports to do. Many organizations do not make any cost-effectiveness evaluation, preferring to regard the EAP as part of the wider organizational internal culture. However, there are many different items to refer to when evaluating the benefits of an EAP and these may include: absenteeism, staff turnover, involuntary early retirements due to ill-health, take-up of the service, and allowing staff to receive counselling for work-related problems from professionals out of the workplace which will result in saving management time.

When collating data the EAP provider must identify with the sponsoring organization the items to be measured, which should also support the reasons for establishing an EAP. The scope of EAP goals and objectives will determine what variables to include in a retrospective analysis. The management reports which collate the usage of the service by employees against company employment data may include such statistical data as: age, gender, department, organizational grade, marital status, number of children (which can identify whether children can contribute to stress), and presenting problems of the individual. It would also be possible to collect data stating either the number of telephone contacts the individual makes or counselling sessions they attend, to identify the level of support they wanted.

Early identification of key issues which are causing high staff turnover or employee stress can be rectified by categorizing and evaluating them. An EAP provides one way of effectively collecting data which identifies the problems and then tries, often indirectly, to reduce staff turnover. The organization can measure the impact of introducing an EAP against, for example, the claims for medical plan costs or against job-related accidents. Absenteeism is a common corporate concern and it may be possible to make correlations between the EAP users and the absentee groups. In 1981, General Motors Corporation reported that absenteeism alone, which was largely the result of employee alcohol abuse, drug abuse, and mental health problems, was costing the company well over one billion dollars per year. In 1986 their EAP was assisting more than 500,000 employees in North America, and about 100,000 employees were using the programme for alcohol and drug abuse problems.

In Britain one in ten of the UK population (largely the adult, working population) suffer from some mental illness in the course of a year which costs UK businesses £3.7 billion per year in lost working days alone. During 1989–90 in the UK, 80 million working days were lost due to one form or another of mental ill-health; 25 per cent of short-term absence from work is estimated to be influenced by stress factors; and Steddon (1991) estimates that 20 per cent is alcohol-related.

MacDonnell Douglas (US) established an EAP in 1970 for its 125,000 employees in the aircraft industry. In 1985 Alexander & Alexander management consultants were commissioned to undertake a review of the programme during 1985–88. The study revealed that the costs of the programme each year, which were deducted from the operating costs, made a total saving of $5.1 million over four years. Johnson & Johnson's EAP, which was introduced in the UK in 1982, showed that the sickness absence rate was 41 per cent down in 1984 and the sickness absence costs were reduced to £300,000 from £520,000.

The Post Office introduced stress counselling over a three-year period. Systematic evaluation of the impact of this counselling service (Cooper and Sadu 1989) found that significant declines in absenteeism resulted between pre- and post-counselling periods:

> During a three-year period, all employees were entitled to counselling for stress. Figures were compared for six months before and after counselling and we found a 66 per cent decline in days lost. This means the Post Office were saving £100,000 for every 175 people counselled at a cost of approximately 15 per cent of the total savings.
>
> (1989: 40)

The Post Office also found that there was a decline in clinical anxiety levels and depression, and there was an improvement in morale and productivity.

Stress management

In March 1988 Liverpool Council's chief environmental health officer wrote a report claiming that the effects of employee stress were costing ratepayers £3 million per year. One of the best definitions of stress is given by occupational psychologist Alistair Ostell (1986: 13–14), who describes it as 'the state of affairs which exists when the way people attempt to manage problems taxes or exceeds their coping resources'. There are many factors that can contribute to stress in the workplace but four key areas which contribute to workplace stress are: environmental factors such as noise, poor lighting, poor ventilation, inadequate childcare facilities; job design factors including conflicting objectives, role conflict, too little or too much managerial supervision; contractual factors, some of which may be part of the contract of employment such as low pay, shift work and job insecurity. The fourth area covers relationship factors. Cary Cooper suggests in *Living with Stress* that poor relationships with colleagues at any level will increase 'stress' litigation, and with the escalating costs of employee healthcare insurance more American companies are providing extensive healthcare programmes for their employees (Cooper *et al.* 1988).

By introducing a new EAP into a company employees with long-term problems may be helped. The programme can therefore potentially make a large difference in work performance. Evaluating results over a long period of time may show a decline in the EAP's impact on performance but this should not be viewed as programme failure (Appelbaum and Shapiro 1989). Many of the studies carried out on EAPs show an annual payoff between three and seven times the cost of the EAP provision (Berridge and Cooper 1993). They suggest that this shows a highly competitive rate of return in both capital outlay and revenue. However, Megranahan suggests that 'there are no standard workplace counselling services available in Britain, which makes comparing costs and benefits difficult' (1990: 256).

Comprehensive evaluation of the administration of an EAP can point out flaws in procedures. When monitored, these problems can be rectified to enable the service to perform at a higher level of efficiency. It is only when management have decided whether they arc going to set up an internal service or whether they are going to employ an external service that the decision can be taken as to the positioning of the EAP within the company. At such companies as B.F. Goodrich and Goodyear Aerospace, mentioned by Shapiro *et al.* (1988), it is the human resource department that is responsible for co-ordinating EAP activities. Midland Bank has a department that uses self-employed counsellors to provide the range of support services to staff and their families. The department head reports to the head of personnel but the feedback from the collected statistical data is given to regional general managers of the Bank to enable them to try to alleviate problems being generated in the workplace.

Key issues

In-house services

In-house services are sometimes criticized for possibly jeopardizing employees' rights as they do not necessarily offer a private location for counselling, and for discussion of information regarding corporate issues which may be fed back to the organization (for example, sexual harassment in the workplace). Some counsellors argue that many employees who need professional help will not use in-house services because they are afraid that management will learn of their problems and hold these against them. It is evident that in-house services may present counsellors with a conflict of interest. On the one hand, professional ethics stress that counsellors must always act in the best interest of their clients. On the other hand, as employees of the company, counsellors may feel compelled to resolve conflicts in the interest of their employer. When counsellors try to resolve the conflicting demands of the employer and the employee, the employees' interests may be compromised.

External services

External services also have a major drawback. Some employee assistance providers may not have a great deal of experience with organizations or their structures. Counsellors' backgrounds often emanate from the public sector and not a commercial context. This may lead the EAP counsellors to emphasize the advantages of available services outside the organization before suggesting to clients that they approach their line or personnel manager who may have the ability to alleviate their concern. Counsellors need to be credible in the eyes of organizations' management and staff alike.

Management of confidentiality

Confidentiality can be a difficult issue for the user of the service, for managers and for the organization. Users will not bring their concerns to an EAP if they feel that there is any likelihood of information being leaked back into the organization. However, line managers are often concerned about their staff and may wish to refer them to the service. If they do refer a member of staff to the employee assistance programme they may also feel that it is appropriate that they are kept informed about that individual's progress. Small companies or departments with only a few staff on-site may also create concern regarding confidentiality as any feedback could easily identify an individual or a particular site. Often the organization considers that as it is bearing the cost of the service it has a right to know the individuals' problems that are being presented to the EAP, as it would then be in a position to review policies or try to sort out some of the issues. Statistical information is usually given to senior management as part of the evaluation process but this should not include information that might identify a specific individual.

Confidentiality is one of the most important issues.

> Confidentiality is a means of providing the client with safety and privacy. For this reason any limitation on the degree of confidentiality offered is likely to diminish the usefulness of counselling.
>
> BAC 1990: B.4.1)

Disciplinary policy

Some organizations include referral to the EAP for counselling as part of their disciplinary procedure. This can cause a serious conflict of interests and organizations must be clear about their policies. Senior management should agree how they would like the EAP policy to interface with the accepted corporate procedures. If an EAP is part of a disciplinary procedure, staff who are instructed to use the service may see counselling as punitive. Those organizations which have chosen not to link the EAP with the disciplinary procedure generally have a higher take-up rate of the service.

The issues of disciplinary procedure and confidentiality within an organization also relate to the voluntary self-referral to or compulsory attendance of the EAP. If the programme is to be seen as independent, confidential and voluntary it should not be used as a management tool for discipline. If the EAP is used as part of the disciplinary procedure, the perception of the service and the take-up from the staff will be reduced due to mistrust.

Location

The location of the services may depend upon whether it is provided internally or by an external agency. It is important that whoever provides the service, company staff and their families' members (if families are included) can gain ready access to it. An external provider will always be off-site and located within easy reach. Some external providers have a wide network of affiliated counsellors, and counselling often takes place in the counsellor's home. However, if the programme is internal, to meet the specification of confidentiality it should ideally be housed in a separate building away from any other staff of the company. It is often located in the occupational health department.

If telephone counselling only is offered to staff, then one site would be sufficient to respond to the needs of the employees. If face-to-face counselling is provided, different locations throughout the country with easy access to public transport or the road system will be necessary to enable users to reach and gain benefit from the service. Therefore appropriate locations of the service will depend upon the kinds of services being offered.

Telephone/face-to-face counselling

Telephone counselling can provide easy and confidential access to a professional counsellor. The service should provide callers with a quick response and enable them to establish an immediate relationship with the counsellor. Travel problems are non-existent when individuals can contact the service by telephone, at their convenience, from home or from work. It also allows users to pre-book calls and some people may find the anonymity of the telephone enables them to talk more freely. Other people will want the more intimate relationship of working on a face-to-face basis.

Client problems or concerns

The typical presenting problem brought to counsellors in EAPs will depend upon the way in which the service is introduced throughout the organization, and vary according to the level of expertise and professionalism of the counsellors. Common concerns as described by Berridge (1990) may include alcohol abuse, bereavement, divorce, family problems, financial distress, marital problems, AIDS, racial harassment, work- or home-related stress, being overweight, violence or career problems. Sometimes the concern is not immediately clear and a person may be confused or uncertain as to what is causing their worry if they have no current upset in their lives. Whichever the case, professional counsellors facilitate the exploration of the problem with the individual and aim to enable them to come to terms with their situation and manage it better within their life context.

Counsellors' response

If an individual has reached the situation where they need help from an EAP counsellor it is important that a response to their enquiry is immediate. Some EAP providers can respond to calls and make an appointment for the individual to meet a counsellor within a couple of days. Depending on the nature of the problem, some callers may need to be referred on to professionals who are not part of the EAP team, such as a lawyer, doctor, accountant or psychiatrist. Sometimes there is the facility for individuals to write to the EAP and letters need to be answered within an agreed time-limit set out in the EAP providers' Code of Practice (EAPA 1990). Organizations who have shift workers may also want to provide a service that can be contacted 24 hours a day.

Counsellors' profile

As described by Shapiro et al. (1988), counselling is a highly skilled business and requires extensive training. Counsellors may often have a social work or similar training background, for example, but to become an accredited member of the British Association for Counselling (BAC), the counsellor needs an appropriate substantial basic training, extensive experience, compliance with an ethical code, and involvement in continuing training, development and supervision. Hoffman (1989), before he would employ anyone to provide counselling, would ask questions such as: Is he or she highly qualified? What is the counsellor's personal track record? How long has he or she been in counselling? What is his or her professional background?

Legal issues

The design and implementation of EAPs must be effected in accordance with current UK law. Counsellors should familiarize themselves with the current law that impinges on counselling practice such as the Children Act (1989), Mental Health Act (1983), Data Protection Act (1994); and also ensure that they are covered by professional liability insurance. Programme policies and procedures should also reflect any organizational regulations see Jenkins 1997.

Future directions of EAPs

According to Masi (1992) there are certain trends in the organization of EAPs in the larger social context that may have implications for EAP programmes in the USA and therefore perhaps the UK. He suggests that companies are setting up EAP programmes to avoid increasing health insurance costs. Companies are beginning to ask their staff to use the EAP to obtain a second opinion prior to the approval of lengthy in-patient hospitalization or long-term out-patient therapy. In the future, EAP staff may be given the responsibility for monitoring the corporate mental health package purchased by the organization. All types of companies, whether they are in the public or private sector, try to reduce alcoholism in the workplace and one way of doing this is by drug-testing, which is considered by doctors to be a reasonable solution. If this happens then EAP providers may be asked to develop policies to implement the testing, which will have implications for extra training for counsellors.

The professional staff in an EAP may also be able to offer managers training in counselling skills and the identification and management of stress and change within the workplace. By enabling managers to feel confident when discussing work-related or personal stress issues with their staff, it may enhance the communication between manager and employee and thereby produce a better working relationship.

Shapiro *et al.* (1988) conclude that by giving widespread recognition of costs of mental ill-health at work there will be a high demand for preventive intervention strategies. They believe that worksite counselling and EAPs are potentially valuable and they endorse their use and development on the proviso that the following objectives are taken into consideration:

- specific guidelines and standards for both service and organizational aspects are set out;
- American methods and systems are adapted to the UK environment and culture;
- audit and evaluation take place to assess programmes in relation to guidelines and standards;

- regular research and development are a part of the programme, to improve the quality, efficiency and targeting of interventions.

Conclusion

EAPs can be a cost-effective, easily accessible and efficient way of supporting employees and their families with a broad range of counselling services. They can provide the confidentiality and neutrality that cannot be obtained from a relationship with a friend or a colleague within an organization. As 'stressors' increase more people may need professional help to manage their personal life and workplace anxieties.

References

Appelbaum, S.H. and Shapiro, B.T. (1989) The ABCs of EAPs. *Personnel*, 66(7): 39–40.

Berridge, J. (1990) The EAP – Employee counselling comes of age. *Employee Counselling Today*, 2(4): 14–15.

Berridge, J. and Cooper, C.L. (1993) *Employee Assistance Programmes – A growing tradition*. London: Coutts Consulting Group plc.

BAC (1990) *Code of Ethics and Practice for Counsellors*. Rugby: British Association for Counselling.

BAC (1992) *Code of Ethics and Practice for the Supervision of Counsellors*. Rugby: British Association for Counselling.

Bond, T. (1993) *Standards and Ethics for Counselling in Action*. London: Sage.

Cooper, C.L. (1991) Counselling for the bottom line. *Counselling News*, 3: 18–19.

Cooper, C.L. and Sadu, G. (1989) *A Post Office Initiative to Stamp Out Stress*. London: Institute of Personnel Management.

Cooper, C.L., Cooper, R.D. and Eaker, L.H. (1988) *Living with Stress*. Harmondsworth: Penguin.

Costello, J. (1987) Employee assistance programme and clinical social work in America. A developmental perspective. *Journal of Social Work Practice*, 2(4): 114–27.

Crichton, A. (1968) *Personnel Management in Context*. London: Batsford.

EAPA (1990) *EAP Code of Practice*. Employee Assistance Programme Association.

Farnham, D. (1984) *Personnel in Context*. London: Institute of Personnel Management.

Feltham, C. and Dryden, W. (1994) *Developing Counsellor Supervision*. London: Sage.

Googins, B. and Godfrey, J. (1985) The evolution of occupational social work. *Social Work*, 396–402.

Health and Safety Executive (1988) *Mental Health at Work*. London: Health and Safety Executive.

Hoffman, S. (1989) Choosing an employee benefits consultant. *Personnel*, 66(7): 36–8.

Jenkins, P. (1997) *Counselling, Psychotherapy and the Law*. London: Sage.

Masi, D.A. (1992) *The AMA Handbook for Developing Employee Assistance and Counseling Programs*. New York: American Management Association.

Megranahan, M. (1990) Employee assistance programmes. Frameworks and guiding principles. *Employee Counselling Today*, 2(3): 29–33.

Moxon, G.R. (1946) *Functions of a Personnel Department*. London: Institute of Personnel Management.

Myers, D. (1984) *Establishing and Building Employee Assistance Programs*. Westport, CT: Onorum Books.

Niven, M.N. (1967) *Personnel Management 1913–67*. London: Institute of Personnel Management.

Ostell, A. (1986) Where stress screening falls short. *Personnel Management*, 18(9): 13–14.

Proctor, B. (1987) Supervision. A co-operative exercise in accountability, in M. Marken and M. Payne (eds) *Enabling and Ensuring: Supervision in practice*. Leicester: National Youth Bureau.

Reddy, M. (1987) *The Manager's Guide to Counselling at Work*. London: British Psychological Society/Methuen.

Reddy, M. (ed.) (1993) *EAPs and Counselling Provision in UK Organisations*. London: Independent Counselling Advisory Service.

Scanlon, W.F. (1991) *Alcoholism and Drug Abuse in the Workplace – Managing care and costs through employee assistance programs*. New York: Praeger Publishers.

Shapiro, D.A., Cheesman, M. and Wall, T.D. (1988) Secondary prevention – review of counselling and EAPs, in *Promoting Mental Health Policies in the Workplace*. London: HMSO Publications.

Steddon, P. (1991) The many advantages offered by EAPs. *Addiction Counselling World*, 2(12): 10–12.

Suggested reading

Bond, T. (1993) *Standards and Ethics for Counselling in Action*. London: Sage.

Carroll, M. (1996) *Workplace Counselling*. London: Sage.

Feltham, C. (1996) *Time-limited Counselling*. London: Sage.

Feltham, C. and Dryden, W. (1994) *Developing Counsellor Supervision*. London: Sage.

Highley, J.C. and Cooper, C.L. (1996) Counselling in the workplace, in R. Bayne, L. Horton and J. Bimrose (eds) *New Directions in Counselling*. London: Routledge.

Jenkins, P. (1997) *Counselling, Psychotherapy and the Law*. London: Sage.

Orlans, V. (1996) Counselling psychology in the workplace, in R. Woolfe and W. Dryden (eds) *Handbook of Counselling Psychology*. London. Sage.

Palmer, S. and MacMahon, G. (1997) *Client Assessment*. London: Sage.

Preston, J., Varzos, N. and Liebert, D. (1995) *Every Session Counts: Making the most of your brief therapy*. San Luis Obispo, CA: Impact Publishers.

Rosenfield, M. (1996) *Counselling by Telephone*. London: Sage.

Useful organizations

Major organizations offering EAPs or employee counselling

Care Assist Group Ltd
Britannia House
50 Great Charles Street
Queensway
Birmingham
B3 2LP
0121 233 0202

Employee Advisory Resource (EAR)
Brunel Science Park
Kingston Lane
Uxbridge
UB8 3PQ
01895 271155

FOCUS
Northside House
Mount Pleasant
Barnet
Hertfordshire
EN4 9EB
0181 441 9300

ICAS Ltd
Radlett House
West Hill
Aspley Guise
Milton Keynes
MK17 8DT
01908 281128

Mentors Counselling Consultants
28 Bedford Street
London WC2E 9ED
0345 030405

Personal Performance Consultants
Florence House
St Mary's Road
Hinckley
Leicestershire
LE10 1EQ
01455 890011

Voluntary sector organizations offering employee counselling

Counselling in Companies
Westminster Pastoral Foundation
23 Kensington Square
London W8 5HN
0171 937 6224

The Norwich Centre
7 Earlham Road
Norwich
NR2 3RA
01603 617709

Relate (National Marriage Guidance)
Herbert Gray College
Little Church Street
Rugby
CV21 3AP
01788 573241

2

Organizational stress: sources and responses

ANDREW BULL

Providing help in organizations makes common sense: troubled employees receive support; counsellors are provided with a forum in which to use their skills; to a manager, it makes sound business sense to bring about a speedy return to productive work; it is a primary function of union representatives; and personnel, welfare and occupational health staff view helping as a legitimate aspect of the human resource function.

In this chapter help is understood to relate to strategies designed to reduce *stress* – which is discussed later. The chapter considers something of the nature of organizations and how this can shape the type of help provided, the causes and extent of stress in the workplace; and provides a framework for implementing stress reduction strategies. It is argued that responses to stress should be unique and require careful assessment rather than a toolbox of techniques – such as stress management training – that may or may not be appropriate.

Organizations

All the above groups have an investment in providing help but each will do so from a particular perspective and perhaps with a different goal. For example, to an employer, an EAP may represent a commitment to the workforce. To a trade union, however, it may be cited as evidence of the unacceptably high levels of stress within an organization. These groups all have one thing in common: they work within the same environment, an organization. It is not a static entity, an empty shell in which people carry out their working lives and fulfil their career aspirations. It has a character which will exert an influence on the type of help provided.

What is an organization? This question has puzzled researchers and theorists for many years and still no single definition exists to cover all types of organization. One way in which organizations are differentiated, which is not dependent on size or product, is in terms of culture, that is, the beliefs, attitudes, norms and values held by employees about their organizations (Brown 1995) and those generated by the organization itself (Reed 1992).

Culture is sometimes assumed to be a homogeneous entity, whereas the reality might be that a variety of cultures exist in any one organization (Hollway 1991). An example of this could be the National Health Service, a vast organization covering a large geographical area. The beliefs, attitudes, norms and values of a big inner city hospital, like the Middlesex Hospital in London, are likely to be very different from those of a small unit serving a rural area. Furthermore, within one hospital, there may be multiple and competing cultures. For instance, the culture might be exploitative and oppressive to low-paid domestic staff struggling to negotiate acceptable wages and conditions. To professional staff, on the other hand, able to advance their careers with relative ease, the culture could be facilitating.

A frequently used typology of culture is given by Handy (1985), who suggests there are essentially four cultures: power, role, task and person. A similar perspective is provided by Van Oudtshoorn (1989) in Lane (1990), where cultures are classified as role, power, achievement and support. It is possible to speculate that the culture itself will exert an influence on the help provided, and the following illustrates this:

- *Role culture* Role culture is associated with an organization that is hierarchical and bureaucratic, for example, a government agency where the counselling service is a system in its own right. Counselling is like a cog in a machine, contributing to the function of the whole but able to exert very little direct impact on other systems and structures within the organization.
- *Power culture* Power resides in the hands of one or a few people. In their negative form employees are ruled by fear or deceit. Arguably, this was the late Robert Maxwell's way of operating. Positively, they are generous and indulgent but in such organizations the counselling function is likely to be strictly controlled to limit any real or imagined impact on the central power base. An effective way to achieve this would be through the use of external counselling services.
- *Achievement culture* Achievement, or task, cultures are likely to involve the counselling service in the organization, which is goal-oriented and organized around project teams. Typically, hi-tech organizations fit into this category, such as computer software manufacturers. The counselling function is part of the project team, hence part of the organization, and

may be used to help employees form a new project team by, for example, facilitating team-building. The impact of a counselling service on this culture may be significant but it may also be the least secure, as the perceived need for help disappears as projects are completed.

- *Support culture* A counselling service may have difficulty establishing itself in a support culture where the organization, such as it is, exists to provide a framework for a group of loosely connected people, such as a firm of architects contracting in self-employed staff. Individual employees will be responsible for getting their own help, in this instance from a counsellor in private practice. Difficulties may be compounded when the organization also has a caring function, such as a drugs rehabilitation agency with employees who have counselling expertise. Here counselling might be restricted to providing specialist help when the necessary expertise is not available in-house, such as during a redundancy programme.

The above illustrates how, with the exception of achievement culture, a counselling service might have little impact on the organization but in all instances the organization has an impact on the help provided. This raises a legitimate question: should the organization be excluded from the 'stress equation'? If it is, the focus of attention rests exclusively on the employee who, to a greater or lesser degree, becomes responsible for the causes and consequences of stress.

Kets de Vries and Miller (1984) argue that ignoring the organization in the stress equation may be not only detrimental but may threaten the organization's very survival. Using a typology of organizations based on the *DSM III*, the standard American diagnostic manual for mental disorders (APA 1987), they suggest that the chief executive's personality is reflected in a dysfunctional organization's systems, structures and culture. For example, the *compulsive* type of organization is a perfectionist place with a preoccupation with detail, dogmatism, obstinacy and control. Rigidity leads to an over-reliance on the manufacture of tried and trusted products which, in turn, relies on a stable and reliable customer base.

In this example, help could be geared to mopping up the casualties of such a rigid, overbearing organization or boss. It could be provided to teach employees better ways of adapting to the organization or the boss's dysfunctional style. For example, staff training could be oriented towards adapting to a particular style of management. A third possibility is that help, such as consultancy, could be used to work with the organization itself. In a large organization this is more likely to be an aspect of its functioning rather than the whole organization, such as inter-departmental communications.

These illustrations highlight how culture can impact on the help provided. It is possible to speculate that the existence or continuity of service provision may depend on its ability to adapt to the host organization's culture. A challenge to providers of help is to understand the culture and the assumptions and values upon which it rests. Without such knowledge the best-intentioned interventions may be doomed to failure if they appear to be inimical to the organization's assumptions and values – see also Agyris and Schön (1978) and Nevis (1987).

Myths

The following section describes the importance of myths in organizations, and how they reveal assumptions and values upon which culture rests. Myths are 'unjustified beliefs . . . which influence how organizational actors understand and react to their social situation' (Brown 1995: 15). Myths arise out of the uncertainty and turbulence of organizational life to provide stability and a framework in which shared meanings can develop (Nijsmans 1992). Unfortunately, there is often a discrepancy between the myth and everyday life.

One reason for the appeal of myths is that they offer plausible and comforting (to some) explanations about organizational life. Boje *et al.* (1982) identify four basic organizational myths, each of which serves a purpose: myths that create, maintain and legitimize past, present and future actions and consequences; myths that maintain and conceal political interests; myths that help explain and create cause and effect relationships; and myths that rationalize complexity and turbulence to allow for taking predictable action.

Myths that create, maintain and legitimize past, present and future actions and consequences

These myths legitimize and rationalize behaviour and its consequences. Stories from the past are employed to legitimize the continued use of techniques, attitudes or values. In an electrical components industry, assembling circuit boards, in Bristol, for example, it was a myth that this work was suited to women because of their manual dexterity. The work was 'sex typed' and so men tended not to apply for these jobs, thus appearing to prove the case that it was women's work – thus the past was used to legitimize the present and the future.

The reality or purpose of the myth could be somewhat different. In the above example, the 'dextrous' women were employed because they did not have a history of involvement in trade unions. This lessened the likelihood of their coalescing into some form of collective action, in support of improved wages and conditions, which suited the manager. He had received a confidential memo from the chairman stating the factory was to be a non-unionized site. Thus, the myth of female dexterity was used to legitimize other practices.

Myths that maintain and conceal political interests

A common myth of this type is the explanation as to why chief executives of large industries need to earn inordinately large sums of money. The myth is that these people possess particular and special skills, knowledge and abilities to lead organizations. It is possible to question whether these special skills exist and, if they do, just how influential they are in generating new markets and increased profits, let alone what justification exists for salaries and pay rises far in excess of those available to the majority of the workforce.

Myths that help explain and create cause and effect relationships

These myths create cause and effect relationships where no evidence of causality exists. For example, a myth exists to explain why women should not be recruited or promoted in organizations (Boje *et al.* 1982): they are unreliable workers who will always sacrifice their careers to the needs of their family. The evidence given for this is the biological fact of female childbirth, *ergo* women are naturally oriented towards childcare. Whether or not women are nature's childrearers becomes a red herring in which an either/or situation is created. It ignores the reality that some women enjoy motherhood, some concentrate on careers, others choose a combination of the two and, for a significant number, childbirth is not a possibility. Whatever the debate it obscures a real issue (that is the reason for the creation of the myth), for example, male hegemony.

Myths that rationalize complexity and turbulence to allow for taking predictable action

These myths create the illusion of predictability and control in the face of random and non-controllable factors. For example, there is a myth of managers adopting a planned and purposeful model of management, whereas decisions are frequently taken 'on the hoof' in the face of competing demands from superiors and subordinates and as a result of extraneous and unforeseen circumstances. A humorous illustration is Captain Mainwaring, of the comedy television programme *Dad's Army*, charging around completely out of control yet reassuring himself, his soldiers and us, the viewer, that he is in total command.

The key point to understanding myths is that in the four examples given they exist to conceal something: an attitude, value or political interest. Myths are not by themselves necessarily stressful, but where the myth is significantly different from employees' realities then stress may result. The myth of decision-making being a rational, planned and well-organized activity is a comforting notion (to many) in Western culture, but its maintenance is potentially expensive and stressful. It requires training programmes, for example, designed to improve employees' abilities at predicting and controlling work and the workplace. However, if organizational life is essentially random and chaotic, training, in this instance, is going to be expensive and unproductive, and it is unlikely to help relieve the anguish and sleepless nights caused by the worry of not being in control of everything.

There is an inherent difficulty in identifying myths. They operate as truths if not facts. It is possible, however, to reflect on some of these *truths* in an organization and to subject them to empirical scrutiny. In the first myth, it is true that many women are dextrous and very proud of it. What of men, are they not dextrous? Male artists use their hands to create delicate and sensitive images of the world around them, and legions of men spend hours under the bonnets of their cars repairing mechanical and electrical systems. All these skills require a high degree of finesse. Men can clearly be subtle and sensitive with their hands, so at a superficial level the myth that only women are dextrous is questionable. Therefore, in the absence of empirical evidence of 'truth' it is possible to consider that the 'truth' is part of a myth.

The foregoing section has attempted to highlight further the importance of including the organization in the stress equation. Strategies which focus simply on the individual may be of limited utility and merely act as psychological band-aids, resulting in a wounded workforce which is unable to give of its best.

Other sources of stress

In addition to the influence of culture in the workplace, five major categories of work stress have been identified (Cooper and Marshall 1976).

1 *Factors intrinsic to the job*: such as working conditions, shift work, long hours, work overload and underload – see Warr's (1987) nine job features below.
2 *Role in the organization*: role ambiguity arises from a lack of clarity over objectives and the scope of responsibilities of a job; role conflict arises from having a number of roles in the same situation, such as a manager acting as a mentor and a line manager.
3 *Interpersonal relationships*: handling interpersonal relationships was found to be the second most important source of job dissatisfaction among head teachers (Cooper and Kell 1993).
4 *Career development*: MIND (1992), in a survey of 109 companies, found that fear of redundancy was the single most important contributing factor to stress in the organization.
5 *Organizational structure*, which poses threats to individual freedom, autonomy and identity, resulting in no sense of belonging, lack of participation, lack of consultation and restrictions on behaviour.

Points 2–5 concentrate on occupational stressors, that is, the totality of the work environment. Warr (1987) identifies nine job features that are responsible for excessive employee stress – where 'job' relates to the tasks an individual carries out at their place of work:

1 *Job discretion* This is the single most important job stressor. It is essential for employees to have a degree of freedom to plan and make decisions about work and to have access to adequate resources with which to undertake work.
2 *Use of skills* There is a clear and positive relationship between mental health and workers who have greater opportunity for skill use. This relationship extends across blue- and white-collar workers.
3 *Work demands* Long periods of repeated deadlines, intense concentration and constant pressure can cause excessive stress. Low work demands also are often a source of stress.
4 *Work variety* Disturbance may arise when there is a lack of challenge or opportunity to learn new skills, often brought about by monotonous work. This is seen particularly in low-level jobs and in mid-career people whose jobs have become over-familiar.
5 *Environmental clarity* There are two main forms: a lack of feedback about performance and desired work behaviours; and lack of information about the employee's and the organization's future.
6 *Pay* Evidence exists that those with low pay (and corollaries such as poor housing and diet) experience higher incidence of ill-health.
7 *Working conditions* Unpleasant environmental conditions, such as extreme heat, physical danger, noise, threats to personal security, crowding and shift work, can all exert stressful effects on employees.
8 *Interpersonal support* Social support and friendship from colleagues acts as a coping strategy and a buffer to stressful situations, as is the need for privacy and personal territory.
9 *Job's value in society* People view their jobs in various ways, one of which is its contribution to society. Warr speculates that the relationship between a job's social merit and health will be particularly significant when the job has a low value.

It is not possible to state categorically that any of the above will be experienced as stressful. This will be mediated by factors such as personality and previous experiences. It is beyond the scope of this chapter to examine these variables, although an example is Type A behaviour – characteristically aggressive, time-oriented, achievement-focused and controlling. There is evidence (Haynes *et al.* 1981) for a relationship between Type A behaviour and coronary artery disease, which is discussed in Chapter 5. What is clear, however, is that the variables identified can be both causes and consequences of stress. For instance, John's relationship breaks down (consequence) after he loses his job (cause). But for Susan the end of her relationship (cause) may result in tardiness and absenteeism leading to her being sacked (consequence). Finally, a deterioration in one factor may cause an improvement in another. For example, Mary is made redundant but her relationship, which was previously in trouble, improves greatly as she and her partner discover a new, albeit painful, shared purpose in rebuilding their lives.

Extent of problem

The very subjective nature of stress and its ambiguity as a term, both describing causal events and individual and organizational consequences of stress, makes it a difficult concept to measure. As stress research has developed, early models, such as that of Selye (1956) which predicts a general response to stress, have been superseded by interactional models which emphasize the role of individual internal processes as mediators between the stressor and the response (Reynolds and Shapiro 1991).

Despite difficulties defining stress and the concomitant problems in its measurement, a body of epidemiological research exists. Out of 1,000 adults, 100–250 have a psychological disorder in any one year (Jenkins 1993). The number of epidemiological studies conducted in the workplace is much lower, but they do show that the commonest disorders in the community, that is, depression and anxiety, also occur most frequently in the workplace. A paradox does exist, however, in that it could be expected that prevalence rates in the community, which includes the unemployed, elderly and ill, would be higher than those in the workplace. In fact, the opposite is true, which may be explained if the studies took place in particularly stressful work environments, but it could point to the inherently stressful nature of work (Jenkins 1993).

There is a reasonable degree of consensus between a number of disparate groups about the size and costs of distress in the workplace. The HMSO document *Mental Health at Work* (1988) states that up to 40 per cent of absenteeism from work through illness can be attributed to mental or emotional problems. Approximately 30 million days are lost annually at work for certified psychoneurotic disorders at a cost of £4 billion (Sadu *et al.* 1989). For every day lost through industrial disputes 30 are forfeited because of stress. Five per cent of the general population are affected by depression during the course of a year, costing £221 million at 1985 prices (Milligan and Clare 1993)

This blanket approach to the measurement of stress overlooks differences between groups in the amount of stress perceived or experienced. For example, uniformed professions, such as police, prison officers and airline pilots, have the highest average stress ratings for broad occupational categories (Cooper *et al.* 1986). Socio-economic factors also affect morbidity – males and females in occupational class V (unskilled manual labour) have a

2.5 times greater chance of dying before reaching retirement age than their counterparts in group I (lawyers, doctors) (Black *et al.* 1990). North *et al.* (1993) found higher rates of sickness absence among less skilled non-manual or manual civil servants, which was not fully explained by risk factors such as smoking, alcohol consumption, work characteristics, including high and low levels of work, and adverse social circumstances.

Davidson and Cooper (1992) reviewed similarities and differences between male and female managers in relation to occupational stress. The specific problems women face include coping with prejudice and sex stereotyping, discrimination from colleagues, employers and organizational structure, isolation and lack of role models. An added stressor is that women also tend to have primary responsibilities in the home and towards child care.

While there is evidence of differences in the incidence of stress and mental disorder between groups, it is not enough to develop strategies solely aimed at a particular group. For example, it would be of little practical benefit for women alone to address the issue of career development when in all probability it is male elites who have the power to influence career prospects. A strategy targeted exclusively at women, in this instance, may well fail and be seen as tokenistic, and increase feelings of isolation. Strategies should be targeted throughout an organization.

Despite conceptual and methodological problems connected with the measurement of stress, Fletcher (1988), in a review of the epidemiology of occupational stress, concludes that psychological factors are 'probably' an important category of stressor in the workplace, experienced by a large percentage of the workforce at any one time; and 'the major sectors of the workforce under strain are those in low level jobs with little support and discretion (or job autonomy)' (p. 38). Thus, organizations with high percentages of employees from lower socio-economic groups can expect to have increased incidence of physical and mental ill-health. Davidson and Cooper's (1992) work suggests that women in the workforce also can expect higher levels of ill-health.

Managing stress in organizations

A number of authors have sought to classify organizational responses to stress. Matteson and Ivancevich (1987) distinguish between preventive and curative strategies. Murphy (1988) categorizes three responses: primary or stressor reduction, which targets policy and working practices, such as increasing worker participation in decision-making; secondary or stress management, which seeks to reduce the likelihood of problem development in the worker; and tertiary, which refers to help for employees in distress, for example, an EAP. Clarkson (1990) adds a fourth domain in which the organization is the client, and its philosophy and policies are viewed as potential stressors for the individual and the community in which the employee lives.

An alternative view is to consider a longitudinal or developmental approach in which the focus or type of help might evolve over time. Bull (1992) provides a model based on an historical account of employee assistance:

1 *Disease stage* Stress and its manifestations are medicalized. Employees are ill and have to be 'treated'. Many American EAPs, particularly those focusing on chemical dependency, adopt this approach.
2 *Employee stage* As a result of the advent of short-term psychological therapies in the post-World War Two years, employees are now encouraged to identify and meet their own needs. Life events and experiences are seen as normal rather than evidence of psychopathology or illness.
3 *Employee–work stage* The workplace is acknowledged as influencing individual and organizational well-being: for example, the design of work tasks, noise pollution, physical proximity of workers. This marks a significant shift from viewing distress as being solely the responsibility of the individual.
4 *Company as client stage* Organizations' policies and philosophies influence the individual, community and the planet, for example, reviewing shift working patterns, noise pollution or reviewing uses of endangered natural raw materials.

In all the above, stress can be understood from one of three perspectives: stimulus, response, integration (Sutherland and Cooper 1990), and each will have an impact on the practical ways in which stress will be addressed within the organization.

Organizations that focus on *stimuli* will be geared towards strategies that identify and ameliorate the causes of stress, such as working conditions or dysfunctional patterns of communication. This risks ignoring ways in which individuals and the organization respond to stressors. The second type will be oriented towards these *responses*, and will seek to remove stress once it is present, for example, work-based counselling services. Third, an *integrational* approach seeks to combine elements of the two, but specifically seeks to explore and understand the subjective experience and meaning of stress.

There are a number of ways in which organizations address the issue of stress: using welfare and occupational health resources; referral to personnel; informal counselling by managers or colleagues; time off to 'sort things out'; disciplinary action; ignoring difficulties; or referral to an internal or external counselling/EAP (MIND 1992; Wheeler and Lyon 1992). MIND (1992) asked UK companies about the perceived causes, consequences and responses to stress at work. The most popular responses were individually focused, giving employees time off (47 per cent) or referral to an external professional counsellor (35 per cent). These findings were supported by Wheeler and Lyon.

Karasek (1992) evaluated 19 studies of stress prevention in the workplace from around the world, and covering a wide range of occupations, such as manufacture, chemicals, service and public sector. His study did not exclusively review individually focused studies but also considered environmental strategies dealing with stress. They were grouped as follows:

- Work environment focus: strategic – such as legislative changes.
- Work environment focus: worker participatory processes – for example, improving problem-solving skills for car assembly workers.
- Work reorganization: expert guided – one initiative studied a shift work change programme for police force.
- Task and work organization: worker participatory processes – this included a project to improve communication in stress-loaded roles among supervisors.
- Task and work organization restructuring: expert guided – for instance, a job enrichment programme to improve learning by doing for assembly workers.
- Person based coping enhancement programmes: expert guided – for example, introducing counselling into a large service industry.

The study identified a number of factors associated with programme success:

- Level of effort – success is generally proportional to the amount of effort put into a programme. All but one of the programmes studied sought to change the work environment rather than focus on the distressed individual.
- Level of management and labour support – the degree of joint support appeared significant in determining programme success. However, union-initiated programmes were more successful than those implemented by management alone.
- Level of worker participation or expert guidance – programmes with strong worker participation in planning or implementation were most successful.
- Type of occupation – four different occupational categories were identified: a) skilled craft/operator, where significant changes were made by combining technical change and developing social processes, for example, discussion groups; b) manager/professional, which reported little change, although many of the programmes for these groups were person-based, such as counselling; c) clerical workers/service (low level), where substantial changes were made, often involving technical changes in the work process; and d) unskilled, which was identified as a potentially very stressful group because of low job discretion (see above) and high workload and physical demands. Person-based programmes showed little effect on working conditions.

- Team composition – projects should contain personnel with skills and knowledge relevant to the change being implemented and the change or outcome criteria. Thus, a team implementing technological change to reduce stress in a manufacturing plant should probably have an engineer on the team, and a doctor/psychologist/nurse if stress is being construed (and measured) in relation to aspects of health.

Karasek (1992) identified joint employee/management support as the most significant factor in the level of success. However, Karasek (1992) and Murphy (1988) found that labour and management can have quite different reasons for introducing stress reduction strategies. According to Karasek, unions identified the reduction of worker stress or illness *per se* as the main reason, whereas managers' reasons included improving employee health; to help employees learn better coping strategies; to reduce absenteeism and turnover; and to avoid company liability for worker compensation claims – stress is one of the fastest growing areas of worker compensation claims (Jee and Reason 1988).

Finally, a number of variables were identified that appear to affect the degree to which programmes become self-sustaining after the research period has been completed:

Facilitating

- enhancing self-worth through a climate that normalizes distress, that is, employees are not victimized or blamed for experiencing stress;
- worker groups are integral to the change process;
- management provides the necessary economic and technical resources to instigate change.

Inhibiting

- programmes that treat individual symptoms when the environment has been identified as the source of stress;
- technical-only solutions that attend to task matters only, rather than process factors, and are imposed by management without fullest worker participation;
- management retains control of the dialogue by inhibiting formation of discussion groups, or limits the group's 'awareness potential', such as where the goals are to learn coping skills rather than implement real change strategies.

Responding to stress

What can be done when the causes, consequences and management of stress appear to be widespread and unknown? Stress is a very real individual and organizational issue, but it would be misleading to treat it solely in terms of psychological causes and manifestations. Stress, it has been argued, also arises in the environment, and bringing about change within the environment can resolve problems. Stress is neither an individual nor an environmental issue, the two affect each other.

An overview of stress management strategies can be found in Sutherland and Cooper (1990), Cunningham (1994), and Ross and Altmaier (1994). It would be convenient to be able to present a checklist of particular techniques for specific situations. Unfortunately, research into stress in organizations is far from conclusive. Workplace stress management studies 'have so far failed to deliver what they have promised' (Reynolds and Briner 1994: 75). This is not necessarily an indictment of stress management techniques *per se* but it is a criticism of the ad hoc manner in which they are often applied.

All strategies dealing with stress should begin with an assessment of need, attending to the unique demands of the moment, rather than relying on a toolbox of techniques to throw at the problem. Through proper assessment it is possible to design realistic and meaningful stress reduction strategies. From the foregoing discussion it is possible to construct a framework for providing help in organizations, and to identify a series of steps to be used when designing and implementing stress reduction strategies:

Framework for providing help in organizations

1 *Focus*
   The individual: sick or healthy, personal or work problems.
   The individual/work interface.
   Working practices.
   The organization – philosophy, policies, role in the community and its impact on the environment.
2 *Functions*
   Primary: problem identification – understanding the situation and implementing strategies to lessen likelihood of problem development.
   Secondary: problem management – strategies to reduce/eliminate a known and present problem.
   Tertiary: problem containment – managing as effectively as possible known, present and chronic problems.
3 *Services*
   Person-focused: counselling – information and advice, training, health promotion.
   Task-focused: content – ergonomics, job redesign.
   Task-focused: process – communications, team composition.
   Work organization – patterns of working, career ladders.

Organization as client – relationship to community, philosophy, working with the boss.

Step 1

This is the assessment of need to identify the extent and the nature of the problem. Prior to this, a commitment to addressing the problem must be present, and the costs of alternative stress reduction strategies should be investigated (Soo Kim 1988). Any existing strategies should be reviewed to assess their suitability for expansion. For example, a counselling service could be provided by an occupational health department with nurses trained as counsellors at marginal extra costs compared to introducing a new counselling service.

Employees should also be consulted about what sorts of strategies they would like to see in place. Anecdotal evidence suggests that many stress reduction strategies occur by chance. For example, a director implements an initiative to address major causes of morbidity and mortality, such as cardiovascular disease, cancer and stress. This is laudable and will undoubtedly have benefits. The issues that are pertinent to the workforce might, however, be quite different. They might be more interested in having crèche facilities, for instance. It is conceivable that the employees are addressing the problems of cardiovascular disease, cancer and stress away from work. Thus, the rate of return on a potentially expensive investment is marginal.

The same director might have paid attention to the general 'buzz' of topics within the organization. From this the seed of an initiative may be planted that, with assessment, may turn into a scheme that has real meaning for the organization and its employees. For example, the 'buzz' might be that employees want a counselling service. The personnel director assumes this to mean a request for a service focusing on personal problems but closer inspection reveals that what is wanted is a service that addresses personal *and* work-related issues.

It will be necessary to enlist key people on to the project team. In most organizations the size and complexity of organizational stress should dissuade any one individual from believing it can be tackled alone. Group membership should be determined by:

- the perceived nature of stress, that is, how it is to be measured;
- the anticipated manner in which it will be addressed, such as changes in shift patterns, technological changes or those with an employee focus;
- stakeholders in the process, that is, union representatives, managers, workers' groups (from all levels) to meet independently and feed back to the project team.

Existing strategies should be identified to determine whether they can be developed further or whether the introduction of a new approach jeopardizes their integrity and existence. For example, the introduction of workplace counselling might undermine a useful and valued pastoral aspect of trade union or occupational health activities.

Step 2

It is during this stage that attention should be paid to the identification of organizational myths. They may well emerge during formal and informal discussions when stories appear about how and why things are done in the organization; what the needs are of particular groups; fanciful explanations for aspects of organizational life emerge; and expressions of rationality and purposefulness are proposed. Workshops and employee discussion groups could be employed to identify myths. Graham (1984) and Reason and Rowan (1988b) discuss how narrative-based approaches to research can be used to identify the meanings people give to life events – see also Boje *et al.* (1982).

Step 3

Having identified a strategy and agreed its goals, a method of monitoring its implementation should be agreed. This is not an evaluation but it should ensure that the strategy is working towards its objectives; provide support for those implementing the strategy; and give feedback to the project team about how it is being perceived and utilized. For example, a medium-sized organization in the service industry instigated a breast cancer screening programme for its female employees over 35 years of age, approximately 65 per cent of its workforce. Patterns of working, a large geographical dispersal and poor personnel records that made it difficult to identify who was over 35 years, necessitated giving the project a five-year life. By the end of year three, 90 per cent of the original target group had been screened. Of the remaining 10 per cent, a number had retired, some refused to take part and there had been a move to less expensive female employees under 35 years. Although it had been a valued initiative, it no longer met its objectives. It had also begun to cause problems because the younger women wanted access to what they believed to be an important benefit.

Step 4

This is the consolidation phase. The strategy has matured and is running smoothly, early 'teething' problems having been dealt with. However, this can bring complacency, resulting in the team resting on its achievements. To offset this, a rotating monitoring group might be employed, such as changing one-third of its membership once a year.

An important function for the monitoring group is to ensure that the project's original objectives are still relevant. For instance, a manufacturing industry in the north of England implemented a stress watch programme, to raise awareness of stress and provide basic stress management skills. It transpired that the people contracted in to run the programme used language that had little relevance to the majority of the workforce. Attendance at the sessions declined and the occupational health department, which had introduced the programme, lost a considerable amount of hard-worked-for goodwill. The monitoring committee were able to discuss this and implement changes to make the strategy more effective.

Worker discussion groups can be used to reduce the risk of valuable resources being underutilized by providing feedback on how initiatives are progressing. This can also act as a method of evaluation, drawing on techniques used in qualitative methods of research – as an introduction, read McLeod (1994), and for more detail Reason and Rowan (1988a).

Step 5

The project is formally evaluated. Soo Kim (1988) provides a developmental model for evaluating EAPs that could be applied to many types of stress reduction strategies. Evaluation might take a quantitative form, for example, a survey or an outcome study employing before and after measures, using as a minimum design a control group and random allocation. Alternatively, a qualitative approach might be preferred, which seeks to explore employees' personal responses to the stress reduction strategy – see Step 4. The evaluation should not be the end of the process but should act as a stimulus to reassess the situation with a view to creating a new agenda for action.

Conclusion

The chapter has sought to show how providing help in organizations is not a matter of possessing a toolbox of techniques. A number of known causes of workplace stress have been highlighted and it has been suggested that culture influences the type of help provided. By identifying myths it is possible to gain an insight into the beliefs, values and assumptions upon which an organization rests. This provides the potential for designing strategies that produce long-lasting change throughout the organization. A framework for identifying stress in organizations has been presented, plus a step-by-step guide for implementing a course of action.

It is often thought that stress and its management is a psychological issue, but this is only one way to conceptualize it. The way work is designed and structured, conditions of work, physical environment and noise pollution, for example, can be causative agents. Focusing on psychological manifestations and consequences alone is not always sufficient. Karasek (1992) showed how a number of non-psychological approaches were used to reduce stress.

Working with myths should identify deep-seated objections or resistances to change, just as counsellors should do with their clients. As with individual clients, the helper in an organization must have the greatest respect for these defences because they are present for very good reasons (if unknown). They exist to protect unacceptable or unpleasant thoughts, beliefs, values, feelings or behaviours, and simply smashing them down will be resisted. If this is the case the scope to disentangle the knots of troubled inner experiences or organizational life will be limited.

A consequence of this fear is that organizations, like individual clients, have the right not to change. No strategy is guaranteed success, and sometimes the reality is that no change is going to occur. Such an eventuality will itself have repercussions, possibly painful for those involved in a stress reduction project. Some might argue that it is better to press ahead and bring the edifice down if it is rotten, but as a counsellor or as a provider of help, I disagree. An analogy with clients is again helpful. It is not my role to destroy clients' psyches, their beliefs, values and assumptions. But herein lies a tension. Should I, because I am a counsellor, construe organizational stress in principally psychological terms? Are there times when direct action would be more appropriate or effective? The best hope we have, perhaps, is to act congruently, to be true to ourselves, and, as such, act as models for what we believe to be fair and equable.

References

Agyris, C. and Schön, D. (1978) *Organisational Learning: A theory of action perspective*. Reading, MA: Addison-Wesley.

APA (1987) *Diagnostic and Statistical Manual of Mental Disorders* (3rd edn). Washington DC: American Psychiatric Association.

Black, D., Morris, J.N., Smith, C. and Townsend, P. (1990) The Black Report (report on the inequalities in health), in P. Townsend and N. Davidson (eds) *Inequalities in Health*. Harmondsworth: Penguin.

Boje, D.F., Fedor, D.B. and Rowland, K.M. (1982) Myth making: A qualitative step in OD interventions. *The Journal of Applied Behavioral Science*, 18(1): 17–28.

Brown, A. (1995) *Organisational Culture*. London: Pitman.

Bull, A.D. (1992) Confidential counselling service. A new breed of EAP?, *Employee Counselling Today*, 4(2): 25–8.

Clarkson, P. (1990) The scope of 'stress' counselling in organisations. *Employee Counselling Today*, 2(4): 3–6.

Cooper, C.L. and Kell, M. (1993) Occupational stress in head teachers. A national UK study. *British Journal of Educational Psychology*, 63: 130–43.

Cooper, C.L. and Marshall, J. (1976) Occupational sources of stress. A review of the literature relating to coronary disease and mental ill-health. *Journal of Occupational Psychology*, 49: 11–28.

Cooper, C.L., Cooper, R.D. and Eaker, L.H. (1986) *Living With Stress*. Harmondsworth: Penguin.

Cunningham, G. (1994) *Effective Employee Assistance Programmes*. London: Sage.

Davidson, M.J. and Cooper, C.L. (1992) *Shattering the Glass Ceiling: The woman manager*. London: Chapman.

Fletcher, B.C. (1988) The epidemiology of occupational stress, in C.L. Cooper and R. Payne (eds) *Causes, Coping and Consequences of Stress at Work*. Chichester: John Wiley.

Graham, H. (1984) Surveying through stories, in C. Bell and H. Roberts (eds) *Social Researching: Politics, problems, practice*. London: Routledge, Kegan and Paul.

Handy, C. (1985) *Understanding Organisations*. Harmondsworth: Penguin.

Haynes, S.G., Feinlieb, M. and Eaker, E.D. (1981) Type A behaviour and ten year incidence of coronary heart disease in the Framingham heart study, in R.H. Rosenman (ed.) *Psychosomatic Risk Factors and Coronary Heart Disease: Indication for specific preventative therapy*. Berne: Hans Buber.

HMSO (1988) *Mental Health at Work*. London: HMSO.

Hollway, W. (1991) *Work Psychology and Organisational Behaviour*. London: Sage.

Jee, M. and Reason, L. (1988) *Action on Stress*. London: Health Education Authority.

Jenkins, R. (1993) Defining the problem: Stress, depression and anxiety: Causes and consequences, in R. Jenkins and D. Warman (eds) *Promoting Mental Health Policies in the Workplace*. London: HMSO.

Karasek, R. (1992) Stress prevention through work reorganization: A summary of 19 international case studies. *Conditions of Work Digest*, 11(2): 23–41.

Kets de Vries, M.F.R. and Miller, D. (1984) *The Neurotic Organisation*. San Francisco: Jossey-Bass.

Lane, D. (1990) Counselling psychology in organisations. *The Psychologist: Bulletin of the British Psychological Society*, 12: 540–4.

McLeod, J. (1994) *Doing Counselling Research*. London: Sage.

Matteson, M.T. and Ivancevich, J.M. (1987) Individual stress management interventions. Evaluation of techniques. *Journal of Managerial Psychology*, 2: 24–30.

Milligan, S. and Clare, A. (1993) *Depression and How to Survive It*. London: Ebury Press.

MIND (1992) *The MIND Survey: Stress at work*. London: MIND.

Murphy, L. (1988) Workplace interventions for stress reduction and prevention, in C.L. Cooper and R. Payne (eds) *Causes, Coping and Consequences of Stress at Work*. Chichester: John Wiley.

Nevis, E.C. (1987) *Organizational Consulting: A Gestalt approach*. New York: Gestalt Institute of Cleveland Press.

Nijsmans, M. (1992) *A Dionysian way to organisational effectiveness*, in M. Stein and J. Hollvitz (eds) *Psyche at Work: Workplace applications of Jungian analytical psychology*. Wilmette, IL: Chiron.

North, F., Syme, S.L., Feeney, A., Head, J., Shipley, M.J. and Marmot, M.G. (1993) Explaining socio-economic differences in sickness absence. The Whitehall II study. *British Medical Journal*, 306: 361–6.

Reason, P. and Rowan, J. (eds) (1988a) *Human Inquiry: A sourcebook of new paradigm research*. Chichester: John Wiley.

Reason, P. and Rowan, J. (1988b) Storytelling as inquiry, in P. Reason and J. Rowan (eds) *Human Inquiry: A sourcebook of new paradigm research*. Chichester: John Wiley.

Reed, M. (1992) *The Sociology of Organisations: Themes, perspectives and prospects*. Hemel Hempstead: Simon and Schuster.

Reynolds, S. and Briner, R.B. (1994) Stress management at work: With whom and to what ends? *British Journal of Guidance and Counselling*, 22(1): 75–89.

Reynolds, S. and Shapiro, D.A. (1991) Stress reduction in transition. Conceptual problem in the design, implementation and evaluation of worksite stress management interventions. *Human Relations*, 44(3): 717–33.

Ross, R. and Altmaier, E. (1994) *Intervention in Occupational Stress*. London: Sage.

Sadu, G., Cooper, C. and Allison, T. (1989) A Post Office initiative to stamp out stress. *Personnel Management*, August: 41–5.

Selye, H. (1956) *The Stress of Life*. New York: McGraw-Hill.

Soo Kim, D. (1988) Assessing employee assistance programs: Evaluation typology and models. *Employee Assistance Quarterly*, 3(3–4): 169–88.

Sutherland, V.I. and Cooper, C.L. (1990) *Understanding Stress*. London: Chapman and Hall.

Van Oudtshoorn, L. (1989) *The Organisation as a Nurturing Environment*. Oxford: Van Oudtshoorn Associates.

Warr, P. (1987) *Psychology at Work*. Harmondsworth: Penguin.

Wheeler, S. and Lyon, D. (1992) Employee benefits for the employer's benefit. How companies respond to employee stress. *Personnel Review*, 21(7): 47–65.

3

Conflict at work

○ LIZ FRIEDRICH

In 1993 the Minister of Health announced that for every 1,000 employees, between 200 and 300 a year would suffer from depression and anxiety. In 1995 the Royal College of Psychiatrists published a pack for employers, *Depression in the Workplace*, as part of their campaign 'Defeat Depression'. In the spring of 1995 the Tavistock Clinic in London ran a conference, 'The Politics of Attachment', bringing together politicians, psychologists, social planners and educationalists to look at John Bowlby's idea that security is the key to human well-being.

In a work intriguingly entitled *The Path Less Chosen: Giving friendship priority over commodities* (Lane 1994), an American professor put forward the view that the feeling of malaise and the failure to experience the 'feel-good' effect of economic recovery together with the increase in depression, especially in younger people, were attributable to the insecurity and loss of sustaining friendships that have followed from the economic changes that are shaping our lives.

These are all indications of a growing concern for the quality of human relationships at work and their importance in maintaining well-being in the workplace, at a time when working patterns are changing dramatically and old certainties are vanishing.

There is a good deal of literature about the nature and functioning of organizations. Much of the early work in the UK was developed at the Tavistock Institute in the 1960s. The next three decades saw a growing literature developing a variety of models of organizational functioning, summarized by Morgan (1986), and Pugh and Hickson (1989). Perhaps the most widely read and accessible analysis of organizations is *Understanding Organizations* (Handy 1992).

While organizational analysts have consulted organizations and groups within organizations, counsellors and therapists have only relatively recently become involved in working with individuals and groups in organizational settings. The employee assistance programmes in the USA, which, as this book shows, grew up to deal primarily with the problems of excessive alcohol consumption, generated little literature that is directly relevant to the much broader-based counselling programmes which are developing in the UK. This is especially true of areas which have only begun to be explored extensively in the last few years: harassment and bullying. Much of what follows therefore draws on reports by professional bodies and trade unions and on anecdotal experience.

Types of conflict

The relationships at work between colleagues, between managers and staff, between the individual and the organization, can provide support, a sense of shared experience, the satisfaction of shared achievement, pleasure in developing talents, and may form the basis of friendship outside work.

A degree of conflict is inevitable at times in any relationship. Provided the conflict is short-lived and is experienced in an environment of trust and shared goals, it can be creative and healthy. Where conflict is acknowledged and differences are worked through, they can lead to stronger working relationships and a greater trust.

When conflict is chronic and especially when it is covert as when, for example, it is expressed through rumour and gossip or the exclusion from the group of an individual who is perceived as different, it can lower morale and the performance of both the individual and the workforce.

Conflict which takes the form of harassment or bullying is distressing and sometimes disabling for the employee, and can also be very serious for the employer. Despite the recession, cutbacks in jobs, an increase in part-time work and short-term contracts, the process (formal and informal) of establishing individual rights has continued, with employees increasingly prepared to take their employer to court to sue for damages caused by stress, for constructive dismissal or to claim harassment. Both managers and counsellors need to keep these developments in mind when considering individual cases.

Conflict with the organization

Breaking the overt 'rules' of an organization, often set down in the contract of employment and/or the policies of the organization invariably leads to some form of disciplinary response. In cases of gross misconduct, failure to carry out tasks or procedures, repeated absence from work or revealing to the public confidential information about the organization, the issues are usually clear-cut.

Most organizations of any size have a disciplinary procedure. Although it often refers to the process as involving 'counselling' this is not the activity referred to in this book. It is a misnomer for investigating, remonstrating and invoking sanctions.

Sometimes the rules are broken not through self-interest, incompetence or criminal intent but through a conflict between the individual's personal beliefs and the culture of the organization. At a time when all organizations are looking to trim costs and maximize profits, employees may feel that values and standards have changed and no longer fit their personal values. Thus in recent years there have been a number of examples of 'whistleblowers' who have felt it their duty to alert the public to what they see as dangerous or unethical practices in areas where they work: doctors and nurses who have denounced dangerously falling standards in the health service; employees working in the nuclear industry who have been concerned about safety; civil servants who have leaked information about dubious government deals.

Such is the growth of these kinds of concerns that there is now a charity – Public Concern at Work – which provides advice and assistance to employees who have serious concerns about public danger and malpractice within the organizations where they work. It also offers support to employers setting up procedures for employees to raise serious concerns without fear of victimization.

A manager dealing with a whistleblower may feel caught between loyalty to the organization, concern about his own position and a degree of sympathy with the individual. He may feel that his role in the organization precludes anything other than a formal disciplinary approach.

A counsellor working with an individual who is thinking of breaking, or has already broken, the organization's rules does not have this ambivalent role. Even if the counsellor is employed by the organization she should be operating within a code of confidentiality that requires her to break confidence only when she believes actions of the client would be a danger to himself or others (BAC 1993). This is usually interpreted to refer to suicide or serious physical injury to others. Whatever the counsellor's personal views, it is not her role either to encourage or discourage the employee, only to help him or her explore fully the consequences – personal, organizational and political of any planned action, not least that the employee is almost certainly putting his job at risk.

An employee's conflict with the organization may also arise from personal characteristics not fitting in with those of the organization. Handy (1992) defines four types of culture: power, role, task, people. Thus an individual whose work style is predominantly task-oriented might be unhappy in a role culture. An employee may feel she does not 'fit' with the organization but not have a way to describe it. A theoretical framework to describe the structure of the organization enables the counsellor to work with the employee to explore and define the dissatisfaction and clarify what changes are necessary or possible for the employee.

Structure as a source of conflict

Problems which taken at face value appear to be interpersonal difficulties between individuals may have a large structural component. For historical reasons the formal lines of responsibility may bear little relation to the way work is actually organized.

For example: a secretary comes to the workplace counsellor complaining that she cannot get on with her boss, the assistant head of department. The difficulties may hinge on problems such as: unreasonable demands by the boss or the secretary's inability to organize her work, or different (unspoken) assumptions of boss and secretary about what the job involves. However, it is always useful to start by asking about the formal relationships in the work group. They are best expressed schematically. A diagram representing the relationships can quickly highlight difficulties. When questioned the secretary in this example reveals that she works for not one, but at least three people.

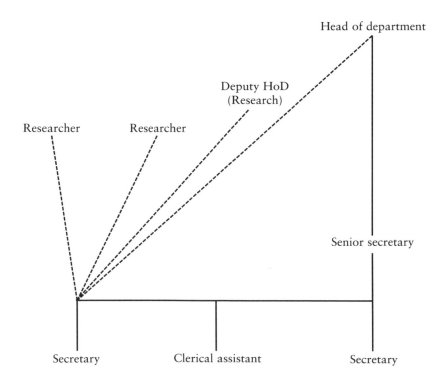

The secretary's immediate boss is the senior secretary – perhaps given this role to recognize long service or provide an increment – but she has no real control over the work of the secretary, though she sometimes asks her to cover her own work in her absence. The secretary works mainly for the assistant head of department – he does not, however, qualify for a secretary entirely to himself and she also works for two researchers who produce work sporadically but always need it done immediately. Sometimes even the head of department will ask her to do some work if the senior secretary is busy.

The senior secretary has no formal relationship with the three people who generate most of the work and no role in prioritizing it. So the secretary who is the most junior person with least power has the responsibility for trying to please everyone, and may well blame herself as well as being blamed by others for expressing conflicts that arise not from her personal qualities, but from the way her job is structured.

In this situation the counsellor has to help the client (the secretary) see the whole situation: is the job do-able as it stands? What changes would make it possible? Who would have to initiate them? Whom can she influence? What changes in her own behaviour might effect a change? Are there skills she needs to develop? If the situation is intolerable and she feels change is impossible, what are her options for changing her job inside or outside the organization?

Situations such as this are often allowed to continue in the vain hope that they will somehow resolve themselves, or else the individual is blamed for not being able to make an impossible situation work. In the example above, helping the secretary improve her assertion and time management skills will undoubtedly be useful but will not solve the intrinsic organizational problem.

In this example the secretary presented the counsellor with a clearly work-related problem. Sometimes individuals successfully manage their intrinsically unmanageable workload by working extra hours, not taking holidays, taking work – and anxiety – home and they then present to the counsellor with relationship problems which can result from this. The counsellor should be sure to explore fully the context of the problem, organizational as well as personal.

Groups and even whole departments can experience similar problems when they are involved in more than one function supplying services or information to different parts of the organization or sharing facilities with others. Again the problem can only be resolved by making lines of responsibility clear and having clear procedures to set priorities and settle disputes. While the counsellor cannot be an advocate for the individual or group, unless specifically asked to act in a consultative role, she can still help them decide what action they need to take and with whom.

Group norms

As well as the formal structure of an organization or department there is also an informal one: groups or individuals who have assumed power that does not necessarily relate to their place in the organization; groups who set norms and on the basis of these, include or exclude others. They can wield considerable power which, because it is not formalized, can be difficult or even impossible to challenge (Egan 1994).

Work groupings form around actual or assumed common beliefs, interests and activities as well as other factors such as age, religion, race, gender, sexual orientation and social background. These groups can provide great support for those inside them but the more cohesive the group the greater its power to exclude and isolate. And their function is not just social: they will discuss and influence the way in which work is carried out, so the exclusion of an individual can have more than personal consequences (Edelmann 1993).

An employee who seeks help in joining a new group or who feels he is being excluded by a group will usually see the group as a homogeneous entity but the norms are set by the most powerful individuals, either the most dominant or the most numerically powerful. A group is seldom as cohesive as it seems. There will be individuals who subscribe to the norms simply to avoid exclusion. Not all policemen are equally keen to drink in the pub after work or to discuss football. Not all female teachers are married, or if they are they do not all want to discuss their husbands and/or children, etc. New alliances around differently identified interests are always possible. Once the outsider can begin seeing the group as a collection of individuals, some of whom will have common interests with him, he will feel less powerless.

Sometimes, however, the group and the individual simply do not fit together. Angela, a secretary, was 56. She had been 'advised' to see a workplace counsellor because she was perceived as 'stressed'.

Angela saw her stress as stemming from the fact that the managers in her department, all considerably younger than her, seemed to reject all her attempts to 'keep up the standards of work' (that of others as well as her own) and were increasingly sidelining her into work that made little use of her skills and experience. She found it difficult to restrain herself from commenting on both the way that work was being done and the way she felt she was being treated. She could not afford to retire early with a reduced pension and knew she was unlikely to find another job.

The counsellor felt that Angela's belief that the group, encouraged by the managers, saw her as an anachronism was probably fairly accurate. At a deeper level it was possible that Angela was carrying for the group a tension it was unable to express: the difficulties of working with fewer staff and a smaller budget, and attempting to retain the quality of work.

Since it was Angela and not the group who was the client, the counsellor focused on helping Angela explore whether she really believed she could change the group; how her behaviour might reinforce their view of her; and, as she felt unable to leave the job, explore ways in which she could concentrate her skills, experience and creativity on activities outside work.

There are times when a whole group presents as a client wanting to deal with some kind of conflict within the group. Groups, especially in public service, will often ask for a 'support group'. The group may have problems centring around interpersonal relationships, organizational change, work itself or any combination of these.

A manager contemplating setting up such a group, or a counsellor thinking of facilitating one, needs to be very clear about: the membership of the group; what problem the group wants to address; what outcome is wanted; should there be a limited number of sessions; how will they be reviewed; what is the relationship between the group and its work and between the group and the organization? All these questions need to be addressed otherwise the group can become simply a vehicle for expressing dissatisfaction and frustration and its members impotent victims. In an effective group, its members will not only be contained but also challenged to explore and understand issues which concern them so they manage their situation differently (Hawkins and Miller 1994).

In dealing with groups, the counsellor needs to be aware of group processes and to have available techniques for conflict resolution: systemic theories (Campbell *et al.* 1991) and transactional analysis (Wagner 1981; Hay 1992) offer useful approaches.

Conflict between individuals

Where conflict between individuals takes the form of open disagreement about an issue there is the possibility of dealing with it and arriving at a compromise. If it is left unresolved, by the time it comes to the attention of a manager or is brought to a counsellor it will have accrued all kinds of stories and beliefs.

If a manager is asked to arbitrate in a difficulty she may consider it appropriate to impose some or all of the solution but it is more likely to stick if it can be negotiated, and facilitating a discussion between the two parties may be the appropriate way to do this.

A counsellor has no authority to impose a solution but has the skills to help both parties, if they are willing to come together, to explore the nature of the conflict. What is the history behind the issue which has triggered the crisis? Is this crisis a culmination of other incidents? Does all or part of the problem stem from organizational problems? What are the belief systems of each? Have both parties taken up positions where they now automatically assume the other is out to thwart or attack them?

Working with both parties to the dispute is likely to be the quickest way to move to a resolution. The results can sometimes be dramatic. Bill was the manager of a large department. He consulted a counsellor because he was concerned about the bad relationship between two of his supervisors, Greg and Jane. They needed to co-operate about arrangements that involved customers but could barely bring themselves to speak to one another. The counsellor had two meetings several weeks apart with Bill and the two members of staff.

It was quickly apparent that both Jane and Greg had made genuine overtures to one another in the past but they had not been seen as such and both had now retreated into a defensive and hostile stance. They seemed to share a belief that their difficulties must be 'someone's fault' and neither wanted to accept the blame. The counsellor acknowledged how hard each had tried and how distressed and hurt each of them seemed. She suggested that it was no one's 'fault', rather a circular system where each difficulty confirmed and shaped their views of one another.

Both Greg and Jane were visibly moved and relieved. In feeling understood and listened to they were also able to begin to see one another in a different way. They negotiated some agreed minimum goals: saying good morning when they met, speaking to one another directly to make arrangements, not sending messages or messengers. They were advised to attempt only minimal improvements so that goals seemed achievable. By the second meeting it was apparent that things were much improved. These improvements continued over the next few months and they needed only one further meeting with the counsellor.

Allowing people to discuss difficulties in a neutral, non-judgemental setting can be extremely helpful. Asking questions about how and who, what and when and 'if this . . . then what?' helps the counsellor and the clients see connections between beliefs, behaviour and relationships, and to explore alternative ways of seeing and doing things differently (Campbell *et al.* 1991). Asking 'why?' tends to keep the focus on the past.

It is important to consider the context of such meetings and who should be invited to attend on the basis of who is affected by the problem. In the situation described above, although Bill did not contribute a great deal to the actual discussion, his presence was important in establishing how seriously he took the situation and in making it clear that it could not continue. He was involved in setting the goals.

When only one person comes to counselling, the other party can be made 'present' by the counsellor constantly asking 'And how would he see that? What would he say or do in that situation? How do other people respond to him, what would they say?', etc.

The aim of the work is to help the client develop some understanding of her own beliefs and the role she herself is playing; to recognize what change might be achievable and what may have to be tolerated. She can then decide what changes in her own behaviour will be useful to alter the dynamics of the situation.

Harassment

> Harassment is unwanted behaviour which others find intimidating, embarrassing, humiliating or offensive. It can occur in many different forms, including:
>
> - physical conduct – unwanted contact including unnecessary touching, patting or pinching, bullying, assault or physical threat;
> - verbal conduct – bullying, threats, abuse, unwelcome sexual advances, propositions for sexual activity, innuendo, mockery, unwanted remarks or jokes;
> - display or circulation of sexually or racially offensive material;
> - use of derogatory sexual or racial stereotypes.
>
> All members of staff have the right not to have to put up with such behaviour, however trivial it may seem to others.

The above is the definition of harassment spelt out in the policy of the Advisory Conciliation and Arbitration Service – *Harassment at Work* – for its own staff (ACAS 1993).

The GMB union, in its model harassment agreement, reflects the growing tendency to identify a very broad range of possible characteristics that might be the focus of harassment, extending the definition to include:

> conduct related to age, creed, disability, nationality, race, religion, sex, sexual orientation or any other personal characteristic and which is unwanted by the recipient or affects the dignity of any individual or groups of individuals at work.
>
> (quoted in Labour Research Department 1994: 30)

Harassment, they suggest, 'may be intentional or unintentional'; harassment may also be seen as exclusion from work or social activities; failure to give promotion and to provide opportunities for training.

Although examples can be given of what may constitute harassment, unlike any other behaviour proscribed by an organization, it is primarily defined by the person who experiences it. Harassment is 'conduct which is imposed . . . It is unwanted, unreciprocated and regarded as offensive by the recipient' (TUC 1991).

Much has been made in the press of the idea that quite 'innocent' people, usually men, might find themselves accused of, for example, sexual harassment for having paid a compliment to a female employee. A survey of 132 employers (Industrial Relations Services 1992) suggested that when complaints of harassment were investigated, nine out of ten were upheld and several employers pointed out that those not upheld were not necessarily found to be false, rather there was simply insufficient evidence.

Charges of sexual harassment are seldom brought on the basis of an isolated incident unless it is something flagrant such as physical molestation. Complaints are usually made only after a series of incidents in which it has been made clear to the harasser that the harassed person is embarrassed, upset or at the very least unresponsive to the behaviour. It may sometimes continue because the harasser is insensitive to the distress being caused, but more usually it is an abuse of power where the harasser enjoys the discomfiture of his or her victim and it frequently occurs where the harasser is in a more powerful position than the victim.

Harassment can be seen as having its roots in social attitudes and prejudice. Both individuals and groups can act out of unthinking prejudice. Often harassment is disguised, as 'just a joke'. While the unacceptable behaviour will be condemned by some of the workforce, the harasser will almost certainly have allies who will agree that it is all 'a fuss about nothing'. Bullying can be seen as a more flagrant abuse of power and seems to have its roots in an individual's psychopathology rather than social attitudes (Adams 1992). It is therefore discussed separately.

The extent of sexual and racial harassment

There have been a number of surveys into sexual harassment. In a survey of 1,700 employees it was found that over half of working women and 7 per cent of men had experienced sexual harassment (Industrial Society 1992). Although cases where men have been harassed by women, or where women have blackmailed a male colleague with threats of claiming harassment, receive huge press publicity they are a tiny minority of reported cases as the Industrial Society figures and similar studies by trade unions and independent organizations have shown. The majority of cases are reported by women and are spread across the entire range of the female workforce.

In a survey conducted in 1987 the types of sexual harassment most commonly mentioned were sexual comments, jokes or verbal abuse. This was followed by sexist or patronizing behaviour and, third, by being touched or brushed against (Labour Research Department 1994). No profession is immune. A study by the Institute for the Study of the Legal Profession in Sheffield University (reported in the *Guardian*, 7 January 1995) showed that 40 per cent of young women barristers had experienced sexual harassment. A few months later in the same year, the paper reported that nearly half of police officers (75 per cent of them women) in Greater Manchester claimed to have been sexually harassed at work (*Guardian*, 19 April).

Despite the large numbers of women experiencing some form of sexual harassment only one in 20 in the Industrial Society survey made a formal complaint. Often an employee fears this may make the situation worse, and with some justification. In 1990 a study of over 100 organizations found that over half admitted that no action was likely to be taken against someone accused of sexual harassment (Davidson and Earnshaw 1990).

However, the situation is changing. A more recent survey of 132 employers (Industrial Relations Services 1992) showed that almost half the organizations had received complaints about sexual harassment in the year prior to the survey. There has been an increase in cases of sexual harassment reported to the Equal Opportunities Commission. Complaints more than doubled in five years, increasing from 317 in 1990 to 775 in 1994. This suggests that, as public discussion and awareness increase, employees may be more willing to report sexual harassment, and both counsellors and managers are more likely to find themselves dealing with this issue.

There is far less documentation about the extent to which lesbians and gay men are subjected to harassment. In a report, *Less Equal than Others* (Stonewall 1993), a lobbying group conducted a survey of nearly 2,000 lesbians and gay men and found that nearly half had experienced some kind of harassment at work. This was most commonly jokes and teasing (79 per cent) followed by homophobic abuse (51 per cent) and aggressive questioning (41 per cent). Threats were experienced by 14 per cent and actual physical violence by 5 per cent.

The extent of racial harassment has not been nearly as well documented as that of sexual harassment. The Commission for Racial Equality had a 27 per cent increase in the number of discrimination cases reported to them in 1992. They find that while racial abuse is a feature of many dismissal cases, it is difficult to collect precise figures for racial harassment. The organization Women Against Sexual Harassment has found that among the women they advise, those from ethnic minorities are over-represented.

The effects of harassment

Whatever the nature of the harassment the effect on its victims is the same: they feel abused, discounted, powerless, angry and often fearful and ashamed. If the harassment goes on over a period of time their work performance suffers as they develop increasing symptoms of stress: inability to concentrate, impaired judgement, depression and mood swings. They come to dread going in to work, may become physically ill and eventually may leave. The longer it continues the harder it is to confront the perpetrator(s). As the victim's self-confidence and self-esteem diminish, they may come to blame themselves for what is happening and for not being able to confront it.

Harassment is expensive for the organization in terms of reduced performance and, if the employee leaves his job, the costs of recruitment and training new staff.

Harassment and the law

Only two areas of harassment are currently covered by legislation: sexual and racial harassment. But consideration is being given at the time of writing to legislation on disability and Parliament is considering an amendment to the Sex Discrimination Act to extend it to cover discrimination on the grounds of sexual orientation.

The Race Relations Act (1976) outlawed all forms of racial discrimination and clearly included harassment. Although the Sex Discrimination Act was passed in 1975, it was not until 1984 that the case of *Porcelli* v. *Strathclyde Regional Council* established that sexual harassment constituted sex discrimination as defined under the Sex Discrimination Act of 1975.

In the areas of both sexual and racial harassment, the legislation makes the employer responsible for any acts of harassment by employees at work. If it can be shown that the employer was aware of the harassment and did nothing, as in *Tower Boot Company Ltd* v. *Jones*, where the company received complaints of racial attack, harassment and abuse against a black employee but did nothing, then the employers will have contravened the Act. Similarly, in the case of *Bracebridge Engineering* v. *Darby (1990)* the employer took no action when a woman complained of sexual assault by two male colleagues. Eventually she left her job and the industrial tribunal upheld her claim for constructive dismissal.

Where a case of unfair dismissal goes to an industrial tribunal the complainant may be reinstated or, more likely in a case of harassment, awarded compensation. The levels of such awards have been rising over recent years and often include a sum to compensate for psychological distress as well as loss of earnings. Since a ruling by the European Court, the ceiling on the level of payment has been lifted – there was previously a limit of £11,000 on compensation payments. In March 1995 a policewoman was awarded £25,000 in a case brought under the Sex Discrimination Act.

In cases of harassment the tribunal may also make a recommendation such as the harasser being moved to another building or department away from the complainant.

The European Commission has a Code of Practice on Sexual Harassment. Although this does not have the force of law, it has been established that industrial tribunals should be guided by the EC code.

Harassment policies

Employees are often unaware of the rights that legislation gives to them. Employers should of course be aware of these. Having a statement on harassment tucked away in a general commitment to equal opportunities or just as part of the disciplinary procedure is unlikely to be taken seriously by employees, and an increasing number of companies are producing specific policies on harassment. The best of these have detailed procedures for investigating complaints both informally and formally, with time-limits for different stages of a formal investigation. They also give examples of the kinds of behaviour which could constitute harassment. The Institute of Personnel and Development has published a model policy, as have several trade unions. The Institute of Personnel and Development (1993) recommends that supervisors and managers likely to be involved in the formal investigation of a complaint should receive specific training.

Trade unions are beginning to take harassment seriously, producing guidelines and training for trade union representatives. Some, such as the Banking, Insurance and Finance Union (BIFU) and the Transport and General Workers Union (TGWU) have special sexual harassment counsellors. These are not, however, necessarily trained counsellors as understood by BAC.

Dealing with complaints

Most policies stress the desirability of dealing with complaints on an informal basis if at all possible. This may mean the recipient of the harassment seeking support from a colleague, from a counsellor, a supervisor or manager to confront the person who is harassing them.

Becoming involved in a complaint of harassment is not a situation any manager welcomes: she will be hearing accusations of unpleasant behaviour against another member of her staff or one of her colleagues. A very natural response may be to query what she is hearing, to make excuses or justify the behaviour or attempt to reinterpret it. However, the person bringing the complaint may have spent many hours, weeks or months agonizing over whether to take the complaint forward: he may feel very embarrassed at discussing it at all or fear not being believed. A manager therefore needs to be sympathetic towards the complainant and their distress while remaining neutral as to what has actually happened until there has been an investigation, formal or informal.

Initially the manager must ascertain whether the complainant wants in the first instance to approach the problem informally or to go through the grievance procedure. The manager also needs to consider whether the nature of the complaint is such that it can be left to the individual to decide whether to pursue it formally, or whether it is of such a serious nature that the disciplinary procedure must be invoked. Such decisions are always difficult.

If the employee requests a formal investigation of the complaint and there are reasonable grounds for believing that harassment has occurred, then it is crucial that action is taken. If the harassment is not taken seriously or no action is taken as a result then the complainant will feel doubly abused, first by the harasser then by the organization.

Sarah, shocked and upset by an incident in which she had been sexually harassed on her way home by a fellow employee, plucked up the courage to go to the company's human resources manager. She was astonished and angry to be told that even though there had been previous complaints about this man, nothing could be 'proved' so it would be dealt with by someone 'having a word' with him. Sarah felt that the organization, apparently unable or unwilling to take any decisive action, was trivializing her experience and reinforcing her feeling of powerlessness.

If an investigation is carried out promptly and fairly and the complainant kept informed of progress, this can help the harassed person deal with their feelings about the harassment.

Absolute 'proof' in cases of harassment may be hard to find. In investigating a case, the Equal Opportunities Department of Midland Bank maintain that unlike a court of law where the evidence has to be 'beyond reasonable doubt', in investigating harassment they are looking for 'grounds for reasonable belief'.

It may be appropriate to transfer either the harasser or harassed if they have to work closely together while an investigation is carried out. The decision whether to simply give a warning or to take disciplinary action will depend on the seriousness of the offence. Whether the harasser and harassed can reasonably be expected to work together again will also depend on the seriousness of the harassment and on how it is resolved. Meeting together with a counsellor or other intermediary may be appropriate or it may be necessary to create a permanent distance between the two employees.

Harassment counselling

Some employers and some trade unions are training 'harassment counsellors' or advisers. These can provide excellent support and advice though this is not strictly speaking 'counselling' as the term is used in this book. There may also be some confusion of roles in that the harassment counsellor may also be a manager or a trade union official. In this instance they should not take any part in a formal investigation.

A counsellor from an employee assistance programme (EAP) or an internal staff counselling service can provide not only support for the distressed employee but also an opportunity to begin to make sense of, and assess, the situation.

On a practical level the counsellor needs to ensure the employee understands the company policy, if any, on harassment (a counsellor employed in a work setting should be familiar with it himself). The employee may need help in deciding how and whether to pursue their complaint.

Since the essence of harassment is the abuse of power, the complainant always feels disempowered, sometimes blaming herself for allowing the abuse to happen. The focus of the work is therefore on re-empowering and restoring self-esteem. If the employee wants to confront the harasser, the counsellor can help with assertive techniques that facilitate this, rehearsing the encounter and anticipating the harasser's response.

The harassed person may need help in deciding who to approach: a colleague, their manager, trade union representative, personnel officer. All or any of these may be appropriate and supportive but they may also have their own agenda and create additional pressures for the employee. A young woman who was being constantly nagged and criticized by several managers in the department where she worked for doing union work, and for absence due to a chronic illness, had received a series of critical letters from her boss when she was off sick and felt at the end of her tether. She found herself being pressured by the trade union to take out a formal grievance. The union had had other complaints about the boss and therefore welcomed an opportunity to take action at last. The young woman however, feeling fragile and battered by the situation, which had gone on for a long time, simply wanted a transfer to another department.

It is not only the harassed person who may need to seek counselling. The person accused of harassment, even if cleared of the accusation, will feel angry and confused. If he is disciplined or dismissed it may mean effectively the end of, or at least a great setback to, his career, and getting another job may be very difficult. Neither harassment policies nor literature on harassment have much to say about how someone accused of harassment can or should be helped.

If the harassment was known only to the two individuals involved there will be a tremendous humiliation for the perpetrator in having it revealed, not just to work colleagues but also to family and friends, some of whom may be supportive but others may withdraw.

The harassment may have been known to everyone but simply not labelled as such: 'She always picks on the new young ones but things settle down after a few months . . .', or 'He does like to make jokes about Asian lads . . . perhaps he goes a bit far sometimes but he doesn't mean anything by it.' In such cases there will be anger as well as humiliation. 'Other people make jokes, why pick on me?' 'It was only a bit of fun at the office party, no-one has ever complained before about a bit of slap and tickle . . .'

Complaints of harassment often begin to be made when social rules change. What was once acceptable or at least had to be endured is no longer so. The harasser discovers this in a very painful way and needs to make sense of the experience and his or her own behaviour. There is also a need to find ways of rebuilding relationships with colleagues and perhaps with family and friends.

It can be very difficult for a manager to have to deal with the cases of harassment and she may herself need some support and an opportunity to think through the best way of handling the situation. A counsellor who understands workplace issues can provide this. Apart from having a good understanding of the organizational aspects of harassment, it is also important that counsellors are sensitive to the issues of oppression of gays and lesbians and experiences of racism, explored in *Pink Therapy* (Davies and Neal 1996) and *Transcultural Counselling in Action* (d'Ardenne and Mahtani 1989; and in Lago and Thompson 1996).

Bullying

Bullying is a term with connotations of the playground, of one person using brute strength against another, of powerlessness and misery. In the context of the workplace it is all these things, though brute force is usually replaced by psychological tactics. Bullying has been defined as 'the improper and frequent use of power to affect someone's life adversely' (Patchett 1992: 7).

Companies with policies on harassment usually refer to the right of employees to be treated with respect both by colleagues and those in positions of authority over them, but often stop short of using the term 'bullying'. While a growing number of companies have policies on harassment, research by the Manufacturing, Science and Finance trade union (MSF), shown as part of BBC2's 'The Business Programme' on 2 June 1994, revealed that just 5 per cent of top companies had policies that referred specifically to bullying. As a result of this research the MSF, who had been involved in producing the programme, launched a campaign later that year against bullying in the workplace. They hope to promote legislation similar to that passed in Sweden in 1994 which made all harassment, especially bullying, an offence.

The extent of bullying

The idea that bullying was an issue at work was first put forward in a BBC Radio 4 programme made by Andrea Adams. The large public response to this programme led to the publication of *Bullying at Work* (Adams 1992), and increasing attention is being paid to what is appearing as a widespread phenomenon. Reporting on a more recent study of bullying in *The Therapist* Adams (1994) found nothing to suggest a decrease in the incidence of bullying. The survey carried out by Staffordshire University took a sample of over 1,000 employees under the age of 45. About half said they had personally experienced being bullied, and 78 per cent said that they had witnessed bullying at work.

What bullies do

Where does 'firm management' or the tough ethos of a company in a highly competitive industry stop and bullying begin? Clearly there is a spectrum of behaviour and management styles. What is acceptable in one industry or organization may not be so in another. The manager or counsellor who is asked to address issues of bullying must always take the context into account. But whatever the context bullies tend to have certain characteristics in common; they tend to:

- lose their temper easily and shout at staff;
- threaten demotion or dismissal;
- give vague and unclear instructions and deadlines so that the victim is set up to fail;
- take credit for the work of others;
- continually criticize and undermine subordinates, often publicly;
- arbitrarily refuse requests for leave or make changes in work arrangements;
- give poor ratings at appraisals, block promotion and training;
- take away responsibilities and diminish people's jobs.

(adapted from Adams 1992; Turnbull 1995)

All this is characterized by unpredictability. The victim will never know when they will be attacked because it seems to bear little relation to their actual work or achievements. Although the bullying will often be apparent to colleagues of the victim(s) it will typically be hidden from the bully's colleagues and superiors.

There are various theories as to why bullies behave as they do. Most authorities would agree that they are abusing power and status to camouflage or compensate for their own inadequacies. The need to control others is usually an expression of fear of lack of control of oneself. Bullies may well have been bullied themselves or have learnt to use aggression to gain attention as children (Crawford 1992).

Bullying is sometimes effectively condoned by the organization. If the organization's culture is purely results-focused, if its policies express the idea that employees need to be curbed and controlled rather than supported and encouraged, if staff are told rather than asked, if aggressive management is equated with effective management, then this is a culture where bullying can flourish.

The effects of bullying

These are similar to the effects of harassment but even more pronounced. Someone who is harassed sexually, or because of their race or religious beliefs, usually knows why they have been singled out, sees some consistency in the behaviour and has the knowledge that the behaviour is increasingly labelled as socially unacceptable. The victim of the bully can see no reason why he is being picked upon. He is confused, loses confidence, becomes fearful or even paranoid. He may begin to perform poorly, to turn his anger on himself, become depressed and even suicidal. He may fear, rightly, that it will be extremely difficult to challenge the bullying. It is likely that, when confronted, the bully will simply deny what is happening and it can prove very difficult to convince superiors. In this situation the victim may take refuge in murderous thoughts about the bully, trying to take control of the situation at a fantasy level. This does not of course change the real situation which may lead to the victim becoming ill and/or leaving.

Dealing with bullying

The discovery of bullying poses dilemmas for a manager. It may raise difficult questions about individuals and about the organization. Where an individual complains of bullying by a superior it is unlikely that the situation can be resolved so that she can remain working for the person of whom she is complaining. The options are to relocate the complainant, which may be seen as unfair and leave the bully to (probably) find another victim; or to tackle the bully. In some cases this may mean disciplinary action or even dismissal, but it may be possible, once it has been made clear that the behaviour is unacceptable, to offer work in a different area, or counselling and training to encourage insight into the behaviour and skills that are lacking.

The counsellor who deals with someone who is being bullied is confronted often with the situation of anyone in an impossible relationship. The longer it goes on, the more self-esteem is eroded and the less possible it is to take action. Normalizing the victim's response to the bullying helps the employee to gain a fresh perspective. Invariably, in attempting to make sense of the situation they will ask 'why me?', and there may well be a childhood experience of bullying which has left a vulnerability to the bully's behaviour. The counsellor may find it useful to explore this but should be wary of the victim's tendency to take their vulnerability as evidence that they were therefore responsible for the bullying and had somehow invited it.

Encouraging victims of bullying to talk to colleagues helps both to validate their experience and to get support. They should be encouraged to keep a record of events and of the effect they have both psychologically and physically. As they begin to feel a little more confident they may need help in deciding how and whether to confront the bully, whether to seek support from the trade union, Human Resources or senior manager, whether they want to take out a grievance, seek a transfer to another department or to leave.

Conflict resolution

Whatever theoretical viewpoint a counsellor brings to helping with the resolution of conflict and whatever vocabulary is used to describe the process, there are certain essential elements to it. There is a need for the counsellor and the employee(s) to analyse the conflict so that they have an understanding of its meaning and context. Parties to a conflict will usually have different views of its meaning and origin but invariably share the belief that its resolution involves one party winning and the other losing. The role of the counsellor is to help create a new way of seeing the situation and the changes that might resolve it without anyone having to 'lose'.

Sometimes it may seem appropriate as part of resolving a conflict to encourage an individual's assertion skills. There are undoubtedly useful techniques that can be learnt that help people learn to say no; deal with manipulation; handle compliments and criticism and so on. Practising these techniques successfully will undoubtedly bolster confidence, but books or courses which claim to develop these without addressing issues of self-esteem may do more harm than good. Assertion techniques cannot be simply bolted on.

A counsellor can help an employee both practise skills and rehearse situations, while at the same time exploring the issues that underlie the lack of self-esteem that leads to non-assertive behaviour.

Conclusion

Few people welcome or enjoy conflict. Tempting though it may be to ignore it in the hope that things will somehow sort themselves out this is seldom the outcome. Where conflict is persistent it invariably undermines the effectiveness of individuals and the organization. The manager who is aware of unresolved conflict first needs to acknowledge it, then persuade the parties to the conflict that it needs resolution – this may not necessarily be seen by both parties to be the case especially in cases of harassment or bullying.

Because a manager is always part of the existing system it is often appropriate to involve a third party. Another manager, someone from Human Resources, a counsellor or occupational psychologist can bring a new view to the most apparently intractable situation. Resolving conflict is always worth while and always profitable.

References

ACAS (1993) *Harassment at Work*. London: Advisory Conciliation and Arbitration Service.

Adams, A. (1992) *Bullying at Work*. London: Virago.

Adams, A. (1994) The unnecessary evil – bullying at work. *The Therapist*, Summer: 16–17.

BAC (1993) *Code of Ethics and Practice for Counsellors*. Rugby: British Association for Counselling.

Campbell, D., Draper, R. and Huffington, C. (1991) *A Systemic Approach to Consultation*. London: Karnac Books.

Crawford, N. (1992) The psychology of the bully, in A. Adams *Bullying at Work*. London: Virago.

d'Ardenne, P. and Mahtani, A. (1989) *Transcultural Counselling in Action*. London: Sage.

Davidson, M. and Earnshaw, J. (1990) Policies, practices and attitudes towards sexual harassment in UK organizations. *Personnel Review*, 19: 23–7.

Davies, D. and Neal, C. (eds) (1996) *Pink Therapy: A guide for counsellors and therapists working with lesbian, gay and bisexual clients*. Buckingham: Open University Press.

Edelmann, R. (1993) *Interpersonal Conflicts at Work*. Leicester: British Psychological Society.

Egan, G. (1994) *Working the Shadow Side*. San Francisco: Jossey-Bass.

Handy, C. (1992) *Understanding Organizations*. Harmondsworth: Penguin.

Hawkins, P. and Miller, E. (1994) Psychotherapy in and with organisations, in P. Clarkson and M. Pokorny (eds) *The Handbook of Psychotherapy*. London: Routledge.

Hay, J. (1992) *Transactional Analysis for Trainers*. Maidenhead: McGraw-Hill.

Industrial Relations Services (1992) Sexual harassment at the workplace 1 & 2. *Employment Trends*, reports nos. 513 and 514.

Industrial Society (1992) *No Offence*. London: Industrial Society.

Institute of Personnel and Development (1993) *Statement on Harassment at Work*. London: IPD.

Labour Research Department (1994) *Tackling Harassment at Work*. London: LRD.

Lago, C. with Thompson, C. (1996) *Race, Culture and Counselling*. Buckingham: Open University Press.

Lane, R. (1994) *The Path Less Chosen: Giving friendship priority over commodities*. New Haven, CT: Yale University Press.

Morgan, G. (1986) *Images of Organization*. London: Sage.

Patchett, R. (1992) Bullying at work. *Croner Employer's Briefing*, 2: 7.

Pugh, D. and Hickson, D. (1989) *Writers on Organisations*. Harmondsworth: Penguin.

Royal College of Psychiatrists (1995) *Depression in the Workplace*. London: RCP.

Stonewall (1993) *Less Equal than Others*. London: Stonewall.

TUC (1991) *Sexual Harassment at Work: TUC guidelines*. London: Trades Union Congress.

Turnbull, J. (1995) Hitting back at the bullies. *Nursing Times*, 91(3): 24.

Wagner, A. (1981) *The Transactional Manager*. Denver, CO: T.A. Communications Inc.

Suggested reading

Back, K., Back, K. and Bates, T. (1991) *Assertiveness at Work: A practical guide to handling awkward situations*. London: McGraw-Hill.

Bramson, R. (1993) *Coping with a Difficult Boss*. London: Nicholas Brealey Publishing.

Commission for Racial Equality (1995) *Racial Harassment at Work: A guide for employers*. London: CRE.

Crawley, J. (1995) *Constructive Conflict Management*. Abingdon: Nicholas Brealey Publishing.

Curtis, L. (1993) *Making Advances: What can you do about sexual harassment at work?* London: BBC Books.
Morris, S. (1993) *Sensitive Issues in the Workplace.* London: Industrial Society.
Randall, P. (1997) *Adult Bullying: Perpetrators and Victims.* London: Routledge.
Reddy, M. (1987) *The Manager's Guide to Counselling at Work.* Leicester: British Psychological Society.
Wheeler, M. (1994) *Problem People at Work and How to Deal with Them.* London: Century.

Useful organizations

Advisory, Conciliation and Arbitration Service
27 Wilton Street
London SW1X 7AY
0171 210 3000

Association for Counselling at Work (ACW)
BAC
1 Regent Place
Rugby
Warwickshire CV21 2PJ
01788 578328

Association for Gay and Bi-Sexual Psychologies (U.K.)
PO Box 7534
London NW1 0LA

Commission for Racial Equality
Elliot House
10/12 Allington Street
London SW1E 5EH
0171 828 7022

Equal Opportunities Commission
Overseas House
Quay Street
Manchester M3 3HN
0161 833 9244

Institute of Personnel and Development
IPD House
Camp Road
Wimbledon
London SW19 4UX
0181 971 9000

Lesbian and Gay Employment Rights (LAGER)
St Margaret's House
21 Old Ford Road
London E2 9PL
0181 983 0696

Public Concern at Work
Lincoln's Inn House
42 Kingsway
London WC2B 6EN
0171 404 6609

Race and Cultural Education in Counselling (RACE)
BAC
1 Regent Place
Rugby
Warwickshire CV21 2PJ
01788 578328

Women Against Sexual Harassment
5th Floor, The Wheel
Wild Court, off Kingsway
London WC2B 4AU
0171 405 0430

4

Career counselling

○ **LAIDON ALEXANDER**

Introduction

Vocational guidance for young people in the USA started in the earliest years of this century, and the National Vocational Guidance Association was founded in 1913. Career guidance for young people has been available for some time in Britain, in schools, further education and statutory settings. Employment conditions created by two world wars led psychologists to devise and refine psychometric testing techniques. There is now significant interest in computer-assisted career guidance (Watts 1989). Applied psychology including counselling techniques is used in career guidance and in recruitment interviewing, some writers endorse the usefulness of counselling skills (e.g. Millar *et al.* 1992). The view that career guidance has reached standards which are either satisfactory or scientific has its critics, however (e.g. Kidd *et al.* 1994).

Despite the need for vocational retraining for adults of all ages, and some lip-service paid to opposing ageism, understanding of career issues for adults and provision for meeting them are not yet well developed. The National Institute for Careers Education and Guidance (NICEC, founded 1975) has made attempts to address this (Watts 1980a; 1980b). Super (1981) and Pemberton *et al* (1994), among others, discuss the issues for adults, but provision is still patchy. In this chapter the hands-on experience of one career consultant is presented, with case examples, as a way of introducing general counsellors and concerned managers to some of the issues facing those who seek to help adults with career dilemmas.

What is career counselling?

Career counselling needs defining because both 'career' and 'counselling' are terms which can be misunderstood. 'Career' can mean progress upwards through an organization or within a profession; usually paid, but not necessarily so (e.g. the profession of politics in Britain before MPs received salaries). But it can also mean simply 'paid work', what people do to earn a living. Such a broader understanding of careers is appropriate for this chapter because it reflects the current reality of career counselling: helping not only people who are pursuing advancement in a profession or in management, but also, to take only a few examples, students thinking about choices of course or first jobs, workers facing redundancy, women wanting to return to work after taking time off to raise a family, and pensioners trying to adapt to retirement. Because people like students, the unemployed and pensioners, who are neither employed nor self-employed, can benefit from career counselling, we can say that the careers that career counselling deals with are not just people's working lives but their occupational lives.

Careers consist of the *activities*, *choices* and *transitions* which make up people's occupational lives; they can be categorized according to their *contexts*; and they are of psychological importance as sources of personal *identity*.

All *activities* in life can be classified as play, learning, work or recharging (feeding and resting are recharging activities), or a combination of these classifications. Careers include all these types of activity (including recharging to the extent that it is essential if one is to pursue the rest of one's career activities effectively). Careers are made up of a variety of such activities, punctuated from time to time by related *choices* (such as changes of role, direction or employer) and *transitions* (from education to employment, for instance, or from earning a living to drawing a pension).

Some career *choices* are freely made by the person concerned; others, however, may be made by the person under powerful influence; or made for him or her, whether by parents (like choice of school or sixth-form specialization), teachers, employers (job reassignment or employment termination), partners, governments or others. All career choices are subject to *constraints*, such as availability of employment, competing priorities such as family or social responsibilities, selection criteria or investment requirements (like buying a franchise); and in the same way as all choices they give rise to *consequences*, welcome and unwelcome.

Career *contexts* include: payment arrangements (paid or unpaid), regularity (full-time or part-time, casual or regular), location (inside, outside or across organizations), dynamic potential (managerial, within the management hierarchy of organizations; or professional, within professional practices or partnerships; or entrepreneurial, building businesses; they can also be static or blocked if, as for a large part of the population, significant advancement is often either not available or not sought), relationship to employer or customer (partly or wholly employed, self-employed or unemployed) and tax status (ditto).

Careers, finally, also serve as potent sources of personal *identity*. 'What are you?' is a question each one of us may be asked. Many of us will give an occupation: a plumber, an accountant, a soldier, a nurse. Others do not, however, experience their primary senses of identity through their careers even during their adult working lives. They may see themselves as British or bird-watchers, feminists or Catholics, graduates or trade unionists, before they identify themselves with a gainful employment. For most of us, nevertheless, the paid occupation in which we are engaged is an important component, sometimes the most important, of how we see ourselves and expect others to see us.

'Counselling' is defined by the *New Shorter Oxford English Dictionary* (Brown 1993) as 'specifically a therapeutic procedure in which a usually trained person adopts a supportive non-judgmental role in enabling a client to deal more effectively with psychological or emotional problems or gives advice on practical problems'. For the purposes of this chapter career counselling is understood as what the career counsellor does with a client, which may include listening, giving information, advising, counselling, training, coaching, testing, encouragement or a combination of one or more of these activities. Career counselling is directed towards helping people, first to acquire greater freedom of choice in their occupational lives, second to develop their capacity to make such choices effectively, and finally to manage their occupation-related problems. Career counselling is most often focused on occupational transitions together with the associated choices, constraints and consequences; but it may also deal with problems related to occupational activities. It is defined by Nathan and Hill (1992: 2–3) as 'a process which enables people to recognize and utilize their resources to make career-related decisions and manage career-related problems. Although focused on the work-related part of a person's life, it also takes into account the interdependence of career and non-career considerations.'

Career counselling clients

Who needs career counselling? Everybody who is old enough to make choices about their occupational activities (or to influence the choices made for them by others, or to decide whether to co-operate with them) can benefit from some sort of career counselling when opportunities for such choices come up. They may not, however, be aware, either that an opportunity for a choice is available to them, or what the long-term implications of the choice may be, or what benefits career counselling offers them.

Who wants it? Generally, people who are faced with career choices, if they are aware that career counselling is available to them. People faced with career choices include students choosing training courses or needing to start earning a living, and unemployed or unpaid people looking for ways to secure paid employment; those who need more money, training, development or personal reputation as means to influence or direct the course of their careers; people afflicted by restlessness, boredom or the wish for change; as well as individuals experiencing deeper needs, for greater stability or autonomy, for entrepreneurial satisfactions or further specialization, or for a commitment to a worthwhile cause; and people wanting to escape unwelcome consequences of choices made for them such as relocation, job loss or compulsory retirement. They may also want counselling to help them manage or find ways out of stressful problems associated with career activities.

Who gets career counselling? Those who want it, for whom it is available and who can pay for it or who may have access to it without paying. Those who may have to pay for it include clients of vocational guidance, career, redundancy or outplacement counsellors; and clients of general counsellors, therapists and psychologists in private practice. Those who may be able to get it without paying include pupils and students with access to careers advice through their school or college; trainees on career development and job-search courses, whether at school or college or in employment; clients of job centres and job-seekers registered with employment agencies; employees offered free career counselling by their employers (where the counselling on offer may be provided by line management, the personnel function, an employee counselling service or independent consultants) and trainees on training courses; clients of general counsellors, therapists and psychologists through the National Health Service or through an employee counselling service; and employees (or customers of life insurance companies) offered pre-retirement counselling. Many people are, of course, offered free career-related information, advice or counselling by family, friends or acquaintances, whether or not these are suitably qualified, trained or experienced, and some of what they are offered may be of as much value as what they would get from professionals. Indeed, good professional advice will often include the advice to make as much use as possible of personal contact networks.

Some clients' experience of career counselling

A few examples of clients' experience of career counselling may serve both to illustrate the range of clients in one consultant's practice and what being a client of a career counsellor may involve.

A high-flying executive in commerce

Helen was a senior executive of a commercial organization. Following a reorganization, but probably also due to a personality clash with her new boss, her employers made her redundant. She had no hesitation about accepting their offer of career consultancy. There was no risk or potential disadvantage and she welcomed the prospect of professional help with the personal and job-related issues involved in redundancy.

She was in a negative frame of mind, angry, hurt, suffering low self-esteem and wavering motivation. In the first few sessions with her consultant they worked on her anger and low self-esteem, building on her natural optimism and the facts of her excellent track record. On the practical side they rewrote her CV as a marketing document and Helen sent letters to some 70 executive search consultancies ('headhunters'), using the consultancy's secretarial support facility.

In the second phase of her campaign she started to go to interviews, mainly with headhunters, and began actively to follow up and extend her network of personal and professional contacts ('networking'). She asked for a practice interview recorded on video-tape. The result was, she remembered later, 'an object lesson in how not to handle yourself in an interview, which was therefore extremely valuable'. She went to five or six headhunter interviews a week for several weeks, and used them to practise her interview techniques.

She needed support from her consultant with respect to networking, which she approached with reluctance. They worked on details of technique, and once she discovered that she was getting positive results she began to enjoy the process as an opportunity to extend her contacts and to bounce ideas off fellow professionals. She started to respond to advertisements. She was feeling better in herself, and could discuss how to answer awkward interview questions without feeling threatened. She looked forward to her regular review meetings with her consultant, which came increasingly to focus more on practical issues.

In the third stage she became involved in selection interviews with potential employers. Her interview technique had improved and she sometimes asked for feedback. This phase was, nevertheless, more frustrating because each interview had a short-term objective – to move to the next stage – and she had to do a lot of chasing replies and waiting to hear outcomes.

Helen started to discuss in greater detail with her consultant the 'buy' stage of the process, how to manage the decision-making necessary between receiving a firm offer and accepting it. She felt more confident, more relaxed about being herself. She could tell whether she wanted to reach the next stage of a series of interviews with potential employers, and whether she was likely to. She wanted to find an organization where her face would fit and her contribution would be welcomed. Just when she was beginning to think that she would never get an offer the first one appeared, in the area which had throughout been her first preference. She accepted it. In the light of her consultant's advice on 'buy side' negotiating she felt later that she had made concessions she might come to regret, but the process gave both sides a chance to find out about each other, she said.

In the event she moved on from the new job to a better one within a year. Her career prospects seem as bright as ever. Helen summed up her view of her experience as a career counselling client as follows: 'The consultants fill an invaluable role as champion to their clients, offering unbiased professional and personal expertise. In addition, a good consultant is a true friend, telling clients good and bad points, and shares the client's objective, that the client should end up with the right job.'

An engineer with a network

The case of Jim illustrates what can be achieved by using your network to get advice and leads, without the intervention of a professional counsellor. Jim is an engineer who became involved in the development of a new product. His combination of enthusiasm and know-how went down well with customers. Introductions led to new business. He felt things were going well and was devastated to be called in by his boss one Friday afternoon and sacked. The business was being sold to Americans who intended to supply European customers through a German subsidiary. They were not offering jobs to anybody in Jim's division. Jim and all his colleagues found themselves out of a job.

Jim was angry and frightened. After 13 successful years with one employer he didn't deserve this. What was worse, he and his wife had recently bought their first house. His wife was pregnant. He took stock. He had good qualifications and useful experience. He got on with customers and was good at bringing in business. He was a hard worker, quick learner, effective team member and an expert on his product range. He had a lot to offer: but who wanted it?

An afternoon in the public library looking through the job ads was not encouraging. He could go back to the drawing board or the toolroom for less money – but it would be a setback. There were no advertisements which asked for the range of know-how he could offer. On the way home, Jim dropped into his local pub and found Henry, another regular, at the bar. Henry offered him a drink and asked how things were. Jim told him. Henry was sympathetic, and asked some constructive questions. He was interested in Jim's experience. It emerged in their conversation that Henry's company used Jim's product and got their supplies from France and Italy. Jim asked Henry why. Henry did not know but offered to ask Mary Robinson, his firm's expert on Jim's product. Jim suggested that he should call her direct and mention Henry's name. He rang her and she agreed to see him.

When Jim turned up for his appointment with Mary Robinson, she asked him why he was interested. He told her that he thought there might be a good opportunity for an enterprising French manufacturer in this area to gain market share in the UK. He wanted to find out which French companies were most likely to be interested. Mary gave Jim a helpful rundown on the main organizations in the relevant French manufacturing scene and some of the key personalities. He commented that she seemed to know quite a lot about one of them, called Dupont, and asked her whether he could mention her name to Dupont when he got in touch with him, as he intended to do. Mary agreed, and suggested a couple of other French contacts. Jim emerged well satisfied with his meeting, from which he had gained useful information and several leads.

He made several telephone calls over the next few days, both to France and within the UK, and ten days later took the evening train from Victoria. In Paris he had an apointment with Jean Dupont, and the same afternoon took another train to Clermont-Ferrand where he visited a second manufacturer. And then . . . what outcome would you prefer?

Jim's story is a composite, including elements from several real stories. The common, and crucial, point is that networking opened up possibilities which led to choices. Jim could have landed up as UK agent for Jean Dupont, or set up as a consultant advising French and other overseas companies about the British market, or gone with the results of his research in the French market to the only other British manufacturer of Jim's product to talk about helping them meet the competition from imports; a range of options opened up by only one chance contact with a casual acquaintance, and one lead arising from the contact. Many people need persuasion to use their personal contacts effectively, and one of the most important tasks of career counsellors is to provide persuasion and coaching toward skilful networking. As it happened, Jim did not need persuading. Not everybody does.

A woman returner

Sarah joined a large retailing organization with a countrywide network of shops after taking an English degree. She worked her way up to store manager while she was still in her twenties, and then got married and decided to start a family. Her employer operated a scheme for extended maternity leave designed to maintain the relationship with women employees who become mothers and to encourage return to full-time employment when the children are older. During her membership of the scheme she worked several weeks each year as a relief store manager.

When she returned to full-time employment she was initially offered an attachment to an area office, working as a relief manager. Within months the area office had disappeared as part of a major reorganization, and so had Sarah's job. Her employer offered her the services of a career counselling organization, which she accepted in a state of some confusion. In her feelings anger was mixed with relief and uncertainty. She felt let down because her membership of the extended maternity leave scheme had not given her the expected return to secure employment, but relieved because she had enjoyed being back at work less than she had expected. The uncertainty was about what she wanted to happen next. She had enjoyed being at home with her young children but the enjoyment was being increasingly overtaken by periods of boredom and frustration. She would prefer to work part-time, or near home with hours which would allow her breakfast and tea with her children; but she was worried that local or part-time work would not be stimulating.

Her counsellor helped her to determine her order of outcome preferences. She wanted to go on working, partly for financial reasons, partly to get out of the house. She learned that her skills were transferable and that they could be useful in sectors other than the one she had experience in. She started to put herself forward for administrative positions with a nearby university, and for paid positions in several voluntary organizations locally. She was eventually successful in obtaining a paid position with the local Citizens' Advice Bureau which she thought would meet her needs.

An apparent failure

Bill was a dealer heading up a dealing team for a commodity trading house. The market for the commodity in which he specialized collapsed as part of a general economic recession, and his firm decided to close the team down altogether. He and all his team were given four months' notice. He had spent all his working life as a specialist dealer and felt that he had no transferable skills and was too old to acquire any. In his view the only option was to keep in touch with the market and wait out the downturn.

He co-operated cheerfully in the initial counselling sessions and home-work. He hated the idea of networking, however. Keeping in touch with his own small market was different, since he was on first-name terms with everybody in it. But he was not prepared seriously to contemplate moving outside it. His campaign never got out of first gear, and after a couple of months had come to a standstill. He stopped coming to see his consultant. Telephone discussions indicated that he was becoming more depressed. His funds were running low, and he turned down all offers of referral to other sources of advice and support.

Bill is a man with many talents: considerable accomplishments in his own line of business, an agreeable personality, practical skills both as a handy-man and as an amateur artist. It may be that fear and anger, never apparent in his manner, lay behind the extreme rigidity of his thinking about the future. His future seemed bleak, both to him and to his consultant. After two years of unhappy unemployment, however, the commodity market in which Bill had specialized became active again. He was re-employed by another trading house in a junior dealing role. He was pleased to be working again, but his confidence and self-esteem have suffered. They may take a long time to recover.

A bright, anxious black accountant

After getting a good law degree Harry started his articles, but decided after a year to switch from law to accountancy. He trained with a well-known firm and then went to work for the finance department of a major corporation. He did well until his boss was made redundant. His new boss took against him, possibly because he was too anxious to please, and started giving him poor reports. Harry was devastated and rattled. By his account it was at this point that his performance started to deteriorate in fact as well as in his performance ratings. Things went from bad to worse, he was given a warning and then the opportunity to resign rather than face dismissal for poor performance. Somebody may have had a bad conscience about his treatment, because he was also offered career consultancy and a period of paid leave before termination.

He arrived with his counsellor exuding anxiety and low self-esteem. He said that it was essential that he should find new employment before his notice period expired, that he had already faced up to the likelihood of having to accept a drop in pay. He was worried, probably with some justification, that his ethnic origin might count against him. He believed that he couldn't afford to tell the truth about the circumstances leading to his resignation. He did not trust his boss to give him a reasonable reference. He could not imagine networking.

Summing up his experience of being a career counselling client later, Harry said that it had taken him time to get over his shock and disappointment, and that initially he found it difficult to build up an effective rate of activity. He found the consultancy's client manual very useful, particularly on interview technique. He had frequent interview rehearsals with consultants, some video taped for later review, and regular review meetings with his own consultant as his campaign progressed; both were helpful in building up his confidence. He continued to find networking difficult, and the offers he eventually secured all arose either from responses to advertisements, registrations with selection consultancies or direct approaches to potential employers. His references were judged satisfactory. The offer he accepted met all his initial criteria. He is still over-anxious.

Career counsellors

Who gives career counselling? On occasion, teachers; also occupational, clinical and counselling psychologists; social workers, counsellors and psychotherapists; career and redundancy counsellors, career and outplacement consultants, career development trainers and educators, and preretirement counsellors. The writings of careers writers and journalists are also sources of information and advice. Family, friends and acquaintances (as already indicated) may all give career advice. Some of these people will give counselling or advice about careers because it is part of their job, others because it seems appropriate to do so, either in general or in the case in question, at the time.

Not all the groups mentioned, of course, are covered by their own professional qualification requirements. Some of the requirements are mandatory and others not (you must not call yourself a psychologist without a recognized qualification but anybody, so far, can call himself or herself a counsellor). Nathan and Hill (1992) suggest that the most relevant qualifications for career counselling are membership of (or accreditation by) the British Association for Counselling, the British Psychological Society, the Institute of Careers Guidance and the Institute of Personnel and Development. They also refer to the qualifications in the guidance and counselling field being developed within the framework of National Vocational Qualifications (NVQ). My own view is that such qualifications are helpful for intending careers counsellors, but not sufficient. Extensive experience of the world of work together with intelligent observation of the way it works are also necessary. Some career counsellors have counselling qualifications not focused on career counselling, but many who practise as career counsellors have no recognized relevant qualifications or formal training at all. They practise on the basis of informal training by colleagues, experience with clients, private study, previously acquired skills or a combination of these.

One career counsellor's experience of career counselling

The only experience of being a career counsellor about which I can write with some confidence is my own. My introduction to career counselling was provided by a partner in a firm of career and outplacement consultants who had been a colleague ten years earlier. After my own redundancy my wife suggested that I would be well suited to counselling. I thought that I knew something about the subject matter and I knew that I enjoyed working with people, particularly one-to-one. Career counselling might be a useful route into counselling because it would use my general experience of organizations and the world of work, and because the training skills acquired as a consultant might prove to be relevant.

In the following five years I developed skills and self-confidence in the work. Some clients were difficult: I learned that a client's initial aggressive approach could mask great distress, that enthusiasm and docility could both mask manipulation, that people who need help can find it difficult to acknowledge their need, that some defences are not only well constructed but take inordinate effort to overcome. Most clients were rewarding. Getting to know clients is a process that rarely fails to arouse my interest, and becoming more deeply engaged with clients is usually enjoyable. I learned from the firm's experience and tradition embodied in the client manual, from the humane values of the founding partner who wrote the manual, from the sardonic wit and deflating logic of the partner who brought me into the firm, from other colleagues each of whom had individual and interesting ideas about the work, and above all from my clients.

My clients taught me other lessons. Time spent on initial self-appraisal by the client and debriefing with the consultant is rarely wasted. Most clients suffer from low self-esteem and respond gratefully to positive feedback, if they believe it. Much of the teaching work is better done by getting the client to read the manual attentively and discuss it later. The major hurdle with many clients is persuading them to make effective use of their personal and professional contact networks. The ultimate responsibility for decisions and outcomes belongs to the client.

The opportunity to develop some of these themes further arose when, following the fifth anniversary of my move into career consultancy, a former colleague invited me to join her in building up an in-house career consultancy for a clearing bank. One of the first tasks was to write the client manual for the consultancy, and all the lessons learned during the previous five years went into it. Among these was the conviction, which had grown since my redundancy from an employment which had lasted 21 years, that most career successes in the next few decades will be gained by people who refuse to be dependent on organizations or to become their victims. This self-sufficient frame of mind may be called the 'permanently self-employed' attitude. The manual preaches the effectiveness, as a strategy for personal survival and prosperity, of the recognition that the employment relationship is primarily commercial and that employees need to take responsibility for looking after their end of the employment relationship with as much care as any small supplier looks after a relationship with a big customer. It links with this the networking philosophy, that 'no man is an island' and that our resources include not only what we have to offer in personal characteristics and know-how, but also who we know and what they can make available to us.

The lessons I preach are open to challenge. My career counselling experience is limited in the sense that it has been entirely with white-collar workers, managers and directors. Will the same lessons apply to unskilled factory workers like those among whom my early working life was spent, to the unqualified unemployed, to youngsters from deprived backgrounds emerging from unsatisfactory educational experiences to face a future with bleak prospects, to all those others to whom life has dealt a weak hand? I do not know, but I believe that anybody in my children's generation who is brought up to value what they have to offer, to treat as a customer anybody who is prepared to pay them for what they have to offer, and to make the best of their resources, internal and external, will do better for this training and have reason to be grateful for it. I suspect that anybody expecting to be looked after in the next few decades by their employers or their trade unions, or by the social services or the welfare system, may be disappointed. If trade unions started treating employers as valuable customers they might be able to serve their members' interests more effectively in the future than they have been in the recent past. They might treat their members more like customers, too. That would be a useful application of both the 'permanently self-employed' and the 'no man is an island' lessons.

My work and learning continue. The pace in the in-house consultancy has been stimulating but strenuous. I have been involved in developing other services which have added variety to the rewards of the job. Having mopped up much of the demand for career consultancy and other counselling services within the bank, the unit has been making its services available externally. The future looks interesting. Most recently, I have taken over management of the unit.

The context of career counselling

Work and careers are important aspects of society, and we live in a society where the rate of change appears to be accelerating. What was meant by work, jobs and careers may have been reasonably clear when people now nearing retirement were starting their working lives some 40 years ago. Even then, self-employment, casual employment and entrepreneurial careers had been around for a long time; but work was widely understood as paid employment, a job was an established employee's role, and a career was understood to imply advancement or the possibility of advancement in the public service, business, management, entertainment, the professions or the arts. Success meant continued advancement.

All this has changed and continues to change. As Kanter (1989: 507) says: 'Not all careers are formed by employment relationships with organisations', and 'employment is only one of the ways in which organisations help form careers'. Informal organizations like social and work-related networks can perform organizational functions too. Helping to find work, publicizing reputations, education, providing accepted credentials, protection and funding are all done informally by colleagues, friends, family and acquaintances as well as by organizations.

Kanter (1989) also points to a variety of distinct but overlapping career patterns: bureaucratic (advancement within a hierarchy); blocked (within a hierarchy but without prospects of advancement); professional (learned and other professions, entertainment and the arts, where advancement takes the form of enhanced reputation and earning power rather than promotion);

professionalized careers in organizations (professionals like teachers and engineers, and consultants employed as internal advisers); semi-professional (such as politicians); entrepreneurial (building a business); entrepreneurial careers in organizations (where the job specification is to add value by growing a business, and rewards are related to the success of the business grown). Such patterns can be mixed within an individual's career. An organization can offer more than one career pattern. Charles Handy's (1984) prediction of an increasing variety of career patterns is coming to look like a description of current trends: more part-time work, shorter careers, more voluntary and co-operative work.

Golzen and Garner (1990) have surveyed some of the changes in career and work patterns. They note, following Peter Drucker (1969), that what employees are primarily selling to employers is knowledge and skills, and that such knowledge is either relevant to the task in hand, or irrelevant. Their suggestions include the following. Traditional expectations of employer–employee loyalty no longer match current realities or can be expected to do so. People need to manage their own careers, continuing to acquire know-how, saving earnings to buy greater freedom of choice, acquiring recognition and reputation to support the same objective. Careers are less likely than they were to consist of progress up a ladder, more likely than they were to resemble a journey across a series of settings. Women may be better equipped than men to manage their careers in the new environment because they have had both more limited expectations of hierarchical progress and more need to choose between priorities. Those men and women, fewer than now, who do get to the top of large organizations will be distinguished by features which include high parental expectations in their childhoods and early experience of leadership, and by evidence of having and communicating clear objectives and of knowing their own strengths and weaknesses. They will be people with above-average ability to judge and take risks, and to pick people, Golzen and Garner (1990) predict. They will be notable for autonomy, decisiveness and energy; and the most important personal characteristics of future chief executives will be flexibility, adaptability and broad cultural empathy, while their most important technical competencies will be strategy, human resource management, marketing and corporate finance. Those who do not share the qualities expected to be required for the top jobs may be reassured to consider that if these predictions are correct they may be better led than earlier generations.

Various writers (for instance, Roger Harrison 1972, Charles Handy 1978 and Gareth Morgan 1986) have grouped organizations by culture ('the way we do things here'). Four types of organization have been defined: autocratic, focused on power, as in 'We'll do it this way'; bureaucratic, focused on roles and rules, as in 'We're supposed to do it this way'; technocratic, focused on task, as in 'It's best to do it this way'; democratic, focused on people, as in 'Let's do it together'. Organization cultures can change, or vary within organizations. People choosing organizations to work in, or with, need to learn to read organization cultures and to decide how far these cultures match their own needs. Women wanting hierarchical progress, for example, are more likely to find it in technocratic or democratic organization cultures.

The content of career counselling

The content of career counselling varies from client to client, depending on need. People's needs from career counselling are varied. Some people may need help in working out what they want out of life, work, learning and play. Some may need to work at understanding their own strengths. Such strengths may include their knowledge of facts, theories, systems and people, as well as their valuable skills, know-how and personal characteristics as demonstrated through their experience and record of achievement and contributions. They should also know their limitations (things they are less good at) and liabilities (aspects of their careers which may tell against them with potential employers or customers) together with their development needs and potential. For others, the urgent concern may be how to evaluate and satisfy their training and development needs, or alternatively how to meet short- and long-term financial objectives.

Some career counselling clients will wish to focus on identifying and understanding the potential job and customer markets for what they have to offer (that is, their experience, strengths and potential) and on learning how to make themselves, and what they have to offer, known in these target markets. Many need to learn how to put themselves across, face-to-face and otherwise; how to identify opportunities for performing well and for achieving reputation and recognition; how to give value, make intelligent choices and time career moves effectively. Learning how to develop and manage a career strategy (objectives, constraints, priorities, plans and reviews) is a task which people who have not done so need to tackle. Some people, however, develop successful career strategies for themselves without ever identifying what they have done as such. Job search tactics are a high priority for those without a job or facing job loss: preparing and using a CV, identifying and responding to opportunities, networking, making job applications, using agencies, approaching potential employers, being interviewed, deploying negotiation criteria for comparing and accepting offers, starting and prospering in a new job. On the other hand, how to start and run your own business as a freelance, professional in private practice or entrepreneur is crucial know-how for those who want to do so.

Career counsellors may be asked by clients to help with problems which might be more appropriately referred to general counsellors or therapists, perhaps because consulting a career counsellor is more acceptable, less associated with mental illness. Coping with stressful problems at work sometimes forms part of the concerns brought to career counsellors. Such problems may include a need for greater assertiveness or for learning how to survive in organizations. Clients may also experience discrimination, harassment, intimidation or violence as career-related problems. Mismatch in organization culture or team goals can often present themselves as career problems. Some clients ask for help in identifying the right time and the best opportunity for a career move to gain better rewards, training, experiential development or visibility. Others are coping with stressful problems of self-employment, dealing with the problems of work re-entry after a career break, coping with redundancy, relocation, unemployment, career blockage or burnout, preparing for retirement or a second career after the age of 45.

Career counselling outcomes

How are these needs currently met in the United Kingdom? Most can be met, but getting them met may not be straightforward. Careers advice for young people, for instance, is not universally available. Careers guidance using psychometric tests is available commercially in major centres for those who can afford it. Help in taking stock of strengths and limitations, identifying markets, marketing and selling oneself (whether as an employee or in a self-employed role) is available through commercial outplacement and career consultancy firms, either paid for by employers or self-funded. In practice these services are mainly used by managerial and professional executives because many employers are reluctant to fund them for junior employees, and they cost too much for the majority of workers to pay for out of their own pockets. Job-search training of a simple sort is made available by some but not all employers, local authorities and adult education institutions to redundant employees. Anecdotal evidence suggests that the quality of what is provided from all these sources is variable and in some cases unsatisfactory.

General counsellors in private practice or in subsidized counselling services may find among their clients some who are anxious, stressed or depressed because of work-related problems. The help they give may not include as much practical advice and coaching as appropriate because many counselling training programmes would not prepare them to do so.

Some employers, and educational and training institutions, offer training courses in career development, interpersonal relationships skills, coping with redundancy, improving personal performance and job-related technical competencies. Some employers and commercial organizations offer pre-retirement, second career or 'third age' training. Training in specific skills is widely available, though it may need searching out.

The worst provision appears to be for the poor, ill-educated and unmotivated. Little or none of the training available seems to be related to a satisfactory general understanding of how careers currently work, or to any developed model of career self-management. Career self-management and how to train people in it, whether initially or later, remains fairly uncharted territory despite some useful and pioneering work that has been done.

Anything, in this field, may be better than nothing. In an ideal world careers education would be about acquiring and maintaining as much sense of direction and effectiveness as possible in managing one's working life in a turbulent and changing environment. It would need to start in the family and be complemented in the educational and employment systems from nursery school onwards.

What sort of career counselling outcomes are currently experienced? I am not aware of reliable studies, and the paragraphs which follow represent a personal view.

The first and sometimes most important career education many people acquire is as a child, from the example of parents and other older family members, and from what these role models say. In this stage expectations are generated and often permanently set. One of these expectations may be that one is going to be looked after, an expectation which can be reinforced by employment as a young adult in a business with a paternalistic employment tradition. Such an expectation may lead to disappointment.

Expectations deriving from family examples are both reinforced and challenged at school. School provides children with the first example of an organization outside the family that most of them encounter, and can easily suggest to bright and motivated youngsters that working hard, getting good marks and keeping out of trouble are the only essential components of a strategy aimed at success. Careers advisers in schools may not have enough personal experience of working outside educational institutions to be able confidently to challenge such unrealistic expectations, especially since they may share them.

Psychometric testing seems more likely to provide a person with new and valuable input to choice-making before the start of working life, or early in its course, than later. For older clients its effect can more often be to provide confirmation of what they have already learned about themselves through many years of experiencing themselves at work. Such confirmation may, of course, be helpful if they are inclined to question their own judgements about themselves, or have become more so inclined as a result of stress. Clients who are temporarily somewhat out of touch with reality because of trauma or psychological disturbance may in some cases find skilful feedback on the basis of psychometric instruments illuminating.

Commercial outplacement and career consultancy firms are well placed to provide good value for their clients, who are often frustrated or shocked, suffering from loneliness and looking for companionship, encouragement and helpful practical advice. A consultant who can offer all three without making unrealistic promises can gain credibility quickly. It may be a more effective relationship when the client is not paying, however, because the economic cost can be a deterrent to the self-funded client who may look for quick results with little client input, and tempts some consultants to make promises which they are not in a position to deliver.

Therapeutically directed counselling related to work and career problems is likely to be helpful in disentangling practical problems from emotional problems, and the emotional impact of practical problems from the disturbances they trigger in relation to the client's past. It will usually need to be supplemented with practical advice and coaching if the practical problems are to be effectively managed. More narrowly focused training courses, with clear and limited objectives, are most likely to be able to meet expectations, assuming that they are prudently selected and well run.

The future of career counselling

The amount of useful research and publications in the field of career theory is increasing rapidly, as evidenced by Arthur *et al.* (1989). The material for developing effective career education and counselling for all stages is likely to improve as a result. The continuing problem in the United Kingdom will probably be funding: who will pay for the development of the training material and the education of the trainers? How will the needs of the most needy be met? Where will the balance be struck between career education and therapeutic counselling?

For students and young adults the lead is likely to have to be taken by the public sector, though private, consumer and voluntary sector pressure may be needed to make it happen. For older people development will probably be market-led with large employers setting the pace. The self-employed and unemployed are likely to lose out unless pressure is brought to bear on their behalf.

References

Arthur, M.B., Hall, D.T. and Lawrence, B.S. (eds) (1989) *Handbook of Career Theory*. Cambridge: Cambridge University Press.

Brown, L. (ed.) (1993) *New Shorter Oxford English Dictionary*. Oxford: Oxford University Press.

Drucker, P. (1969) *The Age of Discontinuity*. London: Heinemann.

Golzen, G. and Garner, A. (1990) *Smart Moves*. Harmondsworth: Penguin.

Handy, C. (1978) *The Gods of Management*. London: Pan Books.

Handy, C. (1984) *The Future of Work*. Oxford: Blackwell.

Harrison, R. (1972) Understanding your organisation's character. *Harvard Business Review*, 50(3), May–June: 119–28.

Kanter, R.M. (1989) Careers and the wealth of nations: A macro-perspective on the structure and implications of career forms, in M.B. Arthur, D.T. Hall and B.S. Lawrence (eds), *Handbook of Career Theory*. Cambridge: Cambridge University Press.

Kidd, J.M., Killeen, J., Jarvis, J. and Offer, M. (1994) Is guidance an applied science? The role of theory in the careers guidance interview. *British Journal of Guidance and Counselling*, 22(3): 385–403.

Millar, R., Crute, V. and Hargie, O. (1992) *Professional Interviewing*. London: Routledge.

Morgan, G. (1986) *Images of the Organisation*. London: Sage.

Nathan, R. and Hill, L. (1992) *Career Counselling*. London: Sage.

Pemberton, C., Herriot, P. and Bates, T. (1994) Career orientations of senior executives and their implications for careers guidance. *British Journal of Guidance and Counselling*, 22(2): 223–45.

Super, D.E. (1981) A life-span, life-space approach to career development. *Journal of Vocational Behaviour*, 16: 282–98.

Watts, A.G. (1980a) Educational and careers guidance services for adults: I. A rationale and conceptual framework. *British Journal of Guidance and Counselling*, 8(1), January: 11–22.

Watts, A.G. (1980b) Educational and careers guidance services for adults. II. A review of current provision. *British Journal of Guidance and Counselling*, 8(2), July: 188–202.

Watts, A.G. (ed.) (1989) *Computers in Careers Guidance*, Cambridge: Careers Research and Advisory Centre.

Suggested reading

Barrow, C. (1982) *The Complete Small Business Guide: Sources of information for new and small businesses*. London: BBC Books.

Bayley, J. (1992) *How to Get a Job after 45* (2nd edn). London: Kogan Page.

Beatty, R.H. (1991) *Get the Right Job in 60 Days or Less*. Chichester: John Wiley.

Bolles, R.N. (1972) *What Colour is Your Parachute? A practical manual for job-hunters and career changers*. London: Airlift.

Golzen, G. (1993) *Working for Yourself*. London: Kogan Page.

Golzen, G. and Garner, A. (1990) *Smart Moves*. Harmondsworth: Penguin.

Gray, D.A. (1985) *Start and Run a Profitable Consulting Business*. London: Kogan Page.

Handy, C. (1976) *Understanding Organisations*. Harmondsworth: Penguin.

Handy, C. (1984) *The Future of Work*. Oxford: Blackwell.

Handy, C. (1994) *The Empty Raincoat: Making sense of the future*. London: Arrow.

Ingham, C. (1994) *Life without Work*. London: Thorsons.

Kemp, D. and Kemp, F. (1992) *The Mid Career Action Guide* (2nd edn). London: Kogan Page.

Leavesley, J. (ed.) (1995) *Occupations*. Bristol: Careers and Occupational Information Centre.

Morgan, G. (1986) *Images of Organisation*. London: Sage.

Nathan, R. and Hill, L. (1992) *Career Counselling*. London: Sage.

Watts, A.G., Law, B., Killeen, J., Kidd, J.M. and Hawthorn, R. (1996) *Rethinking Careers Education and Guidance*. London: Routledge.
Williams, S. (1987) *Lloyds Bank Small Business Guide*. Harmondsworth: Penguin.

Useful organizations

British Psychological Society
St Andrew's House
48 Princess Road East
Leicester LE1 7DR
01533 549568

Career and Educational Counselling
The Tavistock Centre
120 Belsize Lane
Hampstead
London NW3 5BA
0171 435 7111

Counselling and Career Development Unit
The University of Leeds
44 Clarendon Road
Leeds LS2 9PJ
0113 2334911

National Institute for Careers Education and Counselling
Sheraton House
Castle Park
Cambridge CB3 0AX
01223 460277

forget that I had done them. I found myself avoiding doing my job, and I had always enjoyed my work before and been conscientious. The whole of 1990–1991 was an absolute disaster for me professionally and personally. My behaviour with my family was bizarre. I took my wife and granddaughter on a long trip and could not drive over 30 mph. I never said a word. When I got there I walked round and round the coastal path for five hours. When I got back to the house and the kitchen door shut (as I now see it) accidentally in my face, I felt shut out by my family. I just got in the car without saying anything, came home, switched the phone off, shut the curtains, took the photographs of my grandchildren down, and sat in a chair for four days. I have had a lot of help from my doctor and have had counselling. I'm angry for having my working life cut short. I don't feel as though I could work for anyone again, it's knocked my confidence. As regards dealing with people in distress or anguish, I don't feel as though I could help people again. It's only in the last six months that I have started to feel better.

Recent Health and Safety Executive figures state that more than half the number of employees who suffer stress attribute their condition directly to their work. Every year 100,000 people in the UK suffer from stress caused by their work or working environment. This gives rise to the loss of more than 1.5 million working days per annum through work-related stress (HSE 1995).

This figure is second only to loss of days at work from musculo-skeletal conditions. The British Safety Council give an estimated cost of £13 billion lost through absenteeism from stress and stress-related illness each year. Stress, according to Cary Cooper (1981), costs substantially more than industrial injury and more than strikes.

A study carried out by the Office of Population Censuses and Surveys found that one in seven adults experienced a mental health problem in 1993 (OPCS 1994). The four most common neurotic symptoms were fatigue, sleep difficulties, irritability and worry. This study coincided with a study co-ordinated by the World Health Organization (reported in *The Guardian*, 15 December 1994) which said that mental disorders are more disabling, in terms of work lost and daily activities interrupted, than physical conditions such as arthritis, diabetes and back pain.

The well-known response to stress is the fight or flight reaction. Neither of these reactions is necessarily appropriate in the workplace. Physiological effects of such a response are that the muscles tense in preparation for activity. With this tension lactic acid is produced, the products of which have the effect of reinforcing the anxiety and tension felt by the individual. The hormone adrenalin is released, and increases the heart rate in order to service the extra requirements of the muscles. The increase in the heart rate increases the blood pressure. The extra blood for the muscles requires extra oxygen, and the respiratory rate therefore quickens to cope with this as well as to help to expel additional waste products resulting from increased activity. Blood being diverted to potential muscular activity requires the shutdown of some other functions, including reduction in blood through the kidneys as well as the ceasing of digestive functions. This causes the saliva to dry up and the stomach and intestines to stop working. The body's need for additional energy is met by the liver releasing stored glucose into the bloodstream, where the oxygen changes it into readily available energy. Another aspect of the body's defence system capability is that the immune system becomes less active during such arousal, so that infection is more likely.

In the short term, and if the response is adequate, the system will return to its position of status quo. If, however, the arousal is maintained over an extended period of time, the healthy functioning of the body will be impaired, causing chronic complaints. Such a 'general adaptation syndrome', in which the body adapts to repeated and constant stress factors, can cause chronic symptoms to become an accepted way of life. Some common symptoms experienced as a result of such a response may include headaches, dizziness, insomnia, muscle pain, high blood pressure, heart problems, palpitations, circulatory problems, asthma, allergies, indigestion, ulcers, skin rashes, colitis, sexual difficulties, blurred vision, problems with swallowing, depression and irritability. Energy levels and mood are affected by disturbances in the blood sugar equilibrium. If this is accompanied by the excessive use of sugar in the diet and stimulants such as tea, coffee and chocolate, the body's ability to maintain a normal blood sugar level can be severely damaged.

If the arousal mechanisms are maintained in prolonged reaction, it is not difficult to see how potentially destructive this can be to the health of the individual as a whole.

Heart disease and strokes

Some individuals experience pain in the region of the heart and palpitations. On investigation it may be found that anxiety is causing hyperventilation which is responsible for the chest pain.

Heart attacks do, however, account for one-third of male deaths and a quarter of female deaths, which exceeds all other single causes of death, including cancer. Permanent high blood pressure or hypertension can damage blood vessel walls leading to bursting of blood vessels in the brain causing a stroke, or around the heart causing a heart attack. The inability to reabsorb the body fuels released during an extended period of stress response causes fatty acids to build up in the bloodstream creating a deposit on the blood vessel walls and a subsequent narrowing of the arteries. The resultant restriction of oxygen to the heart may cause angina. Evidence as to whether stress does actually cause coronary heart disease is inconclusive. Because of the variation of reactions by individuals it is very difficult accurately to investigate.

The current Whitehall II Study being led by Professor Michael Marmot, Head of the Department of Epidemiology and Public Health, University College London is one project which is trying to gain accurate information on the possible relationship between work-related stress and heart disease. For this study, more than 10,000 men and women working in London-based Civil Service departments are being examined for early signs of coronary and other disease, while also completing detailed confidential questionnaires about their work, lifestyle, domestic, social and financial circumstances. The hypothesis is being professionally tested with support from the British Heart Foundation and the Medical Research Council, to determine whether psychological and social conditions at work and in other areas of life act together with important influences such as cigarette smoking, lack of exercise, diet and high blood cholesterol in the causation of heart disease. What has been discovered in this study is that contrary to widely held belief, coronary heart disease is more common among people in lower-status jobs than among executives and administrators. The first Whitehall Study, begun in 1967, showed a steep inverse association between social class, as assessed by grade of employment, and mortality from a wide range of diseases – the lower the grade, the higher the risk. It was found that the highest grades in the Civil Service, administrators, had one-third of the heart disease mortality of the lowest grade. A correlation with smoking was taken into consideration, but even among non-smokers low grade was associated with higher mortality rates. The Whitehall II study was set up as a longitudinal study to investigate the role of psychosocial and other factors in the aetiology of coronary heart and other diseases. In the 20 years separating the two Whitehall studies of civil servants, there has been no diminution in social class difference in morbidity.

In a study by Alfredsson *et al.* quoted in Warr (1987)

> All cases of fatal and non-fatal myocardial infarction in men aged 40–64 in the Greater Stockholm area between 1974 and 1976 were recorded, together with details of jobs held. For each case at least two matched controls without infarction were selected randomly from parish registers. From interviews with a separate sample of 3876 working men, the 'psychosocial' characteristics of 118 different jobs were determined. The risk of myocardial infarction in jobs with different characteristics was then calculated from the three sets of data. Job monotony emerged as the strongest single predictor of this type of heart attack for the group as a whole.

Musculo-skeletal problems

The Health and Safety Executive's definition of ergonomics is 'about ensuring a good "fit" between people and the things they use. People vary enormously in height and weight, in physical strength, in ability to handle information and in many other ways' (HSE 1994). They go on to say that ergonomics uses information about human abilities, attributes and limitations to ensure that our equipment, work and workplaces allow for these variations. About a quarter of all accidents notified to the Health and Safety Executive every year are connected with the manual handling of loads. There are nearly 100,000 back injuries in Britain every year, with a loss of some 1.6 million working days and a subsequent cost in the order of £60 million each year in lost time. If this relates to reported accidents in the workplace it does not even go so far as to include the vast number of back-related problems that incapacitate but are not the result of accidents.

In theory, all workers doing manual handling work are protected by Section 2 of the Health and Safety at Work Act 1974. This requires all employers to ensure, as far as is reasonably practical, the safety and welfare at work of all their employees, by providing safe systems of work and adequate information, training and supervision. Section 72 of the Factories Act 1961 states, 'A person shall not be employed to lift, carry or move any load so heavy as to be likely to cause injury to him.' In practice, however, these requirements offer only limited help to workers. Manual handling may be defined as the transportation of anything by manual force. This will apply in any work situation, from the office worker to the nurse to the heavy manual labourer. In addition to back pain caused by lifting, spinal problems can also be attributed to modern sedentary working conditions and general lifestyle. The office worker can spend anything from 25 to 40 hours a week in a sitting, working position. Other people at risk are those who spend a large proportion of their working time driving. The National Back Pain Association maintain that poorly designed car seating is a factor in the development of serious back problems in those whose jobs depend on driving, such as sales people, taxi, bus and lorry drivers.

The TUC (1988) states that over 200,000 workers suffer from upper limb disorders, often known as repetitive strain injury, every year. Upper limb disorders affect the joints, tendons, muscles and nerves of the hand, wrist, forearm, elbow and upper arm. Injuries result mostly from one or more of the following factors: poor posture and awkward grip, the use of excessive and continual force, working with hand-held tools producing high levels of vibration, poorly designed tools or equipment and repetition of a simple mechanical task over long periods. Symptoms to look out for include; numbness or tingling in the arm or hand; aches and pain in the muscles or at the joints (especially when the limb is raised, or used for some time); loss of strength and grip in the hand; occasionally, loss of sensation and even whiteness in the finger; or crackling in the joints or muscles (TUC 1994).

The following accounts of sufferers of repetitive strain injury indicate how disabling this can be.

○ It started with tingling and numbness in the hands. I didn't know what it was, and just kept doing my work. Then one day my left hand just froze. The company nurse suggested that it might be something to do with the computers on which I worked with few breaks. That was in 1988. So severe was the injury that it brought my 20-year career in journalism to an abrupt halt. I could not even brush my teeth because of crippling pain. I wore arm splints for nearly two years and was drugged up with various medications for most of the time. I changed from being a happy family person to a depressed person.

○ Symptoms first showed ten years ago. I had operations on both wrists in 1986, and thought I'd been cured. But when I went back to work it flared up, and two days after another operation I was asked to take ill-health retirement. The desks were the wrong height and the chairs were broken. My friends say they've replaced them all now, with proper office furniture.

What is commonly reported by sufferers of repetitive strain injury is that once symptoms have been experienced, the condition is worsened by continuing with the same work. Once the problem has become chronic it is not unusual that sufferers, because of their pain, incapacitation and loss of earnings, feel depressed. As with back pain, prevention is the key. The ergonomics of the workplace need to be addressed as does the manner in which people work. Although employees bear some responsibility for their own health and safety at work, it is up to the employer to ensure that they are not at risk from their work tasks or workplace environment. The TUC guidelines for the prevention of work-related upper limb disorders (WRULD), also known as RSI, advise adequate training and education of the workforce so that any symptoms can be reported as soon as they develop. The knowledge required includes: basic skills of body use; the importance of taking work breaks; the correct use of equipment; basic ergonomic principles; early reporting systems and the importance of reporting symptoms; and where to go for help. The TUC also suggest that Health and Safety representatives and union representatives need knowledge of standards, legislation and union agreements; that they need to know how to identify at-risk workers and implement preventive strategies, with the knowledge of resources and sources of help; and that there should be an awareness of the productivity advantages of work breaks and the economic consequences of WRULD (TUC 1994: 41).

Women's health issues

In the past 25 years, the male labour force has increased by only 3 per cent, whereas the increase in the number of women employed is 43 per cent.

Working women with families can find themselves under pressure from the conflict in roles of trying to be a good mother, partner and employee, sometimes feeling that they are not performing any one of these functions adequately. This then puts even more pressure on to the family, so that time away from work is not relaxing and regenerating. Working women with children also face more career disruption than those without children. Flexible working arrangements can help considerably in supporting women who have childcare responsibilities.

Women workers have a specific need for protection in the workplace. There are a wide variety of harmful agents encountered in the workplace which can pose risks to reproduction. The TUC (1991: 15) lists some of the main sources of work-related risks regarding reproduction: work stress (shift work, night work, long hours); chemicals (e.g. mutagens, teratogens, carcinogens); radiation; micro-organisms (e.g. rubella, chlamydia, cytomegalovirus); lifting and carrying; heat stress; cold stress. Health and Safety law, where correctly observed, protects women in such a vulnerable state. The continuation of care is also necessary towards pregnant women. Women who make the decision to terminate a pregnancy, and women whose pregnancy results in miscarriage, very often suffer a considerable emotional reaction affecting their life at home and at work. Referral for counselling at such a time supports the woman through the difficult phase of loss and sadness towards the ability to face life positively again.

Other conditions that may affect some women considerably and need sensitive understanding are pre-menstrual syndrome and the menopause. Pre-menstrual syndrome, or pre-menstrual tension, refers to the physical and mental symptoms which occur for some women before a period. Some of the common symptoms that are experienced include headache/migraine, breast swelling/tenderness, water retention, fatigue, depression, weeping, irritability and craving for certain types of food.

Pre-menstrual syndrome is not a neurosis or something which women can 'snap out of'. It may be helped by reducing stress, by the use of gentle exercise, by ensuring adequate sleep, and by observing a healthy diet with dietary supplements. It is important to be aware that in spite of the best intentions, pre-menstrual syndrome can affect performance at work. The menopause can occur any time from the late thirties to the early sixties. Before and during the menopause, the production of the two main female hormones, oestrogen and progesterone, decreases and then finally ceases. The common menopausal symptoms are changes in, and cessation of, menstruation, and hot flushes. There may also be bloatedness, headaches, tiredness and because of the loss of calcium, brittle bones. The menopause can make women unwell, but with good health management any effect on work can be minimized. Counselling can help by allowing the time to talk about the feelings that are generated by the physical changes and related emotional issues that may occur at this time in a woman's life.

It would seem important that there is an awareness of health concerns and pressures specific to women at work. However, the dependence of this country on female munition workers during World War Two and the success of women today in highly competitive industries indicates that those special health needs are not a disadvantage in the workplace.

Disability

The British Council of Organizations of Disabled People (BCODP) identify themselves as members of a distinct group with their own particular characteristics of physical or sensory impairment. In their view, the term 'disability' implies being singled out by society for a special form of discrimination. This discrimination, not the impairment, is the disability. They define disability as:

> [t]he disadvantage or restriction of activity caused by a contemporary social organization which takes little or no account of people who have impairments and thus excludes them from participation in the mainstream of social activities.
>
> (BCODP Information Pack: 2)

The Disabled Persons (Employment) Acts of 1944 and 1958 require employers of more than 20 employees to employ a quota of at least 3 per cent registered disabled people. In spite of the fact that people with disabilities enjoy the same legal rights under the employment and employment protection legislation as do able-bodied employees, official figures given by BCODP show that people with disabilities are three times more likely to be out of work than non-disabled people. The TUC (1993) puts forward a model agreement of commitment to equal opportunities for employees regardless of whether or not they have a physical, mental or sensory impairment. In their aims they state that impairments shall not of themselves justify the non-recruitment of candidates, that where candidates for recruitment have special employment needs, due account should be taken of the feasibility of adaptations to buildings, equipment, work organization and other aspects of the working environment using the assistance obtained from the Employment Department's Access to Work Scheme in making such adaptations. The Disablement Advisory Service (DAS) helps employers of all sizes and in all types of industry and commerce, to adopt and implement good policies and practices in the employment of people with disabilities.

Where a person becomes disabled through accident or illness, skilled help may be required to help them come to terms with their personal, interpersonal and social problems. Emotional support and accurate information through counselling and possible contact with a relevant organization may be necessary in making this adjustment.

A positive approach towards health in the workplace

Primary management

Primary healthcare is about prevention and about health promotion. It is an organizational issue, based on observation of legal requirements, as proposed in guidelines set out by the Health and Safety Executive and the TUC. Prevention of avoidable ill-health problems involves a willingness to be aware of the internal functioning of all aspects of the dynamics of the workplace. In order for this to be possible, a basic philosophy and practice of honesty and openness must prevail in which there is a clearly accessible system of channels for communication, as is shown in the following case.

O   One trigger for my problem was in July 1992. My company had lost 25 per cent of employees on voluntary redundancies. The impact on existing employees was that workloads were increased without rewards. My old boss who was a respected man had been made redundant. I was initially unable to recognize the difference with my new boss, I didn't know how to handle him with his barriers and blocking. I started to sink and didn't know how to get out, I couldn't find a way of getting support from my new boss and everything that was happening was invisible to the boss above him. I spiralled down, lost my confidence and self-esteem, not knowing what to do. This lasted a few months, I originally felt that I could sort it out as I had managed to sort out problems before, but then I became hopeless. I had been getting regular flu and colds for six months and I had no energy. I stopped doing sport, lost all interest in life. I would only sit around or go to the pub, unable to contribute to my family. I had bouts of irrational anger, quite out of character for me. I got into a state of feeling scared and out of control, imagining acts of violence to my boss, I wanted to run away. Then I went to my GP and was signed off sick. For the first three weeks I felt physically awful. I stopped drinking. At the end of seven weeks I felt fit and went back to work still not truly understanding what had caused my problem. I had never been ill before. In the second week back work piled on and there were conflicts again. I wasn't the only person who had gone off sick. Anger and emotions flooded back, which I couldn't understand because I was physically well. Still confused with what was happening to me I asked in tears for help from Personnel. I was referred to Occupational Health but there was a waiting list of two to three weeks. I went back to my GP who referred me for counselling.

   The first three sessions felt slow and I wondered what was happening. The fourth and fifth sessions were more valuable and I began to understand what had happened. By the sixth session I felt ready to return to work, I was cycling, going to the gym and doing t'ai chi, I felt great. At work someone new had been found for my old job and there had been reorganization with responsibility taken away from my boss. He did my appraisal which was, as I expected, the worst one in ten years. I took advice from Personnel and followed the company line to write to him. I learned to let go. (I couldn't have done this before the counselling.) The company was also introducing a mentoring scheme, so I was able to choose a senior mentor from the Board to meet with regularly. (This continues.) Now I feel that I have a commitment from my boss and boss's boss, both of whom I trust. I was given a new project to work on and also allowed to look around to see where I might use my talents most usefully. This I discuss with my mentor. I think I would have been picked for the next round of redundancies if there had been a further delay in me getting back to work. In truth if I had been offered redundancy at the time I was off sick, I would have accepted it gladly. Now I am happy and committed to my work.

Drucker wrote

THE MANAGER is the dynamic, life-giving element in every business. Without his leadership 'the resources of production' remain resources and never become production. In a competitive economy, above all, the quality and performance of the managers determine the success of a business, indeed they determine its survival. For the quality and performance of its managers is the only effective advantage an enterprise in a competitive economy can have.

(1977: 13)

In employment situations in which employees feel too pressurized by excessive demands, or undervalued; where they are not utilizing their skills creatively; or where their job position feels insecure, their health may suffer as a consequence. It is also likely that their interest and motivation in their work will also suffer.

It seems obvious that good leadership is of utmost importance; that there is honesty and that those making the decisions are visible and can be believed in. It also seems necessary that managers on all levels spend time in getting an understanding of what is going on throughout the organization. Good management practice shows enthusiasm with good communication skills, so that reward is experienced in the feeling of value.

Good health in a primary sense is clearly associated with good management practice. Problems quickly picked up will usually result in the minimum of disruption both for the individual and for the company. With an openness to address reality within the workplace it is possible to act ergonomically and design jobs around people. If there is a practice of honesty and openness fostered by those in senior management, it could be that managers could meet regularly with each staff member, not with a view to appraising but more to being accessible for enquiring into any problem an employee might be experiencing and then appropriately dealing with such matters as may arise. This is not possible in an environment in which employees feel afraid to show weakness of any kind. Essentially primary health care is about prevention, which is influenced by the management structure, philosophy and approach. The availability of support from external providers may also be an integral part of prevention and health promotion. For example, Osteopaths For Industry, also known as 'the back people', work on multiple levels to help organizations. They offer in-house treatment and consultancy, giving advice on posture, seating and manual lifting. Their service is customized to suit the particular individual as well as individual corporate need. This kind of help is beneficial because it takes place in the workplace so that employees can assess themselves within the reality of their situation.

Health promotion is also about making it possible for the workforce to make good choices about being healthy. If there is a cafeteria, the availability of healthy food is clearly sensible. Guidance from the Health Education Authority is available with the supply of posters and leaflets. The provision of exercise facilities, either on site or by arrangement with a local sports centre, also helps the employees to look after their health. Being fit is not only a powerful destressor, but also helps to keep muscles and joints strong and lowers blood pressure and blood cholesterol levels. Again the involvement of managers is important; if the director is seen to be taking exercise it sets standards throughout the structure of the workplace. Management and unions can also, through occupational health or personnel departments, implement education programmes about alcohol and smoking. People often choose alcohol or increased smoking to help them to cope with levels of unmanageable stress. Any strategy aimed at reducing problem drinking must include a commitment to tackling the cause of stress at work. An employee with a drink problem should be offered counselling and their job protected while they attempt to deal with the problem. Policies on smoking are the responsibility of the organization after health and safety regulations have been observed. Leaflets and videos about smoking can be obtained from the Health Education Authority, and Action on Smoking and Health (ASH). Both ASH and Quit offer seminars and support organizations in adjusting to non-smoking policies thereby helping to minimize any resentment. Quit also offers one-to-one counselling for people who wish to give up smoking.

Primary management is about planning for the future using knowledge from past experience and information from current practice. The asbestos toll is one example of a health problem emerging many years after its original widespread use.

Asbestosis will soon outstrip motor accidents as a cause of premature death with 3000 already dying each year from incurable chest illness, the Health and Safety Executive said yesterday. 'New studies predict the death toll will rise steadily each year to peak around 2020 with a probable 10,000 a year dying from asbestos exposure they suffered in the 1960s and 1970s.'

(The Guardian, 25 November 1994)

The Health and Safety Executive and the TUC work to set safety standards at work with the intention of preventing health problems from arising. *Health at Work in the NHS* (HEA 1992) restates the purpose of the NHS in terms of concentrating on health promotion rather than concentrating only on healthcare. This focus on health promotion and prevention of illness wherever possible is supported by other organizations such as local authorities, voluntary bodies, companies and schools. There is no shortage of support for employers from the statutory and the voluntary and private organizations who wish as a primary task to support and maintain a healthy workforce.

Secondary management

Just as primary management seeks to reduce harmful effects of work or the workplace upon the mental and physical health of the workforce, the approach of secondary management is to reduce further any harmful effects on individuals identified either by themselves or by the organizations as requiring help. Even where an organization puts resources into primary prevention there will always be some individuals who will require assistance of a secondary nature, whether from illness or from problems at home. In such cases the facility of an employee assistance programme is beneficial in offering a helpful arm. Knowledge of the existence of such support can in itself be helpful to managers and employers. Through such a provider confidential help is offered in counselling for emotional problems and possibly also information of a Citizens' Advice Bureau nature. Stress management programmes are widely available, but would seem to be more appropriate where customized to the individual need of the organization. Where staff can see their own behaviour relating to their particular working environment, the value is likely to be much greater and more permanent.

Some aspects of primary management also apply to secondary management or healthcare. Exercise facilities, osteopathic intervention, massage, relaxation classes, yoga, t'ai chi and nutritional guidance, either provided for within the organization, or by arrangement with external providers, not only help to promote good health but are also beneficial in the rehabilitation of health problems. The value of counselling has been demonstrated by Wilson *et al.* (1989), who examine the ways in which insomnia, headaches and obesity can be addressed using cognitive-behavioural therapy. (See also Daines *et al.* 1997).

As secondary management is a response to problems or change of circumstances, one aspect of organization that is widely implemented and of considerable value is the provision of flexible working arrangements for staff members who are disabled, ill or who have family responsibilities or changes to adapt to. This might apply to the type of work carried out, the times of work, the venue, family leave, career break schemes, job sharing and childcare initiatives. Family responsibilities can put considerable pressure on people, often women, who are holding down employment. To be able to take time out from work knowing that your job is secure for you to return to brings the peace of mind necessary to good health. The increase in the numbers of elderly people in this country has brought about a corresponding necessity for many employees to have to balance their work with caring. This presents obvious problems of a conflictual nature. Often the person who is in employment needs to continue to work for financial reasons, not to mention the personal satisfaction that may be gained from their work and the involvement with colleagues. The Carers' National Association believes that carers who are working should be encouraged and supported to remain at work for as long as they want, and has been pressing the government to improve benefits and services to support them.

Oxfordshire County Council (1992) acknowledges that a significant proportion of its employees have caring responsibilities for an elderly, ill or disabled relative. The County Council's social services department has accepted that they have a major role to play in providing support to carers within their employ. It has adopted a Carers' Charter and established a Carers' Advisory Service. All approaches to the Advisory Service are treated confidentially. The County Council has a number of policies which are helpful to their employees who have caring responsibilities, which include a career break scheme offering a break of several years, but remaining in touch with a view to being helped to return when the carer is ready; unpaid leave for up to 12 months; compassionate leave of up to ten days; flexitime to vary starting and finishing times; flexiplace in order to do some work at home; and job sharing or reduced hours.

A survey was carried out in Fife Regional Council social work department in 1993 (Fife Social Work Department 1993) to discover how many staff provided care for an adult friend or relative outside their work, and how they combined this with their employment. As an Equal Opportunities employer, Fife Regional Council aims to create employment conditions which do not discriminate against people on grounds or factors which are not directly relevant to their ability to do a job to the required standard. Seventy-six of the 278 employees who returned survey forms said they had informal care responsibilities (26.8 per cent). It was found that male carers were just as likely to devote all their non-work time to caring as were women carers.

○   Up until February 1992 I had to care for an elderly parent. During this
    time 'flexitime' was not available to me but if it had been it would
    have made the task of caring for my parent easier.
                                                    (Male, full-time worker)

An understanding line manager was the most commonly reported helpful factor for staff with informal care responsibilities, and few staff reported an unsympathetic line manager as a barrier to adjusting their hours. The most frequently reported difficulties were feelings of guilt, either about not being able to provide all the care they wished, or about not being able to do all the work they wished, or both, and pressure of work.

○   The dilemma created by being both an employee (of the Social Work
    Department) and the son/carer of a dependent parent was quite
    intense. I don't know how this conflict of interest could have been
    avoided but I do know that being in that situation, feelings of guilt
    and wanting to do more, are very stressful.
                                                    (Male, full-time worker)

Fourteen staff answered that their career prospects had been restricted by their informal care responsibilities, either by restricting the choice of job that was open to them or going for promotion. Thirteen of the carers said their care responsibilities caused them to worry about their work and seven said they were concerned about how their colleagues perceived them at work. One of the main findings of this research was that the quality of staff relations was the key feature in providing the flexibility within the workplace which was essential for informal carers to meet the changing needs of the people they look after. Employment schemes such as job sharing and part-time working were found to have proven value as a complement to supportive line managers, not a substitute for them.

It is clear that the responsibilities of carers within the workplace is, if anything, going to increase. If the skills and expertise gained by employees through their experience and training are to be preserved, it would seem necessary to be flexible in providing for such needs through the implementation of appropriate work arrangements.

As the health of managers is so important both individually and corporately, the facility of sabbaticals is worth considering. The value of this is to develop awareness for new ideas, skills and motivation. As well as building on the inherent qualities developed from within the organization, there is a distinct advantage in bringing in fresh initiatives from outside.

Tertiary management

Some health problems may be very difficult to resolve, and rehabilitation back into the workplace can be an uphill struggle, or may be impossible to achieve. For chronically sick people, measures as previously described, such as flexible working arrangements, may be appropriate.

HIV and AIDS

Lobbyists and campaigning groups are beginning to target employers for two reasons. First, keeping HIV-positive employees in employment guarantees them the money to maintain their standard of living, and for possible treatment costs as well as keeping morale boosted. Second, by fitting into employers' health promotion programmes, AIDS educators can reach the generation of young people who were too old to receive AIDS awareness training at school. Although AIDS and HIV are often lumped together, in practice they raise different issues. HIV is in effect an equal opportunities issue, one of the main problems being other people's reactions. HIV policies, therefore, are to do with safeguarding HIV-positive employees from discrimination and harassment, and protecting their confidentiality, whereas AIDS policies are designed to offer a fair way of treating an employee with a degenerative disease, balancing their needs with those of the organization. This will raise such issues as medical retirement, pensions and moves to lighter duties if necessary. These problems are not unique to AIDS, but test a company's other employment policies, in particular in relation to long-term illness. It is both a management problem relative to the type of work carried out and a primary prevention agenda in terms of health education. The twin aims of an HIV/AIDS policy, according to the Employers' Advisory Service on AIDS and HIV (ESAH), a Yorkshire-based training, advisory and research service, should be to protect the well, and to behave in a non-negative way towards people with HIV and AIDS.

There is often little consensus as to who within the organization takes responsibility for HIV/AIDS policy. ESAH deplores the tendency to 'medicalization' of HIV and argues that most of the workplace issues raised by HIV are personnel ones, as in nearly all situations the risk of infection at work is minimal. Some employers have a specific policy, while others take the line that their existing policies on sickness, discrimination and other relevant policies are adequate to include AIDS and HIV. Having a specific policy may provoke accusations of special treatment, while existing policies may fail to focus adequately on the specific reaction to colleagues with HIV and AIDS. All employers guarantee the usual medical confidentiality to employees who reveal that they are HIV-positive. Pre-employment screening is rare, but some employers expect employees to disclose if they have good reason to expect that they have been infected with HIV.

Particular employees who need to observe special precautions include researchers who deal with the live virus, some members of the medical profession and post office workers who collect mail from areas where syringes are regularly dumped in collection boxes. Many companies see the greatest risk of infection in their employees who routinely travel abroad, either by sexual contact or by blood transfusion if that became necessary. Briefing and leaflets are given to highlight awareness. Oxaids (an Oxford-based AIDS charity) raises the suggestion that some companies may place their main emphasis on the risks of sexually transmitted infection during foreign travel as a means of denying the existence of a problem nearer home, because the risk of infection is identical in so far as the routes of transmission are identical.

There have been a number of recent initiatives in the field of HIV/AIDS in the workplace including the National AIDS Trust's Companies Act (1992) and the Terrence Higgins Trust's training package, 'Positive Management' (1993). The initiative for the Companies Act came about after a National AIDS Trust survey of advice agencies suggested that there was a strong perception that companies would discriminate against HIV-positive employees. Companies who sign up must have an explicit AIDS/HIV policy judged by the National AIDS Trust to be equitable. The intention is that they should be 'visible witnesses of good practice'. The Terrence Higgins Trust's 'Positive Management' project briefing notes cover:

- HIV and AIDS
- do you need a policy on HIV and AIDS?
- recruitment
- confidentiality and ill-health procedures
- discrimination while in employment
- keeping people with HIV and AIDS in employment
- redeployment and dismissal
- pensions
- first aid
- travel
- HIV awareness
- helplists.

Each section consists of a breakdown of legal considerations and the employer's responsibilities, a checklist of good practice and a set of questions to consider (Incomes Data Services 1993: 11). Most of the potential areas of conflict can be resolved through education and consultation. Counselling available outside the organization is a useful support, whether for people who have been diagnosed as HIV-positive and are on a daily basis having to come to terms with the effects of their illness, or for employees who are finding it difficult to deal with their feelings regarding colleagues who are HIV-positive.

Cancer

Cancer is a term for a large number of different diseases which can strike any organ or tissue, anywhere in the body. All cancers have one thing in common: they involve the uncontrolled multiplication of body cells. If a cell, or a group of cells, continues to divide and multiply in an uncontrolled way, a growth or tumour forms. The tumour may be 'benign' or 'malignant'. A benign tumour is a growth which does not invade or damage surrounding tissue. Tumours of this kind are usually quite harmless, but should not be ignored. Malignant tumours are growths which can invade other body tissues. The difference in the cells of benign and malignant tumours can often only be seen under a microscope. If a malignant tumour is left untreated, some of the cells may break away from the original growth and be transported through the body via the bloodstream or the lymphatic system. The cancer may then form in another part of the body. These secondary growths are called metastases.

The causes of many types of cancer are not known. However, there are specific ways in which risks can be minimized, in particular:

- don't smoke: 90 per cent of deaths from lung cancer are due to smoking;
- don't get burnt by the sun; always use a sunscreen and only expose your skin for short periods;
- follow Health and Safety rules at work to safeguard against contact with dangerous chemicals and radiation;
- eat healthily and limit alcohol intake;
- take advantage of the screening opportunities that are offered.

There are three main treatments for cancer: radiotherapy, in which high energy rays are directed on to a tumour; chemotherapy, a drug treatment which destroys cancer cells in the primary site and in secondary growths; and surgery, in which the tumour is surgically removed. Radiotherapy and chemotherapy cause side-effects requiring time off work. Cancer is a frightening concept because with it comes uncertainty and the possibility of dying. The diagnosis of cancer is usually a devastating one. Typical reactions can be shock, denial and anger. It may not pose the same dilemma of discrimination as AIDS, but when an employee has cancer it may often be difficult to know what to say to them. Managers and fellow employees may be unsure as to whether it is best to speak about it or keep quiet. Of course cancer is not necessarily a tertiary type of problem, as many people take the required time off work to receive the necessary treatment and then go on to return to their position in the workplace while they make a full recovery. In some cases which require frequent surgery or debilitating treatment it may be impossible for an employee to return to their previous position of work so that either more flexible working arrangements are required or the employee must terminate their working agreement. This could be a very difficult thing to do, needing to face the grief that they may die, combined with the loss of the familiarity of work and colleagues. Such situations require sensitive and careful handling.

Inevitably at times, within the working environment there will be intractable problems relating to the ill-health of employees. Davis and Fallowfield (1991) suggest that counselling has a positive role to play in dealing with diabetes, renal failure, disfigurement, head injury, multiple sclerosis, cancer and heart disease. The trauma of illness, disability or death of an employee may cause emotional problems for staff and colleagues alike. Managers may feel helpless in terms of how best to deal with such situations. A counselling referral agency can be invaluable for advice, and can also provide a resource for staff to work through the difficult feelings that may arise.

Conclusion

The workplace is a changing, dynamic structure. People working within this structure are both affected by it, and affect it. The Health and Safety Executive's Working Group (HSE 1993) make the statement that organizations have the opportunity to preserve and promote positive mental health, and that senior managers, when making strategic decisions, should recognize their impact – for good or ill – on the mental health of the workforce. Stress-related problems are not just an employee problem. They may soon be a serious risk liability for employers too. In the recent (1994) case of social worker, John Walker, a High Court judge held his employers liable for a nervous breakdown that ended his career. This is the first case in Britain of an employee suing his employer for stress from overwork. Mr Walker's employers were held liable for damages because of their unreasonable failure to provide a safe system of work, thereby putting stress on the same footing as work accidents or industrial diseases. In future it may be insurance companies who dictate proper procedures to minimize the risk.

There is little trust in an industrial society that operates a 'fear culture', in which people in work are so afraid to be out of work that they can no longer be enthusiastic about their work. It seems likely that work enthusiasts will enjoy better health and be more productive than work addicts.

Alvin Gouldner aptly describes the helplessness that can be experienced by employees who feel overworked and undervalued:

> In short, vast parts of any personality must be suppressed or repressed
> in the course of playing a role in industrial society. All that a man

is that is not useful will somehow be excluded or at least not allowed to intrude, and he thereby becomes alienated or estranged from a large sector of his own interests, needs and capacities. Thus, just as there is the unemployed man, there is also the unemployed self. Because of the exclusion and devaluations of self fostered by an industrial system orientated towards utility, many men develop a dim sense of loss; for the excluded self, although muffled, is not voiceless and makes its protest heard. They feel an intimation that something is being wasted, and that this something may be nothing less than their lives.

(1977)

There are resources for employees to turn to with health problems. Doctors, occupational health staff, counsellors and others need to use each other's resources skilfully, co-operatively and with due regard for confidentiality, for the benefit of distressed individuals. The role of the counsellor can be in assisting the individual to be referred to a suitable medical practitioner; encouraging someone to overcome anxiety about a feared diagnosis; facilitating an individual's need to become more assertive about their rights and needs; helping people to reduce stress factors which may lead to or worsen a medical condition; assisting with the breaking of bad news; offering psychological strategies for chronic pain management; and helping people affected by illness to rebuild impaired self-esteem.

Counselling in primary care settings is being valued as increasingly useful, and enlightened companies such as Johnson and Johnson have long valued the positive contribution of workplace counselling as an integral part of their employee health policies.

References

Cooper, C. (1981) *Executive Families Under Stress*. Chichester: John Wiley.

Daines, B., Gask, L. and Usherwood, T. (1997) *Medical and Psychiatric Issues for Counsellors*. London: Sage.

Davis, H. and Fallowfield, L. (eds) (1991) *Counselling and Communication in Health Care*. Chichester: John Wiley.

Drucker, P. (1977) *The Practice of Management*. London: Pan.

Fife Social Work Department (1993) *Carers at Work. A survey of informal care responsibilities among social work staff in Fife Regional Council*.

Gouldner, A. (1977) *The Coming Crisis in Western Sociology*. Oxford: Heinemann.

HEA (1992) *Health at Work in the NHS* (Action pack). London: Health Education Authority.

HSE (1993) *Mental Health at Work* (IND(G)59L C300 4/94). London: Health and Safety Executive.

HSE (1994) *If The Task Fits: Ergonomics at work* (IND(G)90(L)(REV). Sheffield: Health and Safety Executive.

HSE (1995) *The Costs to the British Economy of Work Accidents and Work-related Ill Health*. London: Health and Safety Executive.

Incomes Data Services (1993) *HIV, AIDS and Employment:* (Study 528). London: IDS.

London Hazards Centre (1994) *Hard Labour, Ill-health and Hazardous Practices*. London: LHC.

OPCS (1994) *OPCS Surveys of Psychiatric Morbidity in Great Britain, Bulletin no. 1*. London: OPCS.

Oxfordshire County Council (1992) *Support for Working Carers*. Oxford: Personnel, Policy and Review Unit.

TUC (1988) *Lighten The Load: Guidelines on manual handling at work*. London: Trades Union Congress.

TUC (1991) *Women's Health at Risk: A TUC handbook*. London: Trades Union Congress.

TUC (1993) *Guidance on Trade Unions and Disabled Members*. London: Trades Union Congress.

TUC (1994) *Guide To Assessing WRULDS Risks*. London: Trades Union Congress.

Warr, P. (1987) *Work, Unemployment and Mental Health*. Oxford: Clarendon Press.

Wilson, P.H., Spence, S.H. and Kavanagh, D.J. (1989) *Cognitive Behavioural Interviewing for Adult Disorders*. London: Routledge.

Suggested reading

Brewster, S. (1993) *The Complete Book of Men's Health*. London: Thorsons.
Northrup, C. (1995) *Women's Bodies, Women's Wisdom*. London: Piatkus.
O'Brien, P. (1993) *Fit to Work*. London: Sheldon.
Sanders, D. (1996) *Counselling for Psychosomatic Problems*. London: Sage.
Shone, N. (1995) *Coping with Cancer*. London: Sheldon.
Smith, T. (1995) *Heart Attacks: Prevent and survive*. London: Sheldon.

Useful organizations

ARMS (Action For Research into MS)
4A Chapel Hill
Stansted
Essex
0170 222 3133

ASH (Action on Smoking and Health)
109 Gloucester Place
London W1H 3PH
0171 935 3519   Fax: 0171 935 3463

BACUP (British Association of Cancer United Patients)
3 Bath Place
London EC2A 3JR
0800 18 11 99, 0171 613 2121

BCODP (British Council of Organizations of Disabled People)
St Mary's Church
Greenlaw Street
Woolwich
London SE18 5AR

British Heart Foundation
14 Fitzhardinge Street
London W1H 4DH
0171 935 0185   Fax: 0170 486 5821

National Backpain Association
16 Elmtree Road
Teddington
Middlesex

Osteopaths For Industry
1 Grove Way
Esher
Surrey KT10 8HH
0181 398 7533   Fax: 0181 398 4864

Society of Occupational Medicine
6 St Andrews Place
Regents Place
London NW1 4LB
0171 486 2641   Fax: 0171 486 0028

SPOD (The Association to Aid the Sexual and Personal Relationships of People with
Disability)
286 Camden Road
London N7 0B7
0171 607 8851

The Stroke Association
CHSA House
Whitecross Street
London EC1Y 8JJ
0171 490 7999   Fax: 0171 490 2686

Debt counselling and financial advice

○ **ROGER THISTLE**

Introduction

Earning money or otherwise creating income is an essential part of life for most people, but it is also the underlying cause of stress for many. Adequacy of personal and family income is a sufficiently problematic theme in itself but individual perceptions of income, material needs, and expenditure generally add further stress. Disagreements about money are a common source of marital difficulties (see Conger and Elder 1990). The personal meanings of money and preferences in how it is to be spent constitute a further problematic dimension (Lunt and Livingstone 1992). Dominion (1995) argues that within marriages and comparable partnerships money frequently symbolizes struggles, not only over real hardship but also over love and power. Money, money management and debt are far from straightforward subjects; economists and psychologists have quite different perspectives on such issues. The American psychiatrist and psychoanalyst Krueger (1992) presents one of a growing number of accounts of how money may be viewed from a psychological perspective. Debt has its undeniable historical and economic dimensions, and Barty-King (1991) provides an excellent overview. Since counsellors and others in the position of providing welfare assistance in the workplace have relatively little specific literature available to guide them practically, the focus of this chapter will be on how individual employees experiencing debt problems can be helped. Also, because a significant factor in the development of individual debt is ignorance, certain fundamental explanations have been included.

Employers who are considering the provision of counselling facilities for their staff may wish to include debt counselling as part of the service.

Others may want to guide employees to sources of professional help outside or encourage employees to develop a credit union. While this chapter offers practical advice to employers on the establishment of such facilities, it will also be of benefit to professional counsellors, personnel managers, social workers, in fact anyone who faces an employee or client with a financial problem. The initial focus here is on practicalities; the psychological effects are discussed later.

During the ten-year period from 1981, total consumer debt (that is, credit cards and loans) rose from £15.5 billion to £53.6 billion, representing around £1,000 worth of debt for every man, woman and child in the UK. In the same period of time, the annual number of homes repossessed because of mortgage arrears rose sharply from 4,900 to 75,500 (HM Government Central Statistical Office 1995).

Shocking as these figures may be, the reality is that people have borrowed ever since trading began. For example, in the biblical story, the Good Samaritan made an advance payment to an innkeeper to care for the victim of a mugging. Although the Samaritan did not have a credit card, he was able to rely upon the goodwill of the innkeeper who shouldered the remaining debt until he returned.

It is probable that banks existed in ancient Babylon, as evidence of financial transactions has been found there, recorded on baked clay tablets at least 4,500 years old. By 350 BC the Romans were using coins, and a thousand years later goldsmiths in the Lombardy region of northern Italy were developing early moneylending and banking systems.

Today, brown envelopes containing quarterly bills drop through our letterboxes, reminding us all (even those who claim not to use credit) that whenever we switch on an electric light or pick up a phone we begin to incur debt.

Bankers and other finance providers will continue to lend as long as the customer's credit is good. A car loan for an individual, a factory for a public company, a major health investment programme for a national government – in all these cases the ability to meet an agreed programme of repayments will be required.

There are a variety of reasons why individuals find themselves in debt and unable to meet their bills or other repayments. Long-term illness may put a strain on budgets. Gambling and drug or alcohol misuse frequently lead to debt as the cost of maintaining an addiction spirals out of control. For some, the need to keep up appearances, perhaps to emulate a successful relative or impress a business partner, may be the driving force in spending beyond their means. There may be ignorance about benefits available. Some local authorities employ people to assist tenants in reducing their rent arrears. I asked one London housing officer about this problem. He told me:

Many people, although eligible, fail to claim housing benefit. Because claims are not normally backdated, arrears can then mount up quickly.

A change in family circumstances such as separation, divorce, imprisonment, accident or death of a partner can mean an abrupt reduction in family income. I wish all tenants would keep us informed so that we can offer help promptly, but they don't and this can eventually put them at risk of eviction.

A period of economic recession such as that experienced during the late 1980s and early 1990s leads inevitably to high unemployment and low wages. Whole communities, especially those dependent upon single declining industries, such as steel manufacture or coal mining, can be plunged into poverty. In turn, this places many of their members at greater risk of incurring individual debt. Parker (1986) draws a portrait of life in a mining community where the pit is under threat of closure. Among his interviews is one with a shopkeeper:

> As far as this business here in this shop goes, I think it will make a big difference if they do shut Red Hill down. If people transfer I think it will take all the stuffing out of the community. Or if they take redundancy, I think before long they will start to drift away. It won't be because they want to, a lot of them have never lived anywhere else; but they'll have to think about their children and what's going to happen to them in the future. There certainly aren't no employment prospects here. It's a very bad outlook.

The pit on which Red Hill is based was closed down three months later.

The shame of debt

Over the years, the English vocabulary has softened, giving rise to expressions such as 'credit facilities' instead of 'overdraft', and 'spreading the cost' rather than 'having to borrow'. The shame of not being able to pay the 'tally man' who knocked on the door on wages day for his repayments has given way to the status symbol of the gold credit card. Even so, personal finance is still regarded as a private subject. We do not readily admit to others how much we earn or the extent to which we are in debt. So are customers honest in their relationship with their bank managers? I asked a retired high street bank manager what he thought. He said:

> Customers frequently try to hide the depth of their financial problems before they seek help. By then repayments and interest costs have escalated, making it more difficult to resolve the problem. Borrowing from one finance company to repay another doesn't change anything (except perhaps the interest rate), but sitting down and having an honest discussion about their whole financial situation is the first step to resolving their problems.

A money advice worker agrees about the need for honesty and told me:

> However difficult the problem, it is never too late to do something. While some people come because their house is about to be repossessed, others are worried about the gas being cut off. You can always be sure that there is more to the problem than one bill, and our task is to help people look at the whole picture. Although large and multiple debts can make us want to put our head in the sand, doing nothing is never really an option.

Prioritizing the debts

When assisting a colleague who has financial problems, whether in a formal counselling setting or when offering informal advice, it is important to develop a plan for dealing with the difficulties. For anyone owing money it may be tempting to prioritize repayments on the largest loans, or in response to the lenders who exert the greatest pressure. However, experience shows that it is far preferable to prioritize according to the seriousness of the steps which each creditor can take.

Harassment of debtors is an offence. No matter how large the amount owned no one has to put up with phone calls at work, vans marked 'Debt Collection' arriving outside the home or threatening calls late at night. Debtors' prisons as such are thankfully a thing of the past (although people in debt often need reassurance on this). It is true that some debts, such as unpaid tax, attract penalties which can include eventual imprisonment, but only where there is proven and wilful non-payment. Neverthless, unpaid tax should be given a high priority alongside rent or mortgage arrears, fuel costs and essential food and clothing. Mortgages are secured against property, meaning that non-payment could lead to the borrower losing their home if it has been used as security. Similarly landlords, including local councils, can evict tenants who fail to pay their rent. In all cases the landlord or mortgage company would need to apply to the court first, which may take time, so whatever the circumstances, the initial emergency advice should always be 'Don't move out – sit tight!'

Unpaid utility bills, for example those for gas, electricity and telephone services, can lead to loss of the service provided and additional charges for reconnection. If the person is taken to court, a record of the outstanding debt and the arrangement agreed for future payment will be entered against their name. This is known as a county court judgment. Once entered this information is available to credit reference agencies, which all lenders use to assess the risks of lending to individuals. So the effect of a judgment is to make it more expensive, more difficult or even impossible to obtain credit in the future.

It is important to respond to correspondence. Lenders may be sympathetic to proposals for the rescheduling of debts over a longer period, but will be concerned if borrowers make unrealistically low offers of repayments, make high offers that are not kept to, withhold information about other debts that they may have, or fail to answer letters.

So it is essential to offer appropriate advice and guidance to anyone in arrears, whatever their type of borrowing. While some people will enter into credit arrangements without thinking about the consequences, many more will tend to look only at the monthly or weekly repayment required without considering the interest rate charged or the length of time the loan will be outstanding. People can be quite ignorant when it comes to basic financial matters, so included below is a brief description of the popular types of borrowing on offer, including details of the ultimate sanctions available to lenders when payments are not forthcoming.

Popular types of borrowing

Mortgages

Most home buyers need to borrow money in order to purchase a home. Mortgages are the means by which a lender can be assured that his money is reasonably secure. The property remains in the possession of the borrower; however, it may be claimed by the lender through legal action in the courts if the loan and interest payments are not met according to agreed terms. The lender is then free to sell the property in order to discharge the debt, paying only the balance (if any) back to the borrower. Before assisting someone with mortgage arrears, it is important to clarify how advanced the problem is. The first sign of difficulty in meeting monthly payments will result in a letter from the bank or building society asking that the account be brought up to date. Encourage the borrower to be realistic, and to explain why the lapse has come about. Two or more missed payments are likely to lead to a threat of legal action, so encourage the borrower to keep in contact with the lender, making some payment and answering all letters even if they are unable to pay in full. Legal action is likely to be taken much faster if the lender does not know why payments are being missed. Lenders can sometimes be helpful in the short term, for example agreeing that the borrower may delay a couple of payments if he or she is in-between jobs or expecting a lump sum, so it is worth asking about this. No one should ever be advised to hand the keys back to the lender and walk away from the mortgage, however bad their financial circumstances. If it does become necessary to sell it is always preferable to maintain control over this. Mortgage repossessed property is normally sold cheaply at auction in order to reduce the lender's liabilities, and in some cases where the borrowing exceeds the value of the property a debt will remain even after the funds from the sale have been used.

Personal loans

Usually a higher rate of interest is charged for personal loans than mortgages. This is because there is no security for the lender to fall back on should the loan not be repaid. Personal loans are offered to people who are reasonably good credit risks, usually for sums between £200 and £10,000. Such loans are often marketed as a means of purchasing expensive consumer items such as hi-fi and cars or even holidays. Although there is no security requested and therefore no risk to the borrower's home, failure to pay could result in legal action and subsequently a county court judgment against the borrower.

Overdrafts

An agreed overdraft is one where the bank allows a customer to borrow up to a certain limit, by drawing more than their actual credit balance. An unagreed overdraft could occur either if a customer drew a cheque for more funds than were available on the account, or for more than the agreed overdraft facility. The distinction is important, because banks usually charge more for overdrafts that are not agreed in advance. In addition to interest charges, an overdraft may trigger bank charges on all transactions during a particular charging period.

Credit cards

Credit cards are simply a means of payment for goods or services but, unlike cheque transactions, cannot be stopped once agreed by the cardholder. In this way payment is guaranteed to the retailer, and the customer is billed monthly by the card company. The cardholder is then able to choose whether to pay the bill in full, at no additional cost; or make a part-payment, in which case interest charges will be made. However, some cards carry an annual fee, and credit card interest charges are normally higher than those for personal loans. Cards are issued by banks, building societies and major retailers such as department stores. Because the credit limit has been agreed in advance, some cardholders may be tempted to spend up to or beyond their means. Cards are widely issued and accepted and they are designed to encourage spontaneous purchases, so it can be relatively simple to run up large debts with a credit card.

When working with someone who has accumulated unmanageable credit card debts they should be encouraged to destroy the cards by cutting through the card numbers (to prevent misuse by others as well as themselves) and to return the cards to the issuer. One way of reducing monthly payments is to apply for a consolidation loan which would bring all the debts into one account, hopefully at a lower rate of interest but certainly payable over a longer term. Some of the card companies and banks are prepared to do this provided the customer is still considered creditworthy. Where this is not a practical option because of the size of the debt, the sample letters at the end of this chapter should be used to request the suspension of interest charges and/or reduction of monthly payments.

One employee managed to run up debts of over £10,000 on ten different credit facilities including cards. Although credit checks are normally taken, he did not have a previous bad record of payment so was able to obtain an average of £1,000 cash from each company over a few months. This money enabled him to hide the fact that he would not otherwise have managed to keep up his mortgage payments. This had been a problem since he was put on to a short-time contract at work. With monthly minimum payments of 5 per cent he was having to find around £500 each month in card and loan payments and even then over a third was going on interest charges. He would have been better advised to discuss the matter early with his building society. As it was, he eventually realized the seriousness of his situation and was fortunate in getting some financial help from within his family to clear some of the debt. He obtained a consolidation loan for the rest, has now moved to a smaller home, and is making reasonable progress in reducing his remaining borrowing.

There is now a wide range of plastic payment cards available, some of which are multi-purpose. In simple terms, all cards carrying the Delta or Switch logo are debit cards which charge payments to bank accounts, while cards bearing just Visa or MasterCard logos offer credit facilities. However, there are some added complications. Some banks issue separate cheque guarantee cards while others combine them with debit or credit cards. Some even issue debit cards bearing both the Delta and the Visa sign, and major retailers issue their own credit cards to encourage customers to shop at their particular stores. Some charge cards issued by companies such as Diners Club and American Express offer monthly billing but no extended credit. Cardholders should be advised to check with their card company if they are unsure of their repayment requirements, interest charges or credit limit.

Catalogue shopping

Mail order catalogue companies are major providers of credit facilities. Some of the larger companies produce comprehensive catalogues offering a wide range of clothing and household items. With catalogue shopping customers have the benefit of ordering and receiving goods without leaving home. Catalogues frequently quote a price for monthly or weekly payments, but the price of the goods normally reflects the cost of providing them on credit, and this is frequently higher than shop prices even when purchasing goods on credit there. Like other debts, unpaid bills from catalogue purchases may be chased initially by the company and subsequently by a debt collection agency. The goods cannot be repossessed; however, if taken to court for non-payment, customers risk a county court judgment being made against them. A debt collection agent told me:

> The worst calls are to single parents living on the top floor of a tower block. You know they've got no money except what they need to feed the kids. Some of them can't keep up the catalogue payments, or maybe they join too many at once. It's too easy and for many of them it's credit they wouldn't get anywhere else. We still have to call on them, of course; if we didn't I guess a lot more of them would try and get away without paying, but I never hold out much hope on these visits.

Hire purchase

After buying a home, the second most expensive single purchase for most people is a motor vehicle. In 1993, the average household spent over £36 weekly on vehicle purchase and maintenance and, significantly, this cost rose to over £49 where the head of household was in employment (HM Government Central Statistical Office 1995). For workers who have no access to a company car or public transport but who need to travel regularly in the course of their work, a vehicle is often regarded as essential. As it is also a major financial commitment it normally requires some form of finance.

Hire purchase is one means of sale whereby a vehicle or other goods are initially hired but then become the property of the customer when final payment is made. Unlike a personal loan, if the borrower does not maintain regular payments, the item (frequently a car) may be repossessed. If a third or less of the total amount owing has been repaid, this may happen without a court order. There may be additional penalty charges for early settlement of an agreement, so it is important to be aware of the small print and make a considered decision whether to risk repossession or treat the debt and the repayments as a high priority.

Vehicles – leased

The user makes regular payments for a set period and enjoys full use of a vehicle which is returned at the end of the agreement. This is attractive both to self-employed people, as no major capital outlay is required, and to companies operating fleets of vehicles, because the leasing agreement may include regular maintenance and running costs of the fleet. There will, however, be rules about mileage covered and vehicle condition on return. Someone in financial difficulty may be tempted to return a vehicle, but as with hire purchase, it is essential to check the fine print and establish the real cost of returning a vehicle early.

Vehicles – option purchase

This is similar to leasing, but after a given term the user has the option to return the vehicle, owing nothing, purchase it at a guaranteed future value or use this value as deposit on a new vehicle. Again, there will be conditions concerning mileage covered and vehicle condition, as well as a date for return of the vehicle, so the agreement needs careful study before any alteration to the arrangement is made.

Leasehold property

Freehold property belongs to the owner outright, although it may be mortgaged to a lending institution. While leasehold property may similarly be mortgaged, a leasehold arrangement gives right of use to the buyer, for a given period, but subject to certain conditions. In a block of flats, for example, leaseholders will have the right to own the property for a given period of time, but pay rent for the land on which it is built, and service charges to maintain the building. The landlord can impose any reasonable charges, and these are likely to increase as the property gets older and requires major attention such as re-roofing or replacement heating systems. Leaseholders have a right to written statements of work planned or carried out by their landlord, but because major bills cannot always be accurately predicted, this is a frequent source of conflict and complaint. It is not uncommon for employees to bring such problems to their employee counselling service, and such disputes can be frustrating and time-consuming. While the potential for such disputes is a clear disadvantage it has to be weighed against the advantage that major repair bills will be shared between the residents of a block or an estate.

Payment arrears

This is not formal borrowing; however, one of the most popular ways of avoiding debt is by using other people's money! Most of us have delayed payment of bills for a few days until the wages have arrived. While sensible budgeting offers individuals a short-term solution to cash flow problems, large arrears on items such as rent or mortgages can quickly mount up to the point where realistic repayments can no longer be sustained. Services such as the telephone may be disconnected if the payment is not made, and an additional charge made for subsequent reconnection. Some people are able to call upon parents, relatives or friends to help out when in a financial crisis. There may not be so much pressure to repay a generous uncle as, say, the gas company; however, the debt still exists, and provided it is not really a gift, and there is an intention to repay, anyone in this position should include such a debt as part of their obligations, albeit as a lower priority

Table 6.1 Types of debt and sanctions for non-payment

Type of debt	Sanction
Unpaid tax	**Imprisonment**

Imprisonment is only a last resort where there is deliberate and wilful attempt to evade payment.

Rent and mortgage arrears	**Loss of home**

Courts will try hard to avoid making people homeless, for example giving families time to try and sell their home in order to move to cheaper accommodation, or to repay rent arrears. In certain circumstances, local authorities may have a duty to rehouse people, but not debtors who are defined as intentionally homeless.

Utility companies' unpaid bills	**County court judgment and**
(gas, electricity, telephone or water)	**disconnection of service**

Most utilities have a clearly defined disconnection policy designed not to increase hardship in cases of genuine need. But they will need to be made aware of the problem promptly. Different legal arrangements apply in Scotland from those in England and Wales.

Personal loans and overdrafts	**County court judgment**
Credit card bills	**County court judgment and loss of card**
Catalogue shopping bills	**County court judgment**
Hire purchase	**Forfeit of goods and/or court action**

Goods purchased under a hire purchase arrangement can be repossessed without a court order if one-third or less of the balance has been paid. There may also be additional financial penalties for an early settlement.

than others. Sometimes, a private arrangement can resolve, in the short term, immediate financial pressure. Discussing such matters at home or within the family is frequently put off for fear of shame and embarrassment. However, once addressed, an honest dialogue can play an important part in challenging unrealistic financial attitudes and expectations.

Types of debt and sanctions for non-payment

Anyone who is in debt and considering which are their priority bills for payment needs to be aware of the ultimate sanctions that various types of creditors can take against their debtors. Table 6.1 is a simple guide together with comments on each item.

The annual percentage rate (APR)

There is a confusing choice of arrangements for the charging of interest. These may be calculated on a monthly or daily basis and special offers on shop prices can include interest-free credit. Because consumers may find it

difficult to make comparisons between finance offers legislation was introduced to ensure that all companies offering credit facilities had to quote a
single annual percentage rate (APR).

Generally, the greater the risk to the lender, or the less security offered by
the borrower, the higher the interest charge or APR will be. Customers can
shop around for the best deal, and rates vary from time to time; however, a
typical range for comparison might be similar to these quoted during 1995:

- first-time buyer's mortgage   6.9% APR
- additional mortgage to move home   7.9% APR
- personal loan from a finance company   15.5% APR
- bank credit card   22.4% APR
- shop-issued credit card   29.5% APR.

With such a wide difference in cost, it would appear at first sight that a
mortgage or remortgage would be the cheapest way of financing borrowing.
However, it needs to be kept in mind that a borrower could lose their home if
they did not keep up payments due on a mortgage or any loan secured on it.
The APR gives a reasonably accurate guide to the cost of credit. It is therefore a
useful tool for working out whether money is being borrowed in the most cost-
effective way. Drawing up a schedule of borrowing like the one suggested at the
end of this chapter will assist in making comparisons on the cost of borrowing.

Debt and work performance

The move towards performance-related pay which has gathered speed in
private industry is now spreading into the public sector as well. As improvements in productivity become financially measurable, employers seek to peg
the remuneration of their staff to the achievement of financial targets. Thus
work performance has a direct effect on an employee's personal financial
gain. But does the reverse apply, that is to say, will a worker be less efficient
at work as a result of financial problems at home?

Such problems may vary in extent from a small overdraft at the end of the
month, to eviction from home or even bankruptcy, and may be caused by
short-time working, industrial action, or other factors outside work. But
because people react differently to apparently similar levels of stress it is
important to consider what the effect is upon each individual.

○   A solicitor's clerk, with multiple debt problems which he kept to
    himself, was particularly depressed when he discovered that his girl-
    friend was pregnant so he falsified some documents and transferred
    cash belonging to a client into his personal bank account. Surprised by
    the ease with which he was able to cover up the fraud he repeated this
    on a number of other occasions. Eventually he was caught by an office
    manager who had become suspicious because the clerk always insisted

on handling a particular client file personally. When confronted the clerk confessed, and he was prosecuted, convicted and lost his job.

This example raises some questions about whether counselling could have helped. The moral responsibility for the clerk's actions lies firmly with him, so why should an employer bother with a dishonest member of staff? Clearly a firm of solicitors cannot risk their reputation by ignoring such a problem but would the clerk have been driven to steal if he had not been so depressed in the first place? Had his employer noticed his depression and referred him to a counselling agency, how would this have improved the efficiency of other colleagues who worked alongside him and who were themselves starting to feel demoralized and depressed by his moods? It cannot be guaranteed that counselling would have had a positive effect; for example, the outcome would depend on the clerk's commitment to using counselling as a means of addressing his problems. But a successful outcome in such a case is not simply about preventing fraud. Providing somewhere for the clerk to talk through his problems with a skilled person could lift his depression and help him to find alternative ways of dealing with them. The improvement in his quality of life could be matched by similar improvements in his relationship with colleagues, which in turn could improve the working environment and efficiency of the firm.

In a private counselling arrangement the client can expect their counsellor to maintain confidentiality in accordance with the British Association for Counselling Code of Ethics (BAC 1993). This lays a responsibility on counsellors to discuss their case work only within a purposeful supervision arrangement and to break confidence only where there is a clear possibility of the client causing harm to themselves or another person. In an employee counselling service this raises two questions. Firstly, who is the supervisor? They should be someone who is completely independent of the management of the company and not responsible for the line management of the counsellor. Without this arrangement confidence in the counselling service will be jeopardized. Second, how should knowledge of potential harm to the company (by allegations of fraud or knowledge of other wrongdoing) be addressed? Here is an example.

O   A building society cashier is married to a man who is self-employed and needs to raise finance for his business. She agrees to a second mortgage on their property through a finance company, although it is against the rules of her employment contract to raise finance in this way. Her husband spends the money on his gambling habit instead of the business. The value of the property falls below the amount outstanding on the two mortgages. She is worried that she has broken her employment contract, and that if she loses her job they will drift even further into debt. It is not in her interest to admit what has happened at work, but she starts to take time off suffering with anxiety and depression.

At a chance meeting with a colleague she is reminded that her employers operate an employee assistance counselling programme. She decides to see a counsellor but only after she has found out that the service is completely confidential and that details of her interview are not made available to her employers. The counsellor is able to reassure her that employees are not instantly dismissed when their partners mishandle money. Together they work out a way of getting help for the husband's gambling addiction, and a strategy which will enable her to approach her line manager and discuss financial matters in an honest and open way. She is disciplined but not sacked. Six months later they are recognizing and addressing their problems. He has joined a Gamblers Anonymous group; she has kept her job and they are making some headway financially.

The issue here is whether the counsellor had the right or obligation to tell the company that the employee had broken her contract of employment. Three things are important. First, when launching and promoting an employee counselling service, the employer needs to ensure that staff feel confident about using the service; in order for it to be successful staff need to use it and they will only do this if they feel it is a safe place to talk. Second, the contract with the counsellor (whether they are themselves employed or self-employed) needs to specify precisely under what conditions, if any, the counsellor should break confidence. Third, the counsellor should make these conditions clear at the beginning of the first session they have with each employee. While the *BAC Code of Ethics and Practice for Counsellors* (1993) offers guidance on these matters, in particular the more extreme cases of potential harm, it is important to consider adopting an in-house counselling code of confidentiality adapted to local circumstances. This is because similar issues will be regarded more seriously in one employment situation than another. For example, a counselling interview that disclosed an employee's strong disciplinarian views on parenting might have no effect on their ability to function as a bricklayer, but could have serious implications in a social work setting. Similarly, some employers might argue that employing a cashier with gambling debts in the family produced an unacceptable risk of dishonest dealings within the company, whereas others would take no view on the matter, leaving it entirely to the employee to sort matters out.

In providing a counselling scheme this employer has recognized that one benefit can be the lifting of anxieties. As long as matters are not dealt with this can be distressing for the employee as well as her colleagues. However, counselling may bring about improvements in work relationships which are likely to translate into reduced absenteeism and greater productivity.

Understanding the psychology of debt

So far we have examined the practical causes and types of debt, but are some people more psychologically disposed to getting into debt in the first place, and what of the emotional effects of debt on individuals?

In a front-page article headlined 'Move to end bank misery', a national newspaper quotes the co-ordinator of the Bank Action Group, Patricia Griffiths, as saying that at times they take 1,000 calls in a week from desperate people, and suicide threats are common. They go on to report that Eddy Weatherill, chief executive of the Independent Banking Advisory Service, claims that over 1,000 people each year commit suicide because of financial worries and cite the tragic example of a pensioner who drowned himself after receiving four letters in one week concerning a small overdraft which he could not repay (Thornton 1994).

Sigmund Freud was one of the first people to propose systematically the theory that we have unconscious as well as conscious motivations for our actions. Could it be that addressing practical solutions alone, however helpfully, will never deal with the underlying and unconscious motivations which create a debt problem for some people in the first place?

To answer this, try examining a series of six practical problems which could lead an individual into debt. For example, the person may:

1 find arithmetic difficult;
2 not understand simple budgeting;
3 not understand how to estimate gas or electricity consumption;
4 have lost a partner who used to pay the bills;
5 not understand how banks work;
6 be unable to fill in a housing benefit claim form.

Now, line by line, compare some suggested and underlying causes;

1 maths teacher at school was a bully;
2 as a child was never given weekly pocket money, but always got everything on demand;
3 mother was afraid of electricity (she once had an electric shock);
4 father did all the household book-keeping and it was an unwritten family rule that this was men's work;
5 family never used banks because they believed that they reported all income to the tax authorities;
6 poverty was considered shameful and not to be discussed with others.

The ability to handle financial matters appropriately is partly governed by education and experience. However, like all things money can take on a symbolic value (Mann 1992). The following case studies demonstrate how unconscious motivation and upbringing affect attitudes to money. It is perhaps useful to bear in mind throughout these examples that it is not only poverty that leads to problems related to money.

O   A boy loses both his parents at the age of 3 in an accident. He grows up in a children's home. There he learns that hard work brings escape from poverty, as well as relief from feelings of isolation and emotional deprivation. As an adult he achieves financial success and runs his own company. By middle age he is adequately provided for, and no longer needs to work; however, he continues to do so. Wanting to retire but feeling unable to, he seeks counselling. Through this he discovers that making money has become not just a means of financial survival, but also his chosen means of escape from early pain and loss. In acknowledging this he is able to let go of his addiction to work.

O   The teenage daughter of a wealthy company director is given everything she asks for. A generous clothes allowance, her own television and stereo and money for entertainment. And yet she is caught shoplifting in one of her father's stores. Her parents are distraught at the embarrassment. It certainly was not a lack of money that caused her to steal, so what else was missing? Could it be that what she really lacked and sought was time with a father who was too busy to notice her?

By way of further illustration, here are some typical extracts from conversations with clients who were seeking debt counselling:

I owe £1500 for the camera. I couldn't really afford it. I felt depressed – you see I'd just missed out on promotion at work. And I always wanted a good camera. I remember my brother getting one for passing his exams. I could have smashed it to bits.

For this client the problem was not just budgeting but self-esteem as well. He would have done anything for that camera, because it was charged with a value placed by his parents on his brother but not on him. Whether his brother really was the favourite child in the family, or not, it certainly felt that way to him, leading to rivalry as a child and debt as an adult.

Here is another example:

My mother drank a lot, so there was never any money left over at the end of the week. My father was always saying he would give us pocket money but hardly ever did. He used to spend it all in the betting shop. I think he earned a good wage but we didn't see it. I was determined that my children wouldn't grow up like that so I've always been generous with them, and made a big thing about Christmas and birthdays. Trouble is things are expensive, and I seem to have overdone it this year.

Here the client wants to make up for her own deprived childhood. Because of her experience she is determined that her children should not suffer in the same way. However, unrealistic overcompensation leads to debt when there is insufficient income to sustain it. So the task here is to enable the client to gain insight into her part in this pattern. The final example emphasizes that wealth in itself does not prevent people getting into debt:

> I've always lived well, nice car, expensive restaurants, that sort of thing. My parents wanted me to have a good education and paid for me to go to boarding school. I went on to university, and they always sent me a generous allowance each term. I got a degree, and now I'm the director of a successful company. The trouble is no matter how much I earn I always seem to be overdrawn at the end of each month.

Most people tend to live up to their income, and those children who have been cushioned financially, may in some cases have unrealistic expectations about adult budgeting. Teaching children how to spend and save, with freely given pocket money from an early age, as well as opportunities to earn extra for specific tasks, may establish in a child's mind the value of goods, an understanding of self-worth and a realistic attitude to earning power.

Employees do not have to be in debt to be in distress over money. The effects of sudden wealth as much as sudden poverty can be equally catastrophic. For this reason the pools companies and the National Lottery contractors provide financial counselling to major winners, encouraging them to think through carefully how they will invest and spend their winnings. Employees who win or inherit large sums of money need independent financial advice from a solicitor, stockbroker, accountant or other independent financial adviser who is properly qualified to offer it.

It is important to recognize that some patterns of behaviour cannot be changed by practical advice alone, but need in-depth counselling or psychotherapy to gain self-awareness of behaviour patterns which are related to money. Some people will want to compensate for poverty in childhood, and treat themselves to purchases they can ill afford, while others may strive to keep up with the financial standards that were set for them by their parents.

For some counsellors, straddling the divide between directive financial advice giving and, for example, a more interpretive or psychodynamic style produces a tension with which it can be difficult to work. The counsellor needs to recognize the financial realities of the client, but where early life experiences are significant, real benefits can accrue for those clients who are prepared to examine their current financial problems as a metaphor for the past.

In summary, then, debt advice addresses only the practical problems of debt. Similarly, psychotherapy or general counselling may help individuals to change attitudes towards themselves and their finances, but won't provide the money management skills that come from a more directive approach. Integrating the two can improve the effectiveness of the help given where the counsellor deals first with the shame and anxiety of the client, and only then with the practicalities of handling debt.

If all else fails

Ever-increasing debt can bring anxiety, depression or a denial of the problem. Employees may simultaneously be experiencing marital or business relationship problems. They may need counselling, advice and support during a difficult time so that they are encouraged to see the problem through to its conclusion rather than vaguely hope it will go away. Where realistic payments simply cannot be met, and it is hopeless to try to come to an arrangement with individual creditors, there are still ways in which someone with unmanageable debts can exert control over their situation.

For example, they can take the initiative and go to court themselves, submitting a list of their creditors and asking for the court to agree what payments are realistic. This may reduce the demands for money to reasonable figures, but where large sums are involved the creditor or creditors may eventually press for bankruptcy. This may sound like a stigma, but it does allow the person to have an income for basic need, respite from financial demands while the case is handled, and a chance to reorganize their life. The courts or solicitors can give further advice. Licensed insolvency practitioners can be approached, either by individuals or at the order of the court. They are specially trained accountants whose task it is to help resolve serious financial problems and put personal or business accounts in order for presentation at court and to creditors.

Credit unions

One practical way in which an employer can help employees avoid the pitfalls of loan sharks and high interest rates is through the establishment of a credit union at work.

These offer accessible savings schemes and low-interest loans and can be particularly helpful to people who would not otherwise have access to credit. A credit union is a co-operative, based on a common bond of its members. This means that they must share an interest, such as local neighbourhood, church or employer. Individual savings are currently restricted to £5000, and members may borrow up to £5000 plus their existing share balance. Membership of schemes is normally restricted to 5000. In the Republic of Ireland, Canada and the United States, it is likely that between a third and a half of all adults belong to credit unions, while in the United Kingdom little more than one in 300 people are members.

The movement is relatively new, the first one being established in the UK in 1964; however, there may be other factors affecting growth. Media coverage has tended to link credit unions to deprived areas and stories of poverty and loan sharks. Start-up funding has been available by government through local authorities, but at a time when overall budgets are being cut and there are competing demands for resources. Useful research has been undertaken by the Joseph Rowntree Foundation (Dibben 1993).

A recent working party convened by the National Consumer Council (Brazier 1993) consulted widely with credit unions and found that the common bond rule was restrictive, that there was insufficient publicity and promotion, and that financial and membership limits set were so low as to stifle development. In spite of this, the common bond rule does include groups of employees, so setting up a credit union at the place of work could be part of a long-term strategy aimed at reducing financial problems among staff.

In conclusion

At the end of this chapter are a set of specimen budget forms, sample letters to creditors, and notes on their use. These have been refined through regular use and offer a practical way for anyone to make an accurate calculation of their income, expenditure and indebtedness. This provides a useful basis for initial discussions with a counsellor. Some employees will require more assistance than others in completing the forms. Expenditure is examined under four headings, namely Home Costs; Personal and Family Costs; Transport Costs; and Borrowing and Payments. A personal schedule of debts and borrowing, which includes comparison of annual percentage rates of interest, is included. Income is calculated including that of a partner. From this information any financial shortfall can be calculated and problem areas of overspending can be defined. Further action can be planned, encouraging the employee to use the specimen letters to creditors as appropriate.

Although employees will not always readily admit when they have debt problems, experience of working in a major employee counselling service reveals that being explicit in publicity about the availability of money advice does encourage clients to come forward. Additionally it enables clients who have come for other reasons, such as alcohol abuse or relationship breakdown, to examine the associated financial problems as part of their agenda. Most people worry about money at some time in their lives, but offering debt advice as part of an employee counselling service can help reduce stress and anxiety at work.

Notes on using the budget forms and specimen letters

- Calculate client's income and expenditure on the budget forms.
- Remember to use monthly or weekly figures consistently throughout.
- Deduct expenditure from income to arrive at available funds, or if expenditure currently exceeds income, deduct income from expenditure to arrive at disparity.
- Establish the highest priorities for payment, for example unpaid taxes, food, housing, clothing, heating and cooking. Ideally payments for these should be maintained at the requested level.
- If this is not possible, begin negotiations with priority creditors to clarify what arrangements will be acceptable to prevent court action, eviction or the cutting off of services. With a mortgage, the lender's consideration of a request to reduce payments will take into account the following factors:
    amount of mortgage
    value of property
    income and expenditure
    any payment arrears
    length of outstanding mortgage
    amount owed on any other loans that are secured on the property
    whether financial problems are likely to be short- or long-term
    age of borrower.
- With rents and charges for services such as gas or electricity, the creditors will want assurance that future payments will be made as they fall due, in addition to some regular contribution towards outstanding arrears, if negotiations are to be successful.
- Use the appropriate specimen letter(s) to explain the position to the lenders.
- Next attend to the non-priority debts.
- Remember that acknowledgement of an old debt for which payment is not currently being demanded can produce a renewed liability, so advise client not to 'reawaken' apparently spent liabilities.
- Advise client to write an individual letter to each creditor.
- Courts have the power to suspend interest charges, and a creditor may agree to do this in advance of any legal action (because they may be more likely to get a return of the original capital sum lent), so it is certainly worth asking.
- The appropriate specimen letters should be used. The figures referred to in them are explained as follows:
    £ (X) is the employee's total income after essential expenses and priority debts have been deducted and calculated on the budget form.
    £ (Y) is the amount that they are able to offer as part-payment of the existing demand.
    As an example take a total non-priority debt of £1000, and a total income available for debts of £100. The employee should be advised to offer one-tenth of the amount requested to each creditor.

BUDGETING FORM – EXPENDITURE

Note: Use monthly or weekly payments consistently throughout

(A) Home costs

Include: All mortgages, loans or advances secured on the home
Exclude: Other borrowing

First mortgage _____ (amount owed) _____ (repayment)
Other mortgages_____ (amount owed) _____ (repayment)
Other mortgages_____ (amount owed) _____ (repayment)
Value of home _____
Rent
Ground rent
Maintenance/service charges
Insurance (buildings)
Insurance (contents)
Insurance (mortgage protection)
Insurance (mortgage payments)
Insurance (life policy as security)
Planned repayment of mortgage arrears
Council tax
Gas
Electricity
Water/sewerage
Telephone/mobile phone
TV/video/cable/satellite/rent/licence
Cleaning/gardening
Property maintenance
Others

Total (A)   £ _____

(B) Personal and family costs

Child support agency payment orders	_____
Other court orders/fines	_____
Self-employment tax and NI	_____
Food/groceries/housekeeping	_____
Milk/paper bills	_____
Clothing (self)	_____
Clothing (family)	_____
Laundry	_____
Prescriptions	_____
School fees and student support	_____
School meals	_____
School trips/events	_____
Nursery/childcare/nanny/babysitting	_____
Children's pocket money	_____
Personal requisites	_____
Christmas/birthdays	_____
Holidays	_____
Subscriptions	_____
Entertainment	_____
Eating out	_____
Alcohol/tobacco	_____
Hobbies	_____
Savings/investment payments	_____
Others	_____
Total (B)	£ _____

(C) Transport costs

Car(s) tax	_____
Car(s) insurance	_____
Servicing/MOT/repairs	_____
Petrol/oil	_____
AA/RAC/breakdown subscription	_____
Transport to work	_____
Transport (social)	_____
Transport to shops	_____
Transport to school	_____
Others	_____
Total (C)	£ _____

(D) Borrowing and payments

Exclude: mortgages and loans secured on home
Include: other loans, credit cards, hire purchase and other finance arrangements, overdrafts, catalogue payments, outstanding bills, borrowing from relatives and friends, unpaid tax and any other borrowing. Use this schedule to compare rates of interest charged in APR column:

Name of lender	APR if charged	Amount outstanding	Regular payment	Final payment due
[_____]	[___%]	[£_____]	[£_____]	[__/__/__]
[_____]	[___%]	[£_____]	[£_____]	[__/__/__]
[_____]	[___%]	[£_____]	[£_____]	[__/__/__]
[_____]	[___%]	[£_____]	[£_____]	[__/__/__]
[_____]	[___%]	[£_____]	[£_____]	[__/__/__]
[_____]	[___%]	[£_____]	[£_____]	[__/__/__]
[_____]	[___%]	[£_____]	[£_____]	[__/__/__]
[_____]	[___%]	[£_____]	[£_____]	[__/__/__]
[_____]	[___%]	[£_____]	[£_____]	[__/__/__]
[_____]	[___%]	[£_____]	[£_____]	[__/__/__]
[_____]	[___%]	[£_____]	[£_____]	[__/__/__]
[_____]	[___%]	[£_____]	[£_____]	[__/__/__]
[_____]	[___%]	[£_____]	[£_____]	[__/__/__]
[_____]	[___%]	[£_____]	[£_____]	[__/__/__]
[_____]	[___%]	[£_____]	[£_____]	[__/__/__]
[_____]	[___%]	[£_____]	[£_____]	[__/__/__]

(Total borrowing)   [£_____]

Total (D)   £_____

(E) Total income

Wages/salary (self)
Wages/salary (partner)
Other part-time income
Income support
Child benefit
Other benefits/pensions
Maintenance received
Lodgers/tenants
Other income

Total (E)   £_____

Total expenses brought forward

Total A: home   £_____
Total B: personal and family   £_____
Total C: transport   £_____
Total D: borrowing and payments £_____

Total expenses (F)   £_____

Now deduct total (F) expenses from (E) income to give either:

surplus funds available   *or shortfall*

+ £ _____ In credit   OR £ _____ In debit

SAMPLE LETTER (1) TO BEGIN NEGOTIATIONS ON PRIORITY DEBTS

To Building Society/Utility Company/Service, etc.
Address

Your name and
Your address

Date

Dear ―――――,

Re: (*Insert your account or reference number*)

I am writing to inform you that, regretfully, I am unable to maintain current repayments on my mortgage (*gas bill, telephone, etc.*). This is because my financial circumstances have altered due to (*specify reason, e.g. unemployment, maternity, divorce, etc.*).

Because of the importance of my (*home, heating, telephone, etc.*) I intend to treat my debt to you as a priority debt and pay as much as I am able.

With the help of (*my employers, a money advice agency, etc.*) I have carefully calculated my income and essential expenditure on the attached form. I now wish to discuss with you ways in which my regular payments to you might be reduced for the time being. May I make an appointment to discuss matters with you in detail? (*or make specific proposals in the letter*)

Yours sincerely

SAMPLE LETTER (2) TO REDUCE PAYMENTS AND SUSPEND INTEREST CHARGES

To finance company,   *Your name and*
Address   *Your address*

                                                         Date

Dear _____

Re: (*Insert your account or reference number*)

I am writing to inform you that, regretfully, I am unable to maintain current repayments on my loan (*credit agreement, credit card, etc.*). This is because my financial circumstances have altered due to (*specify reason, e.g. unemployment, maternity, divorce, etc.*).

With the help of (*my employers, a money advice agency, etc.*) I have carefully calculated my income and essential expenditure on the attached form, which as you can see leaves me with just £ *(X)* each *week/month* to meet my debts. Instead of the current arrangements, I would therefore propose to pay £ *(Y)* each *week/month*. I hope that this will be acceptable, and should my circumstances change I will of course contact you.

Under the circumstances, would you also agree to stop charging interest payments so that the payments I am able to make are all used to reduce my debt?

Yours sincerely

References

BAC (1993) *Code of Ethics and Practice for Counsellors*. Rugby: British Association for Counselling.

Barty-King, H. (1991) *The Worst Poverty: A history of debt and debtors*. Stroud: Sutton.

Brazier, A. (1993) *Saving for Credit: The future for credit unions in Britain*. London: National Consumer Council.

Conger, R.D. and Elder, G.H. (1990) Linking economic hardship to marital quality and instability. *Journal of Marriage and the Family*, 52: 643.

Dibben, Margaret (1993) Credit where it's due. *Search and Social Policy Research Findings*, nos. 38 and 47. York: Joseph Rowntree Foundation.

Dominion, J. (1995) *Marriage: The definitive guide to what makes a marriage work*. London: Heinemann.

HM Government Central Statistical Office (1995) *Social Trends Volume 25*. London: HMSO.

Krueger, D.W. (1992) *Emotional Business: The meaning and mastery of work, money and success*. San Marcos, CA: Avant.

Lunt, P.K. and Livingstone, S.M. (1992) *Mass Consumption and Personal Identity*. Buckingham: Open University Press.

Mann, A. (1992) Debt Counselling: the unfortunate, the incompetent and the profligate, in E. Noonan and L. Spurling (eds) *The Making of a Counsellor*. London: Routledge.

Parker, Tony (1986) *Red Hill: A mining community*. London: Heinemann.

Thornton, Jacqui (1994) 'Move to end bank misery', *Daily Express*, 21 February.

Suggested reading

Ellis, A. and Hunter, P. (1991) *Why Am I Always Broke? (How to be sane about money)*. Secaucus, NJ: Lyle Stuart.

Wolfe, M. and Ivison, J. (1993) *Debt Advice Handbook*. London: Child Poverty Action Group.

7

Family and relationship problems

○ **CLARE TOWNSEND with DENISE NELSON**

The traditional view of the family as one consisting of parents with children is changing. As nearly half of all marriages in Britain now end in divorce one might question whether marriage is a viable institution and this is perhaps why so many couples cohabit. Taking a broader view it is clear that family structures have undergone enormous changes in the past 40 years and that there are many different kinds of family arrangement to consider. For example, not all couples choose to or are able to have children. Many people who choose to marry again after divorce will live in a family which consists of their partner's children by their first marriage, their own children and any new children produced by the second marriage. Single-parent families represent 20 per cent of all families with children in Britain today (Church 1994). A typical Asian family may look different from a Caucasian family because it is a common practice for the bride in certain cultures to live with her husband's parents. Caucasian couples do not usually do this on a long-term basis but may do so for a short time for economic reasons. There are many adults living alone today. Gay and lesbian couples also need to be included in any discussion of 'what is a family'.

These patterns of family arrangements are huge topics in their own right, so because of limitations of space we are going to concentrate mainly on long-term traditional relationships. The reasons for change are also complex and include changes in social values and attitudes, changes in population trends and life expectancy, and economic changes. For example, with relative economic prosperity in the developing countries women have been able to concentrate on education and postpone marriage and starting a family. In Western Europe, the average age at which women have their first child has risen sharply. Many women with children now work, creating quite a contrast to the traditional picture of the family where the man goes out to work and the woman stays at home to look after the children. Some of these changes in partnership patterns will be discussed in more detail later on.

Much attention has been paid to these changes which culminated in the United Nations General Assembly designating 1994 as the International Year of the Family. Its aim was to promote the family through a series of initiatives which would encourage the shaping of social policy to support the changes and diversity in family structures. At the centre of its objectives has been the fundamental belief that the family plays a pivotal role in ensuring the well-being of society.

In an employee counselling service family and relationship problems are likely to receive considerable attention because many employees are at that particular life stage when putting down roots, and consolidating personal arrangements in both career and family terms is likely to be a priority. A student counselling service, by comparison, would be unlikely to have the same proportion of married or cohabiting clients.

This chapter will take as its focus the interface between work and family life. Are the environments of work and family independent from each other, or do the demands of one spill over on to the other? Family problems may arise, for example, if a man's work makes considerable demands on his time so that his wife and children rarely see him. Evans and Bartolome (1984) point out that there is increasing evidence that work, marriage and parenthood become pressing concerns at different phases in life and that this is part of the process of adult development. Their study of 44 British and French male managers indicated that for these men, work came first at a time when the demands of family life would be considerable, when their children were still very young. They placed more importance on family life in their mid-forties. Priorities for work and family life do not necessarily complement each other. Women, from biological necessity, may plan more effectively. Some women have their children first and then build a career, and others wait until their career is established before having children.

Before looking in detail at the nature of family problems and the impact of such problems on the workplace, the meanings of work and the family will be briefly reviewed and a conceptualization of the relationship between the two will be suggested. The second half of the chapter will concentrate on methods of dealing with relationship and family problems. Particular attention will be paid to the role of professional counselling.

Family and relationships

Although there is a high divorce rate in this country, marriage remains popular, with the average marriage lasting ten years. Thirty-five per cent of all marriages are remarriages, where one or both partners are marrying for the second or third time (Griffin 1987).

What is it about long-term relationships that continues to be of central importance to so many people? In some ways marriage mirrors the relationship that young children have with their parents. Marriage is at best a secure base from which people can grow and develop, enjoying times of closeness and intimacy. If the relationship is secure both partners will feel free to enjoy pursuits which do not necessarily involve each other, such as work, friendships or hobbies, for example. Attachment theory (Bowlby 1971) tries to describe the nature of the emotional bonds or relationship that is made between people. The need to make strong affectional bonds continues throughout life but there are different patterns of attachment behaviour which depend on the individual's age and circumstances. For example, a child under 3, and particularly between the ages of 1 and 2, will tend only to venture a short distance away from their mother or attachment figure. Similarly, courting couples will often spend long periods of time together, but this pattern may change several years into the relationship.

Attachment theory suggests that people have a need to be in relationships with one or several significant people, for example mother, parents, partner, and that the significant attachment figure is not easily replaced. The work of Bowlby (1989) has been enormously influential in putting forward the viewpoint that many forms of emotional distress are a result of unwilling separation or loss of a special person. This experience of loss can represent a concrete event like bereavement, or may appear to be less tangible. For example, I (CT) recently interviewed a client in a workplace setting who was concerned about her 15-year-old son, who was involved in minor offences. She expressed a lot of devotion for her son and described his relationship with her second husband as close. His father, her first husband, had lost contact with his children when they divorced. As we talked I felt convinced that some of her son's current problems were to do with the experience of loss of his father, at a time when children are most prone to blame themselves when distressing things happen.

Employees are going to be affected by significant changes in their social relationships; getting married (a positive stress), bereavement or divorce are just a few examples. It is important to recognize that attachment behaviour – the propensity to make strong relationships and to be distressed if something happens to disrupt that bond – is different from dependent behaviour. This difference can be observed in adults and children. The attached child is normally secure enough to make forays into the world, knowing he can return to his parents. The dependent child, however, will not share the same self-reliance, often because he feels anxiety about the nature of his secure base. A child who cannot rely on his parents will often exhibit clinging behaviour. Many studies have examined the formative experiences of adults who demonstrate self-reliance. These experiences include belonging to close-knit families and developing the ability to ask for help (Bowlby 1971).

Social networks and support systems are very important in alleviating stress. It is the general practice of counsellors to assess the nature of the client's support system in order to make some diagnosis about the client's vulnerability. The many manuals for employers and others on how to survive stress all include the need to have a strong social network (Wycherley 1992). Such is the importance of affectional bonds that they can influence a person's physical as well as emotional health. McCormick (1992) describes studies in which the presence of a loved one during intensive care lowered electronically measured blood pressure by as much as 20 points.

The study of the family and comparable relationships is a huge task, and we have briefly outlined the viewpoint of one theory which has had enormous influence on many branches and schools of psychotherapy. We hope to continue to demonstrate how relevant and important such relationships are in the life and well-being of the employee. We also want to show that employers need to pay attention to the interaction between work and family life in order to get maximum efficiency from their employee as well as for ethical and health reasons.

The meaning of work

One interesting characteristic that features in much of the research literature on the relationship between work and family life is that it is usually work problems which spill over and cause concern to the family arrangements, rather than vice versa. Another significant factor is the amount of research carried out on male rather than female employees.

It is beyond the scope of this chapter to go into a detailed review of the meaning of work in all areas of society, but generally men tend to place more emphasis on work, while women typically continue to see relationships and the family as more important even though many women now work. This is not a sexist stereotype; it is merely stating that some issues are gender-specific to one degree or another. Nevertheless, many exceptions can be found: there are women whose principal source of identity is found in their work, and clinical experience shows that there are many who are concerned with family issues.

Certainly work has several obvious and very necessary functions – the provision of income, of status and identity, the structuring of the day, opportunities for shared experiences and social contacts (Jahoda 1979).

Some of the most interesting research done on the meaning of work has come through looking at unemployment (Mattinson 1988). Many men, as shown in the following quote, see work as a confirmation of their gender identity: 'The fact is that after I felt sure of myself as a welder, I felt sure of myself in everything, even the way I walked' (Mattinson 1988: 21).

Work is also a channel for sublimation. Some people, notably, are naturally more aggressive than others. This aggression can be sublimated in work. Mattinson cites the example of a man who when employed could exhibit the caring, sensitive side of himself in his marriage. However, when he was made redundant he became increasingly hostile at home, where previously he had been described as a 'caring father'.

If a person finds his or her principal source of identity in work, it is likely that the career will be put first and this may involve a sacrifice at home. This may not be a problem for the employee, but it may be a considerable one for their spouse and children.

As well as providing a sense of identity and a source of sublimation, work is also important in providing a time structure. Many couples coming for counselling wrestle with the issues of finding the right amount of intimacy and distance in their relationships. Work can sometimes help people who particularly need to maintain some distance in their relationships. Some jobs require the employee to be absent from home intermittently, either for short or long periods.

The question needs to be asked, why, when choice is available, do people choose occupations which take them away from their families for extended periods? Some people choose such occupations because it limits their involvement with a partner. They thus choose occupations which have a secondary function of structuring the amount of intimacy in their relationships.

Lastly it is worth noting that work has a containment function for some people when they are experiencing distress from other sources, of one kind or another. Employees often report that throwing themselves into work helps them to keep going during a major crisis, such as bereavement. Perhaps in some cases work can be too successful as a containing function. Notably, for some people work can be a way of trying to escape from problems which do need attention.

The relationship between the environments of work and family

It has already been pointed out that in examining the influence of work on home life and vice versa people appear to be more willing to state that work problems affect family life rather than vice versa. This may be a way of saying indirectly that work is more important than family life for some people, but it may also be something to do with organizational influences. There is often the lurking fear in an employee that if he or she admits to having problems at home, it might be considered a sign of weakness or of not being a fit employee. We are reminded of a telephone call one of us had where a young woman was making enquiries as to alternative accommodation because she had split up with her boyfriend of three years. She was in tears. When I (CT) gently suggested she might like to come in to discuss the emotional effects as well as the practical details of breaking up a long-term relationship she readily agreed. It was as if she needed permission to discuss the emotional impact of her problems.

Much clinical evidence supports the theory that actively expressing the effects of relationship problems, for example expressing concern, sadness or anger, is in the longer term more beneficial than harmful. Behaving in this manner is actually an indicator of strength, that is, facing something rather than burying it, particularly as emotional problems which are 'buried' have an amazing propensity to emerge later in other problematic ways. It is not being advocated that employees should inappropriately allow their family problems to influence their work, but if the right attention is given, perhaps in the form of a counselling service, there can be much benefit to employers and employees.

The meaning of work and family life, including each person's current stage of adult development, needs to be considered on an individual basis. Evans and Bartolome (1984) have arrived at five main ways of describing kinds of relationship between work and home. These will be considered briefly before discussing in depth some of the implications.

Spillover

Work and home each affect the other in a positive or negative way. If a person is satisfied at work this will contribute positively to his or her family life, while if a person is dissatisfied with work the effect on family life will generally be negative. In a similar way satisfaction with family life may affect feelings about career and home.

Independence

Work and home life exist side by side yet for all practical purposes are independent of each other. It is quite possible to be successful and satisfied in one's career and home life, in one or the other, or in neither.

Conflict

Work and home are in conflict with each other and cannot be easily reconciled. Success and satisfaction at work will necessarily entail sacrifices at home; or vice versa.

Instrumentality

Work and career are seen primarily as ways of obtaining the means to build and maintain a satisfying home life or vice versa.

Compensation

Work and home are used as ways of making up for what is missing in the other.

Spillover from work into family life

In the previously mentioned study of 44 managers, nearly half described the relationship as one of spillover from work into family life (Evans and Bartolome 1984). Another issue that arises from this discussion is that of balance. In many ways the goals of working and loving are equally important, yet problems can occur when there is spillover or conflict.

It was Freud who originally stated that the ability both to work and to love contributes to a person's mental well-being. In talking of love and work he was speaking of a general occupational productiveness which would not preoccupy the individual to the extent that his or her right or capacity to be a sexual and loving being would be lost (Mattinson 1988).

What are the main factors in working conditions that contribute to problems in family life? There are some occupations which can be described as greedy in the demands they make on their employees. Relocation can be a significant problem when families have just put down roots and children have settled in schools and made friends only to have to move again. Long hours contribute to the 'absent father' problem – absent emotionally as much as physically. This may not be intentional, in the sense that the father may be too tired to participate in family life once he arrives home!

Partnership patterns

Many partners who both work and combine this work with a family have problems in juggling their commitments. An interesting way of looking at marriage and partnerships has been provided by Charles Handy (1978). He studied husbands and wives in terms of their needs for achievement, dominance, affiliation and nurturance. He found four patterns which reflect fundamental approaches to life. To arrive at particular marriage patterns he combined the husbands' orientation with that of the wives.

The first pattern was of a 'thrusting husband and a caring wife'. Here the husband is the breadwinner and the wife is the home-maker. His goals of success are her goals as well and all her efforts are put into making the home comfortable. These marriages create the least stress and therefore may fit the 'independence' category that Evans and Bartolome put forward. However, this pattern may create a problem when the children have grown up, as the wife can no longer meet her own needs secondhand through looking after the children. This could be the reason why some women start divorce proceedings when their children are teenagers, often to the surprise of their partners. The teenage children in such cases are often deeply distressed.

The second marriage pattern is the pairing of two 'thrusters' where both the husband and wife have high needs for achievement and dominance. Domestic arrangements can often become chaotic, with neither partner willing to do the 'caring'.

The third pattern is the partnership of two 'involved' people. Although the husband and wife are both high achievers they also place a high value on caring and belonging. Such couples tend to set very high standards for themselves, and their stress levels tend to be very high, as there is no compromising in either area. Both these categories fit into the 'conflict' description suggested by Evans and Bartolome.

The last pattern is an 'involved' husband with a caring wife. Here the husband is highly achievement-oriented but values the caring aspect of relationships. The husband is likely to be under a great deal of stress because he is not only ambitious but also worries about others. Handy (1978) suggests that these relationships are less predictable than the other patterns he describes because there is so much effort put into reworking roles in marriage.

In dual career marriages there is likely to be less stress where there is an 'accommodator' pattern (Cooper et al. 1988). The accommodator pattern usually has one partner who has a high career involvement and a low home involvement while the other partner has a high home involvement and a low career involvement. The difference between this pattern and the traditional family one is that either partner can play either role.

Perhaps what this research is indicating is that in spite of the principle of 'equality of opportunity', partners cannot share roles equally all the time, and that there has to be some adjustment at different stages in their working lives.

Spillover from family to work

What of the spillover from family life into work life? So much of the literature indicates a bias of work spilling over into family life that one could hypothesize that it is this neglect of the importance of family issues which is the main problem for employees. With this in mind the phrase 'family friendly' has been coined by the United Nations Year of the Family (United Nations 1993).

Several stresses exist in family life that affect work, as shown in the following list. The care of pre-school children is very demanding and this will affect both men and women. Even if there are traditional roles the husband will not be immune to the effects of disturbed nights. Children's sickness is another stress, particularly if one of the partners is sick at the same time. Adults who were sexually, physically or emotionally abused as children carry the psychological scars into their working life and from time to time their confidence may be seriously impaired. Domestic violence is a family problem which will spill over most unhelpfully into working life, particularly where a battered wife or partner is coming into work covered in bruises or taking a great deal of time off work.

Another main contributor of spillover from family into work life is separation. The impact of separation and divorce and its aftermath is enormous, which is perhaps why so many people seek help from counselling services. Couples often tend to think that they will go to a counsellor to get help in order to stay together. In reality counsellors take a neutral position and much constructive help can be given by a counsellor in helping couples to separate as well as stay together. Nevertheless many people seek advice about issues to do with maintenance, property and contact rights to children. This demonstrates how much an aftercare service for separating families is needed.

Relationship breakdown

The impact of relationship breakdown on couples who were married and those who were living together is very similar. However, in legal terms 'common law' marriages are not recognized so division of property can be more problematic. People living together have no automatic immediate rights to equal ownership.

Married or not, the impact of separation has far-reaching effects. It is often described as the next worst stress-producing life event after bereavement. A good recovery from divorce can be characterized, as can bereavement, by a painful period of mourning, after which good memories are often able to rise to the surface again.

Couples and families need a great deal of help in separating constructively, and often it is the way people divorce as well as the event itself which causes harm. For separating families with children, preparation and care can reduce the stress; trauma in childhood does not have to be viewed automatically as a cause of failure and distress in adult life. What counts a great deal is the way traumas and crises are handled; for example, in the experience of both bereavement and divorce children need to be allowed to express and talk through the hurt that arises from these events (Holmes 1993).

Research indicates, however, that parents often know little about the process of divorce and how to organize their children's future. A recent study (Cockett and Tripp 1994) sought the views of both children and parents concerning their experience of divorce. The study found that children whose families had been 're-ordered' by separation or divorce were more likely than children from intact families to have encountered health problems and to suffer from low self-esteem. Only a small minority of children – one in 16 – had been prepared for an impending separation or divorce by explanations from both parents. Fewer than half the children in re-ordered families had regular contact with the other non-resident parent (usually their father). Most children, when interviewed, said they wished their parents had managed to stay together. One should not infer from this study that parents should stay together in unhappy circumstances rather than divorce. It is important to note again, however, that children generally prefer to have one parent of each sex and that one parent cannot simply substitute for the other. Parents interviewed in this study felt that what they needed most was easier access to services that offer support to families close to breakdown. The purpose of mediation services, intended to help parents reduce conflict, was found not to be fully understood.

The current divorce laws contribute to the difficulties in separating because they are adversarial. However, the Lord Chancellor McGregor has recently brought in some new proposals which should change this. Before those changes are discussed we might reflect on who typically initiates divorce. Seven out of ten divorces are started by women (Griffin 1987). It is generally believed that this is because women have higher expectations than previously, and not because marriages are worse than they were 50 years ago.

At present the grounds for divorce are irretrievable breakdown of marriage. This includes adultery, unreasonable behaviour and desertion. Contested divorces are rarely if ever successful, as the law is quite pragmatic on the matter: if one person thinks there is a problem, then that is sufficient. Nevertheless, at present grounds for divorce have to be found, which means that divorce can become very confrontational between the two partners.

Under the proposed new terms, which come into force in 1998, couples will be required to wait a year to 18 months before they divorce. They will also be required to attend a mediation service which will give them time to prepare themselves and think through their decision (see *Family Law Gazette*, 26 June 1996). The original aims of the Family Law Bill were to simplify divorce proceedings by introducing the concept of no fault, and to reduce unhelpful confrontation. Nevertheless, some solicitors fear the bill will result in new complications. A waiting period of 18 months may cause greater uncertainty and insecurity for children. Compulsory attendance at mediation services may exacerbate the problems of some couples who are resistant to this kind of help. Additionally how will increased mediation services be funded? It is yet to be seen whether the new law will be a blessing or a curse.

Methods of help

This next section will look at methods of help, both informal and formal, for families with problems. It will be divided into three sections: help for separating families; help for children and lastly help for couples who want to stay together.

Help for separating families

The National Association of Family Mediation and Conciliation Services began in Britain in 1979 and grew out of the belief that separating families need assistance both legally and therapeutically. Nevertheless, these services are still not widely used. The view is that separating couples seeking help have the opportunity to meet with a solicitor and a counsellor who work together to help the couple decide over issues like property and children.

Up until now solicitors have often been reluctant to refer their clients to the mediation services because they view them as competition. However, this is not so, since couples will need their own independent solicitors to represent them. Nevertheless, when the new divorce laws come into existence the influence of mediation services may rapidly increase. Conciliation services usually employ a counsellor (rather than the combined help of a counsellor and a solicitor) to work with couples who are separating.

One way in which couples can help themselves in this process is to talk through all the issues involved before solicitors are approached. Unfortunately, couples are not always able to do this constructively. Some find ways of punishing the other partner for the hurt felt. Some women, for example, will obstruct their partner's desire to have regular contact with his children.

The wider family is not always able to help, people often take sides and cannot view matters objectively. In many Asian families it will frequently be the grandparents' advice that is heeded. However, Asian families may often take sides and become entrenched in conflict over issues to do with children and property (Atmar 1994).

Sometimes the only way to help yourself is to get professional help. As well as working within mediation and conciliation services, counsellors experienced in working with couples can help those who are trying to reduce the stress of separating. A young couple had been married for five years; the husband had already moved out of the marital home but was not sure whether he wanted to make the separation final. Both partners wanted to try to understand how the marriage had broken down and had eight sessions to explore their feelings and experiences. Although this process challenged both of them a great deal and there was some temptation just to 'cut and run', each partner felt they had gained something from the process of counselling and both felt stronger as a result. They did decide to divorce.

Couples who are separating do not have to see a counsellor together if they do not want to. We frequently work with one of the partners of a couple who are in the process of a divorce.

Help for children

For children under 16 there are many avenues of help. The problem for the parent is often assessment: will my child grow out of this problem or should I ask for help? Of course there is a wide variety of books on child care which are useful: Penelope Leach (1988), for example, gives excellent advice.

But how does a parent know if his or her child needs professional help? As a rule of thumb, if the problem is causing the family distress and has been continuing for more than three months it is wise at least to seek an assessment. There may be nothing seriously wrong but fears can be allayed. A 10-year-old girl and her family were referred to a child psychotherapist, for what is generally a very common problem: sibling rivalry. However, the hate this child felt for her younger brother was of an unusual and disconcerting degree. Most siblings have periods of fighting and periods of enjoying each other's company. This girl had hated her brother intensely since he was born. The family and school were becoming increasingly concerned, and relieved when the family could see a child psychotherapist privately fairly quickly. We heard from this family that psychotherapy was proving to be beneficial.

The other alternative would have been to ask their doctor to refer them to their local child guidance clinic where children up to the age of 16 are seen. However, they would have had to have waited for about three months. Some hospitals offer family therapy where the whole family is seen if children are having problems. There are independent institutions like the Institute of Family Therapy where a sliding scale of fees will be charged.

There are several non-statutory counselling services for young people aged 14–25. Here a young person can see a counsellor independently from their family, and in confidence. Some employee counselling services employ counsellors who are experienced in working with children and who can help with assessment and referral.

Help for couples

An employer or manager can greatly help staff who are experiencing relationship problems, if he or she takes the attitude that family life is of equal importance to working life and that the two environments cannot ultimately be kept separate.

People seeking help are often afraid of what others think, as well as having their own, individual misgivings about the process. Creating a climate where it is 'normal' to get professional help for relationship problems, in the same way as it is 'normal' to consult a doctor about physical problems, can enable staff to resolve problems before they become intractable and begin to have a serious impact on their work performance.

What then is the kind of help that couples can get from professional counselling, and what makes 'couple counselling' different from counselling individuals?

Couple counselling

Couples often come to a counselling session at a time when they are in crisis and when their relationship is in jeopardy. One or both may have committed adultery; they may not have talked to each other for many weeks. They may feel their needs and interests are incompatible, although they can still remember how they felt about each other when they first met. They often both feel very hurt and guilty.

Probably the most widely known specialist couple counselling agency is Relate, but Relate often has long waiting lists of between three and six months. In general a long waiting time is not advantageous for a couple in crisis. A specialist couple counselling agency that offers long-term marital psychotherapy has a policy of keeping waiting lists to a minimum for this reason.

Many employee counselling services offer help to the families of employees and can be a real resource for couples in providing short-term counselling for a period of six to eight weeks. Many couples going to Relate (1992) expect to be seen for a similar period although they can be seen for a longer time.

The main difference between couple counselling and individual work is that in the former it is the relationship that is the focus. Couple counsellors have a special skill in being empathic towards both partners even when the partners are expressing enormous disagreement and it would be easy to take sides. Couple counsellors pay attention to particular aspects of the relationship, in particular how the couple communicate with each other and if they listen to each other carefully.

Despite the theory that opposites attract, couples often choose a partner who is similar in one respect or another. Robin Skynner describes an exercise he conducts for trainee family therapists. He asks a group of people who do not know each other to circulate around a room and to choose two or three people to form a small group. He finds that people quite unconsciously choose others in the group who are like members of their families (Skynner and Cleese 1983: 20). Couples bring to their relationship both conscious and unconscious expectations, based on the experience of their own families. This experience provides them with an internal working model of how families should be. Often there are distortions which need to be corrected.

A couple one of us saw came from apparently different backgrounds. In the woman's family there was a lot of emotion expressed, and terrible uncontrollable rows. In the man's family all emotions were 'blanked off'. Although coming from different backgrounds they shared the same belief system – that it was not safe to express vulnerability and that one must approach life as logically as possible in order not to get hurt. They achieved this by leading rather separate lives, pursuing different activities.

This was satisfactory until they had a child. The parenting of this child gave them enormous pleasure. The experience of closeness they gained from their relationship with their child led to a desire to experience a similar kind of closeness with each other. Both partners worked full-time and held senior positions in their respective organizations. The focus of the counselling work with them was their attitude to emotions and how they both had a tendency to trivialize them.

It has been stated elsewhere in this chapter that we all need to be looked after from time to time, and that needs for nurture are applicable to all stages of life development. The problem for some couples is that they get stuck into one way of relating, for example one partner will tend to parent the other. In healthier relationships partners are more flexible in their roles and can take turns in looking after each other when needed.

Peter and Susie came for counselling because Peter had had an affair but they both wanted to stay together. Adultery has an enormous impact on couple relationships. Susie wanted to go over and over with Peter all the details of his relationship outside the marriage to the extent that he wondered how he could convince her that the relationship was over.

Both found counselling helpful because they had a place to explore their anger with each other in a way that felt safe. The counsellor was able to acknowledge Susie's deep feelings of betrayal and help them both realize that it would take time for trust to be re-established.

There are always reasons why couples have affairs. In this instance, Peter, who had always felt somewhat inferior to Susie, had needed to affirm his self-value by getting attention outside the marriage. This couple was able to explore more directly in the counselling sessions their love for each other and to find ways of acknowledging and affirming each other's needs for recognition and acceptance.

The following case study, of Joe and Marion, gives a more detailed description of what happens in couple counselling. The focus is the relationship between work and family life. This study usefully draws attention to the kinds of problems that occur when work preoccupies the individual to the extent that his capacity to be a loving person is impaired.

O   Joe made contact with the counselling service by telephone, reporting that he was very stressed, seriously concerned about work targets that he had no hope of achieving, and anxious that because of his personal stress, his marriage and family life were being negatively affected. He wished to see a counsellor, and his wife was willing to attend sessions with him. As a couple they were offered an initial appointment three days later, after working hours, so that neither had the embarrassment of taking time off work.

At the first session, Joe appeared very stressed and anxious, while Marion seemed concerned for his welfare. Joe reported that all had been going reasonably well until about the year before when two significant things happened, namely, his mother died and, three weeks later, the sales targets for the next year for his branch were given to him. He felt these targets were unreasonably high, but as he was unaccustomed to making his feelings and opinions known, he simply buckled down to finding ways of attempting to achieve them, with an ever-increasing fear of failure. Around the time of his mother's death, he had also felt a loss of interest in sex, had difficulty falling asleep at night, or would fall asleep easily, but wake up very early and fret. During this time Marion had been very supportive, putting the loss of sex drive down to grief. Now, a year later, the situation had worsened with irritability and some degree of insomnia for both of them, and arguments were quite frequent, although not of a serious nature. Joe's relationships with their 19-year-old son and 16-year-old daughter were very strained, and this too was a recent development. Closeness and intimacy between Joe and Marion were less and less apparent, since some months before Joe had not been able to perform sexually, and this had caused him to feel a sense of failure.

In the first session the history of these recent feelings of stress and failure was established. Joe clearly felt a great deal of performance pressure, particularly in his work context, and this was profoundly affecting his self-esteem and feelings of self-worth. On further questioning, Joe talked of the pressure to achieve that his parents had always maintained in his regard, with no reward for success, simply spurring him on to higher things.

The counselling work was effected on two levels:

1 An exploration of ways of enabling Joe to be more assertive with his senior managers regarding the targets that had been set for his branch.
2 Working on Joe's feelings of inadequacy and failure, and building up the communication at all levels between himself and Marion and his two children.

First, looking back at all that Joe had achieved in both his work and personal life, he was able to give himself the affirmation that he deserved, and this served as a reference point for subsequent work. There was clearly some grieving that Joe needed to do for his mother, and for the first time he was able to acknowledge feelings of hurt, anger and disappointment towards her because, although he valued her discipline, he also felt hurt that she had never acknowledged his successes, nor shown him much affection. In order to help him focus his feelings more sharply, it was suggested that he write her the kind of letter that he would always have wanted to write during her lifetime, expressing not only his love and regard for her, but also his feelings of hurt and disappointment. Marion was very supportive of Joe, recognizing that she too influenced his feelings of loss of esteem by not affirming his obvious dedication to providing the best for his family. She acknowledged too that from time to time she had played a game of 'one-upmanship' with Joe in regard to her own work achievements and promotion. Joe wrote the letter after the first session, and derived considerable cathartic benefit from the exercise.

They had quite readily, as a couple, slipped into concentrating on their individual concerns, and not paid sufficient attention to spending periods of quality time with each other. A programme of exercises was suggested to them during which sexual intercourse was 'banned', so as to remove the performance anxiety from both, and instead the time was spent caressing and giving each other pleasant sensory experiences. This necessitated spending time together at least two or three times a week, and this proved to be a starting point for improved communication and mutual affirmation.

As Joe's feelings of self-esteem were built up, and Marion gained insight into her part in the near-breakdown of their relationship and mutual regard, so Joe was enabled to be clearer and more assertive about his need for another member of the sales staff to be appointed; and to his delight, and that of other branch managers in the area, sales targets were reviewed and set at a more realistic level. This was achieved in the main by Joe, who called a meeting of other managers similarly affected, who then collectively decided to present their views to senior management.

Joe and Marion had seven counselling sessions in all, over a period of 12 weeks, the first four being weekly, and the last three being spaced over two- to three-week intervals as they gained more confidence and insight into their problems. By the sixth session, Joe had not only regained personal confidence, but was able to perform sexually once more, and understood that if on occasion he experienced some sexual difficulty, it was likely to be only temporary, and due to immediate stress, not anything more serious.

The door was left open for Joe and Marion to return at any time in the future for a follow-up session, and both independently telephoned to report two to three months later that their relationship was much improved and they had spent a very happy week away together, without their son and daughter, and all was well.

Conclusion

This discussion on couple counselling has drawn attention to the kinds of problems couples present and the way they are handled by the couple counsellor. Whether there is a direct bearing on the relationship between work and family life, as in the case of Joseph and Marion, or not, much useful help can be given by employee counselling services.

This chapter points out the importance of relationships in the life of the employee and suggests that the environment of family life should not be neglected by organizations which are seeking to enable their staff to work productively.

References

Atmar, R. (1994) 'All in the family'. BBC Radio 5, 4 January.
Bowlby, J. (1971) *Attachment and Loss*. Harmondsworth: Penguin.
Bowlby, J. (1989) *The Making and Breaking of Affectional Bonds*. London: Tavistock/Routledge.
Church, J. (1994) *Social Trends 24*. London: HMSO.
Cockett, M. and Tripp, J. (1994) Children Living in Reordered Families; *Social Policy Research Findings*, no. 45. York: Joseph Rowntree Foundation.
Cooper, C.L., Cooper, R.D. and Eaker, E.H. (1988) *Living with Stress*. Harmondsworth: Penguin.
Evans, P. and Bartolome, F. (1984) Work and family. *Journal of Occupational Behaviour*, 5: 9–21.
Griffin, T. (1987) *Social Trends 17*. London: HMSO.
Handy, C. (1978) *The family: Help or hindrance*, in C.L. Cooper and R. Payne (eds) *Stress at Work*. Chichester: John Wiley.
Holmes, J. (1993) *John Bowlby and Attachment Theory*. London: Routledge.
Jahoda, M. (1979) The impact of unemployment in the 1930s and 1970s. *Bulletin, British Psychological Society*, no. 32.
Leach, P. (1988) *Baby and Child*. Harmondsworth: Penguin.
McCormick, E. (1992) *Healing the Heart*. London: Optima.
Mattinson, J. (1988) *Work, Love and Marriage*. London: Duckworth.
Relate (1992) *What is Marital Counselling?* Rugby: Relate.
Skynner, R. and Cleese, J. (1983) *Families and How to Survive Them*. London: Methuen.
United Nations (1993) *1994 International Year of the Family*. London: United Nations Dept of Public Information.
Wycherley, B. (1992) *Stress at Work*. St Leonards-on-Sea: Outset Publishing.

Suggested reading

Beattie, M. (1989) *Beyond Codependency*. Center City, MN: Hazelden.
Beck, A.A. (1989) *Love is Never Enough*. Harmondsworth: Penguin.
Danziger, D. (1995) *Lost Hearts: When marriage goes wrong*. London: HarperCollins.

Dominian, J. (1995) *Marriage*. London: Heinemann.
Fisher, B. (1992) *Rebuilding: When your relationship ends*. San Luis Obispo, CA: Impact.
Freeman, D. (1990) *Couples in Conflict*. Milton Keynes: Open University Press.
Garlick, H. (1994) *The Which? Guide to Divorce*. London: Consumers Association.
Gough, T. (1994) *Couples in Counselling: A consumer's guide to marriage counselling*. London: Darton, Longman Todd.
Litvinoff, S. (1994) *The Relate Guide to Better Relationships*. London: Vermilion.
Murgatroyd, S. and Woolfe, R. (1985) *Helping Families in Distress*. Milton Keynes: Open University Press.

Useful organizations

Divorce after care services

Family Mediators Association
1 Old Forge Close
Stanmore
Middlesex HA7 3EB
0181 954 6383

National Association of Family Mediation and Conciliation Services
9 Tavistock Place
London WC1H 9SN
0171 383 5993

Solicitors Family Law Association
PO Box 302
Keston
Kent BR2 6E2
01689 850227

Couples

London Marriage Guidance Council
76a New Cavendish Street
London W1M 7L8
0171 580 1087

Relate
Herbert Gray College
Little Church Street
Rugby CV21 3AP
01788 573241

Tavistock Institute for Marital Studies
Tavistock Centre
120 Belsize Lane
London NW3 5BA
0171 435 7111

Families

Institute of Family Therapy
43 Cavendish Street
London W1M 7RG
0171 935 1651

Kensington Consultation Centre
47 South Lambeth Road
London SW8 1RH
0171 793 0148

Marlborough Family Service
38 Marlborough Place
St John's Wood
London NW8 0PJ
0171 624 8605

Young people 13–25

Youth Access
Magazine Business Centre
11 Newark Street
Leicester LE1 5SS
01533 558763

Children

Association of Child Psychotherapists
120 West Heath Road
London NW3 7TU
0181 458 1609

8

Common mental health concerns

○ **COLIN FELTHAM**

Bob Slocum, the central character in Joseph Heller's novel *Something Happened*, makes various deadpan observations about the company in which he works:

> I think that maybe in every company today there is at least one person who is going crazy slowly . . . We average three suicides a year: two men, usually on the middle-executive level, kill themselves every twelve months . . . People in the company like to live well and are usually susceptible to nervous breakdowns . . . Nervous breakdowns are more difficult to keep track of than suicides because they are harder to recognize and easier to hush up.
>
> (1975: 27)

Depending on the organizational culture, work may be experienced by some employees as enhancing their mental health and by others as undermining and damaging their mental health. Freud made the distinction between ordinary unhappiness, which perhaps everyone suffers, and neurotic misery. In this chapter, in contrast to Jane Fawcett's, the focus is on the kinds of everyday problems and concerns experienced from time to time by a majority of people, and almost certainly by a majority of people at work. Many clinicians accept that there is a scale of neuroticism and psychoticism, the former applying to the kinds of phenomena to be discussed here, the latter to more severe mental health problems, or mental illness. It is not easy to distinguish clearly between certain kinds of behaviour, however. The police inspector who apparently cracked under pressure and shot up a gypsy encampment in 1985 may be regarded as reacting wildly to extreme stress and anxiety, but was he mentally ill? He was an experienced officer who was coping with heavy job demands as well as with a sick wife (Ainsworth and Pease 1987).

Most people have probably felt the touch of transient depression and anxiety. Most of us experience critical life stages, for example those in mid-life, when we may become susceptible to self-doubt, problems of self-esteem, self-image and what has been called developmental dys-synchrony, or not having achieved what we had expected (Budman and Gurman 1988). Bereavement is universal, both in the sense that we all, and increasingly as we age, experience the loss of close friends and relatives through death, and also in the sense that many of us lose relationships, homes, jobs and other 'objects' that give our lives meaning. Although such concerns may not drive us to seek professional assistance, they often preoccupy us and they are all potentially concerns which can fester and develop into more serious mental health or psychosomatic problems. It is widely recognized by GPs that a good proportion of visits to their surgeries (up to 33 per cent, or according to some anecdotal evidence, up to 75 per cent) concern emotional and psychological problems rather than physical illness (Oldfield 1983).

We should remember too that psychological distress still carries a stigma for many who probably 'somatize' their distress (suffer from headaches, back-aches and non-specific illnesses) instead of identifying it to themselves or doctors as emotional distress. Indeed, many GPs seem to employ the global terms 'stress-related illness' or 'post-viral fatigue' when writing sick notes for patients who are actually depressed or anxious, but who do not wish to declare such conditions to their employers. People who are inclined to dismiss personal, emotional problems as trivial, attention-seeking or malingering in nature (including some diehard, macho-style managers) may not be easily convinced that these conditions are real, serious and deserving of study and help, but it is hoped that the following account may go some way towards explaining why they are indeed worth understanding and acting upon.

Depression

Depression is a condition affecting mood, motivation, thinking and physi-ology. It may be characterized by apathy, hopelessness, feelings of mean-inglessness, guilt, worry, loss of concentration, negative outlook, lethargy, disturbed sleep, appetite changes and other biological alterations (Gilbert 1992). It may be considered a form of deep unhappiness out of which the sufferer cannot voluntarily shake him or herself. It varies greatly in intensity from one individual to another. Depression has been understood and de-scribed in many different ways. When people refer to themselves or others as being 'a bit down', 'run down', 'out of sorts', 'under the weather' or 'fed up', they are often referring to moods which may also be described as mild depres-sion. When they persistently describe themselves, others or life in general as bleak and meaningless and claim that 'there's no way out' and 'there's no point in anything', then such statements may indicate more serious depression, sometimes called 'clinical depression'. Another important distinction to make is that between brief bouts of depression which are often associated with particular, recent life events (e.g. loss or rejection), and protracted low moods which appear not to stem from any identifiable event. The terms 'reactive' and 'endogenous' have been used in psychiatry to refer to these two kinds of depression, the latter implying a biologically determined condition. Critics of such labelling argue that they are meaningless and unhelpful.

How prevalent is depression?

Accurate figures are hard to come by because mental health professionals use different measures and diagnostic procedures cannot always discriminate accurately. The editors of the specialist journal *Depression* suggest that over 100 million individuals worldwide suffer from some form of depressive illness (Nemeroff *et al.* 1993). Across the lifespan males have an 8–12 per cent risk of *major* (clinical) depression and females a 20–26 per cent risk (Gazzaniga 1992). For various reasons, women are twice as likely as men to be *diagnosed* as depressed. Women are of course more vulnerable to specific depressive reactions following miscarriage, abortion and childbirth. They are also more susceptible generally to the kind of demoralization accompanying the isolation from other adults involved in childrearing and homemaking. It is small wonder that many women choose to work part-time even when their income barely exceeds what they must forfeit on tax, fares and childcare arrangements.

In recent years great concern has been expressed at the rise of depression among young males. It has been estimated that depression and anxiety occur among 15–30 per cent of the UK working population at any one time (CBI/Department of Health 1992). A study by Jenkins (1985) revealed that 33 per cent of executive officers in the Home Office were suffering from 'minor psychiatric morbidity'. The likelihood that depression is both under-diagnosed by doctors, and largely unreported to employers under that name, means that we may never know its true prevalence or its actual effects on work performance.

What causes depression?

Theorists dispute whether depression or a tendency towards depressive reactions may be innate. Gazzaniga (1992) suggests that there may indeed be a genetically determined basis for major depression but that environmental factors play a large part in triggering, or not triggering, the tendency. He suggests that there may be some adaptive purpose in mild to moderate depression, in the sense that the person withdraws and conserves energy, ready for future challenges. This may be particularly the case in so-called seasonal affective disorder (SAD) when sufferers withdraw in winter. It has also been argued that human life itself, or at least in its present stressful form, is intrinsically depressing, and that depressed people may have a more realistic perception of it than others! It has often been believed that a depressive, manic or otherwise eccentric proclivity is almost a prerequisite for the creative professions.

There are some reports of childhood depression which often imply some form of innate predisposition. People often assume pessimistically that if a parent or other close relative has suffered from a mental health problem, then it 'must run in the family'. Although there is some evidence for this view, it is often more likely that growing up in a largely depressed, joyless or unexpressive family 'rubs off' on the person but that later insight and hard work, with or without professional help, can emancipate him or her from such influences to a reasonable degree.

Certain psychoanalytic theorists argue that a sad or somewhat depressive mood is an inevitable part of early childhood as each of us experiences temporary losses of and imperfections in our caregivers. With good-enough mothering or caregiving, most of us develop normally. Deprived of minimum necessary care (severe disruptions in parenting, abuse and neglect, death of a parent or caregiver at a critical time), anyone might gradually develop a stubborn tendency towards later chronic or recurring depression. Certainly it is borne out in clinical experience that when a client initially reports that there is no reason for them to be depressed, it often transpires during the course of counselling that early emotional deprivation existed and has continued to exert an unrecognized but pervasive influence. When clients in counselling make contact with the forgotten sad or angry parts of themselves, progress often follows.

Other explanatory models of depression point to a variety of environmental stressors. Brown and Harris (1978) looked at the social origins of depression, particularly among women, and suggested that a combination of personal vulnerability and provoking factors in the environment accounted for symptoms of depression. As suggested above, it may be the case that many of us 'learn' to be depressed, hopeless or helpless in bleak family situations or in countries where oppressive regimes or chronically adverse weather conditions exist, or in apparently inescapable marriages or monotonous jobs. A great deal of depression can be explained by one's perception of events, how much control one has over them, and one's coping skills (Ormel and Sanderman 1989). Indeed behaviour therapy and cognitive-behavioural therapy rest on the observation that we have learned and can relearn adaptive behaviour quite consciously (Blackburn and Davidson 1990; Gilbert 1992). Often, simply out of lifelong habit, we continue to think and act in ways which reinforce our experience and belief that life and its challenges are miserable and overwhelming. The underlying principle in most approaches to counselling and psychotherapy is, of course, that there is usually at least some room for re-examining and remaking aspects of our lives.

Particular connections between depression and work

Is there such a thing as a depressing job? It is easy to assume that any work related to death, such as that performed by hospice workers, pathologists, mortuary technicians and funeral directors, is intrinsically depressing, but workers in these fields do not necessarily report them as such. Counsellors are often told 'Your job must be terribly depressing, listening to people's misery all the time; doesn't it get you down?' Of course, it doesn't. Counsellors tend to be fascinated by people, deeply interested in the differences between them, and responsive to the painful and distressing complexities of each of their clients' lives. The work is absorbing, gripping and rewarding, and counsellors recognize the need to look after themselves and not to take on more work than is healthy.

As Warr (1987) and many of the contributors to Steptoe and Appels' (1989) accounts of stress and adaptation have shown, there are some clear connections between aspects of work and mental health which should command our attention. It is important to bear in mind that some depression is certainly context-free, that is, it is not affected for better or worse by the person's surroundings. One aspect of the relationship between work and depression concerns life stages, in particular mid-life (and mid-career) and pre-retirement and retirement, at which points consciousness of lack of achievement or disengagement from a lifelong career can precipitate depression (Kets de Vries 1995). Specifically job-related depression is complex and therefore difficult to quantify, but the following job features have been shown to be likely indicators of how it develops:

- having little or no influence on the planning of work;
- having little or no say about the work setting;
- having little opportunity to maximize or develop skills;
- having minimal influence over the timing of breaks, holidays and flexible hours;
- having a monotonous work schedule and no opportunity to voice or change this;
- having little or no discretion regarding making private phone calls or personal visits when necessary.

Many of these features are present to a greater degree for unskilled or semi-skilled workers than for professionals. Often they will be referred to imprecisely under the umbrella of 'boredom'. Warr (1987) places job-related depression at one end of a depression–enthusiasm scale. Clegg and Wall (1990) found that poor mental health among assembly-line workers was associated directly with the nature of their work, but only when they felt they were not using their skills and when they were aware of 'cognitive failure' (e.g. daydreaming instead of concentrating).

Managerial and professional workers are also likely to experience job-related distress, including depression. In a study undertaken by Firth and Shapiro (1986), the personal problems of 53 such workers requiring clinical attention included: difficulties with colleagues; loss of self-confidence; feelings of inadequacy; sense of career failure; role ambiguity and work overload; difficulty making decisions; concentration and memory loss; loss of creativity. The more global terms of burnout and exhaustion are also applicable here. Professionals may be more likely to suffer from the effects of work overload and taxing diversity than from monotony, but ultimately the experiences of moderate to severe depression will be similar regardless of the actual job. Firth and Shapiro acknowledge that it is very difficult to pinpoint whether intrinsic job stress changes people's liking for and ability to cope with their work or their experience of distress colours their perception. Employers with significant numbers of distressed staff or small numbers of highly valued, but highly stressed, employees obviously need to discriminate between individually located sources of distress (perhaps requiring counselling) and organizational sources of stress (requiring other remedies: Argyle 1989).

It had been predicted a few years ago that technological progress would lead to greater leisure time and the wealth to enjoy it. Advanced technology has certainly changed working patterns and freed many people from their jobs – often involuntarily in the form of redundancy. David Nicholson-Lord, in an article in the *Independent on Sunday* (29 January 1995), asked 'Does work make you stupid?' His argument is that the work involved in symbolic analysis (which much information technology is about) divorces employees from real contact with others, customers or colleagues, and offers simply another version of alienation. VDUs diminish us and cause subtle 'soul damage'. Furthermore, it looks as if we are heading for greater wage slavery rather than greater leisure, with an average 67-hour week for those lucky enough to have work being just around the corner. According to Nicholson-Lord, fear of losing work in a climate of high unemployment leads to the phenomenon of employees enduring soul-destroying tasks and avoiding complaining or making creative suggestions. If this view of developments is accurate, it is a recipe for impaired mental health. Debates on the balance between the likelihood of our entering a cyber-social liberation or a technological nightmare are found in Finnegan *et al.* (1987).

How can people who are depressed be helped?

There is now ample anecdotal, clinical and research evidence that talking about depression is likely to be of benefit. Not only that, but there is an increasing demand for counselling from those who experience depression. Severe and chronic depression may be highly resistant to counselling or psychotherapy, but even here it can often be effective in conjunction with medication. While no real evidence exists to demonstrate that any one kind of approach to counselling has superior results in treating depression, cognitive therapy has been commended as particularly suitable (Blackburn and Davidson 1990).

A brief digression into the theory of cognitive therapy may be useful, since it has taken as its particular focus problems of depression and anxiety. This approach builds on the view that our current thought patterns play a very large part in determining how we feel and act. We are not the helpless and neutral victims of circumstance but we actively process the meaning of events. In other words, whatever has happened to us, is happening to us or is about to or may happen to us or around us, is always in some way mediated by our own interpretation of it. We are often not consciously aware of it, but usually there are certain automatic thoughts going on which colour our perceptions. We often think that events are more adverse than they really are, we underestimate our ability to cope with problems, we make assumptions about what other people think about us, and so on. For some of us, our negative thoughts have gone on so long that they appear to be unquestionable realities. 'Nobody likes me' and 'I'll never do well at anything' are classic examples. There are very few, if any, people who are actually disliked by everyone, or who have absolutely no redeeming abilities! The task and skill of the cognitive therapist (or counsellor using a cognitive approach) is judiciously to challenge such beliefs and to suggest gradual experiments with thought-monitoring, trying out new beliefs and new actions until positive changes begin to occur. Table 8.1 shows an example of how a secretary construes a simple workplace event and how this may lead to symptoms of depression or anxiety.

In addition to formal counselling or psychotherapy, depressed people can certainly often benefit from support from friends, carers, colleagues and relatives. The instinctive 'cheer up' approach may not work very well, but a willingness to listen, to be available and to offer any necessary practical help can go a long way. There are a number of self-help groups for those who suffer from depression. There are also many valuable self-help books available, sometimes written in a work-book format, which give clear descriptions of what depression is and how it can be overcome or reduced by gradual self-challenges. Often depression is best overcome by taking slow and realistic steps towards better functioning, rather than aiming for dramatic improvement. Physical exercise sometimes helps far more than simply talking about the depression and its possible sources. Employers can help by being flexibly supportive, offering counselling and time off for any necessary appointments. The most devastating action for most depressed people is to be summarily rejected. According to Dr David Baldwin, speaking as part of

Table 8.1   Examples of information processing errors in depression and anxiety

---

Situation: My boss laughed at two typing errors that I had made in a draft.

1 *Selective abstraction:* The patient selects one aspect of a situation and interprets the whole situation on the basis of this one detail.
   Interpretations:
   He dismissed two hours' hard typing with derision. (*depression*)
   I keep making mistakes. (*anxiety*)

2 *Arbitrary inference:* The patient reaches a conclusion without enough evidence to support that conclusion or even in the face of contrary evidence.
   Interpretations:
   He thinks I am a poor typist. (*depression*)
   I must be really clumsy. (*anxiety*)

3 *Overgeneralization:* The patient draws a general conclusion on the basis of one aspect of a situation which has been arbitrarily selected from a whole context.
   Interpretations:
   Nobody appreciates me. (*depression*)
   I should never have become a secretary. (*anxiety*)

4 *Magnification and minimization:* The patient exaggerates the negative aspect of a situation and minimizes the positive aspect.
   Interpretations:
   What is wrong with me? I make nothing but mistakes. (*depression*)
   I can't cope with this. What if he gets angry? (*anxiety*)

5 *Personalization:* The patient relates to himself external events when there is no basis for making such a connection.
   Interpretations:
   No wonder he looks so harassed all the time. He cannot even rely on me to type his work correctly. (*depression*)
   I am being ridiculed. (*anxiety*)

Source: Ivy-Marie Blackburn and Kate Davidson, *Cognitive Therapy for Anxiety and Depression*, 1990, Blackwell Scientific Publications, p. 25.

the Royal College of Psychiatrists' 'Defeat Depression' campaign, employers all too often fire depressed employees, presumably on grounds of incapacity. Not only is this painful for employees but expensive for employers and, given the relatively low cost of treating depression, misguided (reported in the *Daily Express*, 10 December 1994).

O   *Case example 1*
    Sonia, an administrative assistant of 28, reported that she lacked the confidence that her colleagues appeared to have. She felt 'different' and often burst into tears at work. She had briefly seen a psychiatrist in the past but had not felt helped. She had a secure relationship with a man,

functioned well at work, but failed to make due progress in her career because she was perceived as under-confident. Sonia was intelligent and attractive but could not believe this. She was aware that sometimes she was straining the sympathy of the one or two close friends she had by constantly craving their reassurance, then rejecting it when she got it.

The counsellor who saw Sonia was prepared to help her identify to what extent her concerns were deeply rooted in the past or of more recent origin. It seemed that she had had a particularly poor relationship with her father, who was often absent from the home, but was cold and scathingly critical when he was there. Sonia believed that her sister and brother suffered similarly from the father's behaviour and also had problems of low self-esteem. Her mother seemed to have been fairly warm, but unable to stand up to her husband. Sonia had a certain perfectionism in her psychological make-up, yet however hard she worked her achievements were somehow eroded by a nagging sense of worthlessness. The initial assessment, agreed on by the counsellor and Sonia together, was that she had deep-seated problems of self-acceptance relating to her father, which might take some considerable time to overcome, but that she also had some reasonably circumscribed concerns which could probably be focused on beneficially in a brief counselling contract.

With help, Sonia described certain specific difficulties relating to her work. She was not being given certain responsibilities, she believed, because she came across as shy and awkward. She felt unable to talk candidly with her line manager, even though she could admit that he was very approachable. She also felt isolated at work and avoided going to lunch with colleagues. The counsellor encouraged her to ask a colleague out to lunch and to tolerate her feelings of vulnerability. At the same time, Sonia agreed to keep a diary in which she entered her observations of how she behaved at work and what her typical self-defeating thoughts were. By persevering with such tasks, she was able, within a relatively short time, to begin changing some of her daily relationship patterns and, to some modest extent, her low self-esteem. She agreed that during this time she had not felt any acute depression and she identified for herself a link between depression and avoidance of social contact. She resolved to maintain an agenda of initiating such contacts, noting the content of her underlying thoughts in social situations and, whenever helpful, tracing these to the way she felt about herself in relation to her father. At the end of six weekly meetings with the counsellor she reported feeling significantly better. A follow-up meeting was scheduled for three months later, at which she said that she was applying for a promotion and had also joined a local group of people who were exploring their depression with the assistance of a transactional analyst.

O   *Case example 2*

Jean, a junior manager in a health authority setting, often found herself somewhat idle at work. She worked in a small department and had the feeling that her appointment had been primarily a 'political' one intended to protect funding. Her job description was unhelpfully broad and her line manager was usually quite evasive when she asked for specific guidance about what expectations there were of her. Very well qualified, well paid and with a young child, Jean knew how well paid she was, could not find comparable employment elsewhere and could not afford to give up the job. Yet on a day-by-day basis it was, she said, 'driving me mad'. She often worked alone and this isolation increased her feelings of demoralization. She came to dread going in to work every day, often experiencing free-floating anxiety. Apparently nothing much was expected of her, and when she complained to friends they simply joked that they should be so lucky. Anxiety and depression alternated within her and she finally sought counselling for help. During counselling it became even clearer that she was in a trapped, paradoxical position, but one in which her health was progressively suffering. She tried rehearsing statements to her boss and her husband, and applied these with limited success. Gradually she came to accept that her strategy had to be to endure her position as well as possible, meanwhile making strenuous efforts to find alternative, more fulfilling employment, even if it paid a little less.

Anxiety and stress

Anxiety has a range of meanings from the very general to the clinically precise. We may say that we live in an age of anxiety, that we are anxious to complete a deal and that we are filled with anxiety. We may say that we are dreading a forthcoming confrontation or commitment or that we are feeling tense or stressed. We also say that we are afraid of people, afraid of making mistakes and so on. Anxiety, stress, worry, nerves, tension, agitation, fear, dread and apprehension have overlapping meanings. When there is no obvious reason for these feelings, psychiatrists sometimes refer to them as constituting a 'generalized anxiety disorder'. I include the term stress here because I believe it is often used synonymously with anxiety or as a euphemism for anxiety (Powell and Enright 1990). In other words, it has become more acceptable to declare oneself 'stressed' than to reveal that one is anxious or afraid. Anxiety, like stress, often expresses itself somatically. Because anxiety and depression are often found together or as alternating moods, and together they constitute the most common mental health problems, I have already implicitly covered at least some of the issues and I shall therefore have less to say about anxiety than about depression.

What kinds of anxiety are there?

There is, of course, the kind of excited, anxious apprehension before a feared or important event which may be considered natural, universal and even helpful. We sometimes talk about an 'adrenalin rush' in positive terms; being somewhat tense, aroused and expectant can improve our performance. However, the degree to which acceptance of such anxiety is healthy is open to debate. Many actors admit to feeling sick and vomiting before performances. Many, if not most emergency service workers experience frequent stop-start anxieties; although these have in the past been regarded as simply part of the job, questions are now arising about the possible negative, health-damaging cumulative effects of such stress. Prolonged-duress stress disorder is the name suggested for this phenomenon. But continuous pressures are also found in working environments which are not literally concerned with life and death, for example in financial dealing (Kahn and Cooper 1993) and in academia (Fisher 1994). Tracing the relationship between career choice and objective, job-specific anxieties is outside the scope of this chapter, but Hood (1995) has pointed interestingly to the effects of anxiety among one typically perfectionistic group of workers – creative perfumers. It is not only deadlines and life-threatening situations which induce anxiety, but also the pre-existing personality traits of certain professionals.

Apart from generalized anxiety, we may consider mild to moderate social anxiety such as shyness or fear of public speaking; simple phobia (e.g. fear of spiders, snakes, etc.); and panic disorder.

Social anxieties may be said to include shyness which reaches debilitating proportions or which seems to force the person to avoid almost all social situations; public speaking anxiety or stage fright, not only in large public events but perhaps even in small business meetings; and anxieties related to apparently small and simple activities involving others, such as fear of writing or signing cheques in the presence of others (sometimes called scriptophobia), or fear and avoidance of the telephone (sometimes known as telephonophobia). Obviously, these latter two problems may seriously hamper sufferers' careers. Very often these anxieties are specific to young people or to absence of practice, for example, in public speaking. Those beset by acute fear of embarrassment may 'successfully' order their life in such a way (living alone, remaining unemployed, or opting for work which involves little or no contact with colleagues or the public) that the severity of the problem is hidden for years. Alternatively, they may attempt to disguise their anxiety by pretending to far greater extroverted characteristics than they really possess, or they may consume alcohol to excess to disguise their social anxiety.

Simple phobias, so-called because they are usually singular and easily identified, include fear of spiders, snakes, cats, birds and so on. Again, sufferers may manage to organize their lives in such a way that nobody learns of their terror. Since most workplaces, for example, are free of animals, someone suffering from a cat phobia can probably hide their problem completely while at work; the strain of having to avoid cats altogether, however, may show up eventually in generalized stress or tiredness at work. Animal phobias often stem from childhood. Other familiar and not necessarily severe phobias include fear of flying and fear of dental treatment. Agoraphobia is the most common serious phobia and, by definition, is not frequently encountered in relation to employee counselling, unless perhaps triggered by a traumatic event such as an assault, accident or rape. Employees subjected to an assault at work may well develop an apparent 'phobia' in relation to the workplace itself. Someone witnessing a fatal accident at work may feel genuinely unable to return to that place for some time.

Anxiety attacks, also referred to as panic attacks or panic disorder, are characterized as discrete episodes of acute fear with palpitations, chest pain, breathing difficulties, dizziness, feelings of unreality, hot and cold flushes, sweating, trembling and a terror of impending death, madness or loss of control. An individual may experience several, but not necessarily all of these symptoms and may experience 'simple panic attacks' or chronic, recurrent attacks. The age of first onset is often, but not invariably, in the late teens or twenties. Attacks are most likely to occur when queuing, ruminating on personal problems, in a dense crowd, when tired or ill, or when alone or away from home, but some people also experience spontaneous attacks apparently unrelated to circumstances. Use of certain recreational drugs, or rather withdrawal from them, may trigger anxiety attacks. Although some attacks may follow an identifiable event, many appear to come from nowhere. Once experienced, panic attacks seem to play on the mind of the sufferer so that they may constantly anticipate and perhaps 'create' further attacks by interpreting tiny meaningless body sensations as catastrophic, self-fulfilling images of impending doom. Agoraphobics invariably experience attacks but this does not account for all panic attacks. Typically, sufferers will try to hide or disguise their problem, feeling ashamed of it and associating it with madness; therefore the condition often goes untreated for many months or years. A thorough analysis of the factors involved in panic attacks can be found in Baker (1989).

What causes anxiety?

The so-called 'fight or flight' response is well known: when confronted by a fearful object or situation, we are programmed to deal with it appropriately, perhaps aggressively, or to take evasive action, perhaps by running away or even momentarily freezing. In modern society, however, we are often challenged by myriad minor fearful objects or situations that cannot be avoided or fought; in addition, many of our fears are internalized ones. In other words, the powerful memory of a past experience of fear or even terror (perhaps as a small child) may be reactivated in the present. We may respond physiologically as if we are actually being threatened, even when we are not. If you have been raped or seriously assaulted, for example, many years ago, it is understandable that the terror associated with that event may be easily triggered by any event which even faintly resembles it. Arousal as part of appropriate preparation for a forthcoming challenging event is considered normal, healthy and helpful, but over-arousal, worry and panic are clearly counterproductive and unhealthy.

Psychodynamic counsellors are likely to interpret anxiety in the light of early separation anxieties (birth, weaning, everyday partings and traumatic partings) and other internal, unconscious conflicts. We develop mechanisms to deal with our anxieties but when these defences fail us or become obstacles to our growth, greater anxiety may result. Cognitive therapists generally point to the role of thinking and its errors, as described in the section on depression and in Table 8.1. According to this understanding of anxiety, we both create and perpetuate our anxiety by self-reinforcing negative thoughts and worries. Anxiety is generally related to fear of impending events, whereas depression is often related to the past and to loss. Behaviour therapists are likely to emphasize the role of bad habits, family traits and counterproductive avoidance in the perpetuation of anxiety and phobias. Particular anxieties are sometimes traceable to specific past events and sometimes not. Once established, certain phobias take on a life of their own and seem immune to insight or willpower.

Anxiety, stress and work

> For fear of shaking, a secretary may become unable to take shorthand dictation or to type; a teacher may stop writing on a blackboard in front of a class and cease reading aloud; a seamstress will stop sewing in a factory; an assembly line worker will find it impossible to perform the actions necessary for assembling a product.
>
> (Marks 1980: 99)

Obviously, certain jobs are intrinsically stress or anxiety-engendering. Broadbent (1995) paints a clear picture of some of the relationships between anxiety and job pressures. Hales *et al.* (1991) take an interesting look at military life from the perspective of combat factors, alcohol and substance consumption, divorce, mobility and other features of army life. Police officers face quite specific stressors and according to one analysis items such as witnessing the death of a working partner, taking someone's life in the line of duty, pursuing a violent criminal, and dismissal rank highly (Ainsworth and Pease 1987: 152).

In some cases, as mentioned, people may choose their careers consciously or unconsciously to match, disguise or defend their pre-existing anxieties (Hood 1995). The highly anxious technical repair person whose work demands constant attention to detailed wiring systems, for example, may have chosen this career path in order to avoid intimacy; later in his career he may suffer a crisis which forces him to seek counselling and to remember his childhood decision to steer clear of close relationships. (Of course, I am not at all suggesting that all career choices are made neurotically!) Finally, it is most likely that a combination of occupational and domestic forces, personality factors, timing and other dynamics will be responsible for outbreaks of temporarily unmanageable anxiety. Evans and Coman (1993) have attempted to discriminate between specific and non-specific occupational stress. Sheikh (1995) outlines some of the possible legal ramifications of workplace stress and suggests that anxiety, depression, abnormal eating habits, panic attacks and phobias can all stem from, or be exacerbated by, occupational stress.

How can people with anxiety problems be helped?

Probably the more generalized the anxiety is, the more likely it is to respond to almost any one of a whole range of therapeutic approaches, most of which aim to facilitate the person in exploring the nuances of anxiety, discovering its roots and possible solutions or coping strategies. Minor tranquillizers are less prescribed than they once were and many counsellors are averse to their use, since they do not, of course, help people to identify the source of their problems, nor do they promote the learning of better coping techniques. But many non-traditional or complementary medicines such as hypnotherapy, aromatherapy, massage, homeopathy and acupuncture address themselves to the alleviation of anxiety. The kind of treatment offered to those with problems of anxiety will depend on clinical training, beliefs and settings, and therefore clients should preferably prepare themselves with some knowledge of the different beliefs and structures of mental health agencies and practitioners in advance of receiving treatment (Dryden and Feltham 1995).

Anxiety management is the term often used by clinical psychologists to refer to a package of education, self-help and treatment for anxiety. Descriptions of anxiety and its emotional, cognitive and physiological components may be given, enabling clients to recognize exactly what is happening to them, to learn to accept that anxiety is common and not life-threatening and to begin to gain some mastery of their reactions in the face of anxiety. Relaxation techniques are taught, as are helpful 'self-statements' (unvoiced healthy and positive thoughts), and sometimes tape-recordings are made which clients may listen to at their leisure later. Sometimes anxiety management is conducted in small groups, enabling participants to help each other

and to learn that they are not alone. Not all clinicians agree with a generalized anxiety or stress management programme, however (Hallam 1992).

Social anxieties may best be overcome using a combination of cognitive
therapy (examining distorted beliefs about oneself and social situations and
changing these), social skills and assertiveness training (learning how to
improve one's social interactions) and, possibly, practising and experiment-
ing with new behaviour in either real-life situations or in purposefully convened groups. Certain approaches, for example rational emotive behaviour
therapy, advocate a challenging combination of questioning one's irrational
thoughts and fears, and undertaking moderately frightening challenges in
everyday life, such as deliberately exposing oneself to potential embarrassment in order to learn that it is not, in fact, the dreaded 'end of the world',
but simply uncomfortable.

Arguably, the more specific and acute the fear, such as phobias and panic
attacks, the more are behaviour therapy interventions indicated. Behaviour
therapy begins with careful assessments of actual problems and objectives
and often includes graded targets, drawn up in the form of a hierarchy of
anxieties, for example. When asked how anxious you feel on a 1 to 10 scale
when contemplating a major public speaking engagement, you may decide
on a 9; your anxiety in relation to speaking at a small dinner party may be 7;
and so on. One approach is to tackle the least fearful scenarios first, often
combined with newly learned ways of relaxing and talking yourself through
difficulties, gradually moving on to more challenging tasks only when you
have overcome the previous hurdle. This can be done in reality or by imag-
inative exercises and is known as systematic desensitization. Exposure
therapy, or facing the very situations you are anxious about, is recommended as the most effective solution to severe anxieties (Marks 1980;
Baker 1989). The alternative to graded exposure is outright confrontation.
Given the nature of fear and terror, however, a majority of people probably
opt for gradual exposure. Where this is the approach used, it is important
that it is carried out systematically, and in general the sufferer benefits more
from concerted confrontation within a short time-span.

Self-help is often effective in cases of anxiety, especially in combination
with strong social support and bibliotherapy (reading and following instructions in self help texts designed to help you overcome anxiety). Some good
examples are given as recommended reading at the end of this chapter. Most
such books advocate careful analysis of your precise problem scenarios, and
an active approach towards conquering anxiety. Many suggest that a diary
of troubling events and irrational thoughts is kept and monitored, thus
encouraging greater self-knowledge and giving a concrete sense of progress.
Self-help groups can often be found which are composed of people with
similar anxieties and which allow for progress and relapse to be reported
back to the group. Even long-standing anxieties can be overcome in a very
short time, given the right clinical input and support (Baker 1989). Many

clients are helped with transient worries, perhaps gaining insight into their tendencies to avoid fearful situations, with counselling. Those involved in EAPs may need to consider what expertise or mechanisms for referral are required for particular anxiety problems, since they do not always respond well to talking therapy alone and may demand special resources. Palmer and Dryden (1995) present a useful multimodal (systematically eclectic) understanding and treatment approach for stress, anxiety and depression.

○ *Case example 3*

Anxiety and depression may be found together, or someone may be considered to be simply very 'stressed'. The following example demonstrates perhaps that an exact diagnosis is not always possible or even necessary. It also demonstrates that success in counselling terms is not necessarily success in commercial or employment terms.

Christopher, a middle-aged managing director, experienced a series of difficult life and professional events within a relatively short space of time, culminating in being a witness to a traumatic accident in which his wife's life was endangered. On developing various symptoms – early morning waking, chronic headache and temporarily impaired confidence – he took time off, fully supported by the company. A regime of anti-depressant medication, relaxation training and counselling helped him within about three months to feel able to function more or less normally again and to return to work. The business was flourishing and he looked forward to an imminent return to full helmsmanship of the company. Unfortunately, his period of time off work and association with compromised mental functioning fuelled the company's own insecurity and Christopher was abruptly presented with his own redundancy. Such can be the stigma of stress, anxiety and depression, especially in cruelly competitive times, that employers may lack due compassion and sound business judgement in a case like Christopher's. In fact, Christopher was an extremely talented man with an enormous amount to offer and it was the company's loss that they had evidently panicked. If there was a silver lining to this story, it was that Christopher regained contact with his emotional life, his relationship with his wife improved greatly, and he would think twice before again setting himself up as what he called a John Wayne manager in a fickle commercial environment.

Life stages and events

My intention here is simply to refer briefly to some of those, usually obvious, stages or maturational points in our lives, such as mid-life and retirement, which may have a particular impact on our mental health at work, as well as those life events, such as accidents and bereavement, which un-avoidably impact on our functioning. Major life events do not, however, necessarily have a greater negative impact on us than the sum of never-ending daily hassles, as argued interestingly by Brown (1974). Counsellors generally, but certainly those working in EAPs and with adults of mature age, should be acquainted with theories and findings on life-span develop-ment and how these impinge on the counselling process (Budman and Gur-man 1988; Thomas 1990; Knight 1992). Managers and others involved in employee welfare should consider the relationship between the age-related issues within their workforce and the kinds of welfare or counselling pro-grammes they introduce, and by whom these should be staffed.

Work and life-span development

In Britain people may be employed in one form or another of work between the ages of 16 to 65, or longer. Laidon Alexander's chapter in this book looks at different working patterns. Women are likely to have more inter-rupted careers, but even here the current pace of change makes generaliza-tions problematic. For most of us, work is an arena we enter after leaving school or higher education and our entry into the workplace may be fraught with anxiety and uncertainty; our career developments may be punctuated by good and bad choices and shaped by sheer good or bad luck. There is a continuous interrelationship between personality and job-fit, and the impact on individuals of success or failure, resulting in possible enhanced or chal-lenged self-esteem (Budman and Gurman 1988; Furnham 1994). Many have entered careers for safety, expecting a long association with a particu-lar employer, and of course such expectations are now being thwarted. Most writers on career development and chronological age agree roughly that early working life is characterized by making choices, errors, compro-mises and consolidation or, for some, beginning a clearly defined, upwardly directed professional career. It is thought by some that 30 is a classic age to stop in one's tracks, to ask questions about the meaning of life and, some-times, to enter psychotherapy, either to gain perspective on one's personal past or to consider existential or transpersonal matters.

Mid-life

Since social norms and patterns have changed so much, one cannot accu-rately claim that all or even most workers experience similar developmental stages. However, mid-life generally has a particular significance for both women and men. The term 'mid-life crisis' (coined, according to Kets de Vries [1995], by the psychoanalyst and organizational sociologist Elliott Jacques [1965] may have no proven basis but does compel popular belief. For women, the years from the late thirties often press home the message that fertility is time-limited. Recent trends in first conceptions show that many women are delaying having children until their late thirties or even early forties, partly in order to consolidate a career. Such choices are not an unmixed blessing, since one consequence is that the children of older parents may be experienced as more challenging and exhausting. For those women who have had children in their twenties, mid-life is often associated with the so-called empty nest syndrome, when adjustments to the loss of a busy household and the prospect of greater loneliness have to be made. Depression and suicide are in some instances associated with this stage of life.

The impact of mid-life on women may be interpreted in relation to social traditions and feminist and sociological critiques of these traditions, and it is not inevitable that women will experience emotional turmoil simply because they reach middle age or their children leave home, or indeed because they may have no children. Similarly, reactions to menopause differ. For some women, the menopause is highly disruptive and unwelcome, biologically, psychologically and socially. One woman complained to her counsellor that although she had not wished to 'give in' to it, she felt compelled to request hormone replacement therapy (HRT) to deal with her hot flushes, sleeping difficulties and mood changes. In an ideal or even moderately compassionate workplace, recognition of the needs associated with the menopause (rest periods, time off and even simple respect for natural emotionality) would go a long way to help.

Whether men genuinely experience a menopause is still debated, but it is often remarked that many men during middle age find themselves trying sometimes recklessly to recapture their lost youth and dreams in ways which may threaten their close relationships and their livelihood. The amusing term 'menoporsche' has been coined for those who feel a sudden need to purchase and drive fast cars designed to deny the reality of the ageing process. One survey of over 1000 male professionals suggested that five out of six of them had had an intense age-related crisis often beginning as early as the late thirties (Schultz 1974). It is well documented that certain physical and intellectual characteristics or abilities begin to become problematic in middle age, for example in the areas of weight gain, stamina, fitness, sexual appetite, performance and fertility, baldness and intellectual flexibility. Moral and political views may narrow from mid-life onwards particularly, and willingness and ability to master cognitive skills such as those required by new information technology may be reduced.

Awareness of declining powers and failure to achieve desired career and lifestyle results can lead to depression for some, but Kets de Vries (1995) suggests that depressive reactions are far from inevitable. The psychotherapist Carl Jung regarded the later years as filled with potential for mature reflection, truth-seeking and the opportunity to offer accumulated wisdom. Indeed, a majority of counsellors in Britain are over 40 years old and some psychologists suspect there may be a demonstrable positive correlation between wisdom and mature age (Sternberg 1990). By the year 2000, 40 per cent of the workforce will be over 45 and there are signs that employers are slowly changing their attitudes towards older employees, partly encouraged by the Department of Employment's campaign for appropriate and equal opportunities for older people (DOE 1994).

Enlightened employers may wish to anticipate the effects of mid-life on valued employees, not only for the sake of those employees individually but because unaddressed problems within the mature and more experienced sector of the workforce may create problems elsewhere in the organization. The effects of redundancy on middle-aged workers are more likely to be devastating than on younger employees, but the 'survivors' of downsizing are also prone to guilt and anxiety which may negatively influence the organization (Noer 1993). Kets de Vries (1995: 155) argues that proactive counselling has a vital role to play:

> In advocating a greater use of counselling, we are not only thinking of intervention in instances of severe crisis, but also of a more preventive form of counselling at a time when 'repair' is less difficult. We observe that usually counselling is sought for cases of breakdown while no steps are taken to help the much larger number of demoralized.

Those resistant to the introduction or use of counselling for facilitating organizational change may prefer to think in terms of a mentoring programme, which in fact is often simply another kind of counselling (O'Brien 1995).

Pre-retirement and retirement

Retirement is running at the rate of about 600,000 a year. Anyone who has worked for up to 50 years, especially but not necessarily in the same organization, will face the challenge of adaptation and loss. Indeed it is well known that a significant proportion of people whose career had meant everything to them fail to adapt to retirement and die relatively prematurely following retirement. Retirement can also mean a change in financial fortunes and lifestyle, particularly for those who have been unable to make extra pension arrangements for themselves; a third of pensioners live at or below the supplementary pension level. In combination with advanced age, retirement often entails changes in relationships, in health and mental agility, in housing and in the sense of self-worth. Given increasing life expectancy, a substantial proportion of people may be officially retired for decades. It is for these reasons that preparation for retirement is increasingly considered to be so crucial. Since many employees now take early retirement in their fifties, employers who are genuinely concerned with this issue need to think carefully and strategically about the implementation of pre-retirement training packages or individual counselling or assistance.

In asking 'is there life at retirement?', Kets de Vries (1995) suggests that retirement itself needs to be purposefully managed. Isolation, inertia and apathy should be guarded against. Although many people are delighted to retire, particularly if they feel they have served their time in a less than satisfactory job, retirement frequently coincides with declining health and stretched finances. A tendency towards hypochondriasis and depression is not unknown. It is important to remember that, in spite of assumptions to the contrary, there actually is no compulsory state retirement age and some older people prefer to remain engaged in part-time or voluntary work and consultancy. Others may turn to travel or study.

Enlightened organizations will wish to provide preparation for this stage of life if possible, by means of counselling, training, flexible or phased retirement. Individuals not offered such amenities would do well to seek some such assistance themselves.

Bereavement

Every year in Britain approximately 600,000 people die. According to Cruse, the major voluntary organization working with the bereaved, this means that around 1.5 million people experience major bereavement each year. Cruse deals with 90,000 enquiries a year and in 1993–94 counselled approximately 29,000 people. Death in Britain is traditionally still avoided as a subject of open conversation, and the grief and sadness it generates is more often than not experienced with some embarrassment and even denial. The older one is, the more likely it becomes that one will have lost or will soon lose parents and other loved ones. Unfortunately for many, the sudden, premature and unexpected deaths of friends, relatives and colleagues from accidents, illness and suicide may be experienced well before they seem due or fair. Whatever comfort anyone draws from religious belief or social support, most of us are likely to suffer some shock and various emotional reactions. Furthermore, the news of a death and its effects tends to cause ripples of sadness or disequilibrium around the person, so that in the workplace, for example, news of (or even witnessing) a colleague's death may have widespread, if subtle, emotional repercussions. The emotional effects of the loss of a job, partner, home, good health or other significant pieces of our personal identity and landscape, often mimic the effects of bereavement by death.

Normal grief is thought to follow, more or less, a course of shock, denial, numbness, confusion, longing, anger, fear, sadness, guilt, despair, loneliness, acceptance and adjustment, though not necessarily in this order for everyone. People may experience physical symptoms such as insomnia, headaches, nausea and exhaustion. How grief is experienced will depend on personality factors, relationship with the deceased, nature of the death and so on. There is no 'normal' period of mourning but there are many myths about how long or short a time it should be before someone 'gets over it'. It is quite common for a bereaved person and/or their friends to insist that they 'should have recovered by now', after a few weeks. Certainly many employers fail to recognize just how long recovery can take. Some spouses report that they never, in fact, completely recover, living the rest of their life with some degree of sadness and sense of loss. It has been recorded, perhaps contrary to popular expectations, that some people who are bereaved actually feel worse (more irritable, more inclined to smoke or drink to excess, for example) a year or so after the death (Stroebe *et al.* 1993). Anniversaries of deaths are also particularly poignant for many. There is some evidence of gender differences in styles of coping with death, with women being perhaps more inclined to show overt grief (Littlewood *et al.* 1991). It is also important to remember that there are more bereaved female partners in any one year than males; in 1993–94 there were approximately 3,200,000 widows to 750,000 widowers. Among men in particular, it may be that lack of overt grief does not indicate absence of inner sadness, nor does the copious display of outward grief necessarily signify greater difficulty in coming to terms with the death.

Bereavement may become problematic when the stage of denial cannot be passed, for example when someone insists on believing that her husband is not really dead. Those who cannot bring themselves to dispose of belongings or to redecorate the bedroom of the deceased person may exacerbate their difficulties. People who feel guilty for a prolonged period may not allow themselves the need to continue meaningfully with their own life, for fear that they may be perceived as betraying the deceased. When death occurs without any possibility of seeing the person, saying goodbye or putting the record straight, complex upsetting feelings may result and become protracted. The most common problem following a bereavement is depression, which may be regarded as a refusal to experience and express loss with due sadness or anger; feelings, both negative and positive, may remain frozen thereafter. At its worst, depression following the loss of someone loved, particularly a lifelong partner, may result in suicide or premature death from a 'broken heart'.

Employers and colleagues can and should assist bereaved employees both practically and emotionally by offering practical help, time off, the chance to talk, and formal counselling where appropriate. A sensitive path must often be trodden between not pretending that it hasn't happened and not forcing the person to talk about it. Charles-Edwards (1992) presents a succinct description of the issues pertinent to the workplace.

Conclusions

Mild to moderate mental health concerns such as those presented here occur frequently in the population at large and certainly feature widely within the workforce, sometimes independently of occupational factors, sometimes stemming directly from them. In addition, unavoidable and problematic life events and stages contribute to the overall stress levels to be found in any working environment. Although hard to quantify, these concerns certainly cost both individuals and corporations dearly in psychological and financial terms. Counselling has been shown to be a relatively economical and effective way of addressing such concerns, and humanitarian and business interests alike are served by companies providing access to counselling help.

References

Ainsworth, P.B. and Pease, K. (1987) *Police Work*. London: British Psychological Society/Methuen.

Argyle, M. (1989) *The Social Psychology of Work* (2nd edn). Harmondsworth: Penguin.

Baker, R. (ed.) (1989) *Panic Disorder: Theory, research and therapy*. Chichester: Wiley.

Blackburn, I.M. and Davidson, K. (1990) *Cognitive Therapy for Depression and Anxiety*. Oxford: Blackwell.

Broadbent, D. (1995) Job demands and anxiety, in P. Collett and A. Furnham (eds) *Social Psychology at Work*. London: Routledge.

Brown, G.W. (1974) Meaning, measurement and stress of life events, in B.S. Dohrenwend and B.P. Dohrenwend (eds) *Stressful Life Events: Their nature and effects*. New York: Wiley.

Brown, G.W. and Harris, T. (1978) *The Social Origins of Depression*. London: Tavistock.

Budman, S. and Gurman, A.S. (1988) *Theory and Practice of Brief Therapy*. New York: Guilford.

CBI/Department of Health (1992) *Promoting Mental Health at Work*. London: CBI.

Charles-Edwards, D. (1992) *Death, Bereavement and Work*. London: Centre for Professional Employment Counselling.

Clegg, C. and Wall, T. (1990) The relationship between simplified jobs and mental health. A replication study. *Journal of Occupational Psychology*, 63: 289–96.

DOE (1994) Getting on, in *Too Old – Who Says?: Advice for older workers*. London: Department of Employment.

Dryden, W. and Feltham, C. (1995) *Counselling and Psychotherapy: A consumer's guide*. London: Sheldon.

Evans, B.J. and Coman, G.J. (1993) General versus specific measures of occupational stress: An Australian police survey. *Stress Medicine*, 9(1): 11–20.

Finnegan, R., Salaman, G. and Thompson, K. (eds) (1987) *Information Technology: social issues. A reader*. London: Hodder and Stoughton.

Firth, J. and Shapiro, D.A. (1986) An evaluation of job-related distress. *Journal of Occupational Psychology*, 59: 111–19.

Fisher, S. (1994) *Stress in Academic Life: The mental assembly line*. Buckingham: Open University Press.

Furnham, A. (1994) *Personality at Work: Individual differences in the workplace*. London: Routledge.

Gazzaniga, M.S. (1992) *Nature's Mind: The biological roots of thinking, emotions, sexuality, language and intelligence*. Harmondsworth: Penguin.

Gilbert, P. (1992) *Counselling for Depression*. London: Sage.

Hales, R.E., Cozza, K. and Plewes, J.M. (1991) Normality in the military, in D. Offer and M. Sabshin (eds) *The Diversity of Normal Behavior*. New York: Basic Books.

Hallam, R. (1992) *Counselling for Anxiety Problems*. London: Sage.

Heller, J. (1975) *Something Happened*. London: Corgi.

Hood, V. (1995) Work-related counselling – a psychodynamic approach. *Psychodynamic Counselling*, 1(2): 239–52.

Jacques, E. (1965) Death and the mid-life crisis. *International Journal of Psychoanalysis*, 41(4): 502–14.

Jenkins, R. (1985) Minor psychiatric morbidity in employed young men and women and its contribution to sickness absence. *British Journal of Industrial Medicine*, 42(3): 147–54.

Kahn, H. and Cooper, C.L. (1993) *Stress in the Dealing Room*. London: Routledge.

Kets de Vries, M.F.R. (1995) *Organizational Paradoxes* (2nd edn). London: Routledge.

Knight, B. (1992) *Older Adults in Psychotherapy: Case histories*. Newbury Park, CA: Sage.

Littlewood, J.L., Cramer, D., Hoekstra, J. and Humphrey, G.B. (1991) Gender differences in parental coping following their child's death. *British Journal of Guidance and Counselling*, 19(2): 139–48.

Marks, I.M. (1980) *Living With Fear: Understanding and coping with anxiety*. New York: McGraw-Hill.

Nemeroff, C.B., Schatzberg, A.F., Weiss, J.M. and Cohen-Cole, S.A. (1993) Depression (editorial). *Depression*, 1(1): 1.

Noer, D.M. (1993) *Healing the Wounds*. San Francisco: Jossey-Bass.

O'Brien, J. (1995) Mentoring as change agency – a psychodynamic approach. *Counselling*, 6(1): 51–4.

Oldfield, S. (1983) *The Counselling Relationship: A study of the client's experience*. London: Routledge and Kegan Paul.

Ormel, J. and Sanderman, R. (1989) Life events, personal control and depression, in A. Steptoe and A. Appels (eds) *Stress, Personal Control and Health*. Chichester: Wiley.

Palmer, S. and Dryden, W. (1995) *Counselling for Stress Problems*. London: Sage.

Powell, T.J. and Enright, S.J. (1990) *Anxiety and Stress Management*. London: Routledge.

Schultz, D. (1974) Managing the middle-aged manager. *Personnel*, 51: 8–17.

Sheikh, S. (1995) Pressure of work. *Guardian Gazette (Journal of the Law Society)*, 92(11): 18–19.

Steptoe, A. and Appels, A. (eds) (1989) *Stress, Personal Control and Mental Health*. Chichester: Wiley.

Sternberg, R.J. (ed.) (1990) *Wisdom: Its nature, origins and development*. Cambridge: Cambridge University Press.

Stroebe, M.S., Stroebe, W. and Hansson, R.O. (eds) (1993) *Handbook of Bereavement: Theory, research and intervention*. Cambridge: Cambridge University Press.

Thomas, R.M. (1990) *Counseling and Lifespan Development*. Newbury Park, CA: Sage.

Warr, P. (1987) *Work, Unemployment and Mental Health*. Oxford: Clarendon Press.

Suggested reading

Burns, D. (1990) *The Feeling Good Handbook*. Harmondsworth: Plume.

Charles-Edwards, D. (1992) *Death, Bereavement and Work*. London: Centre for Professional Employment Counselling.

Dryden, W. and Gordon, J. (1993) *Peak Performance: Become more effective at work*. Didcot: Mercury Business Books.

Hilderbrand, P. (1995) *Beyond Mid-life Crisis*. London: Sheldon.

Marks, I. (1978) *Living With Fear: Understanding and coping with anxiety*. New York: McGraw-Hill.

Noer, D.M. (1993) *Healing the Wounds*. San Francisco: Jossey-Bass.

Palmer, S. and Dryden, W. (1995) *Counselling for Stress Problems*. London: Sage.

Potter, B. (1980) *Beating Job Burnout*. Berkeley, CA: Ronin.

Powell, T.J. and Enright, S.J. (1990) *Anxiety and Stress Management*. London: Routledge.

Stubbs, D.R. (1986) *Assertiveness at Work*. London: Pan.

Useful organizations

British Association for Counselling
1 Regent Place
Rugby
Warwickshire CV21 2PJ
01788 550899

British Psychological Society
St Andrews House
48 Princes Road East
Leicester LE1 7DR
0113 549568

Centre for Stress Management
156 Westcombe Hill
London SE3 7DH
0181 293 4114

Cruse Bereavement Care
Cruse House
126 Sheen Road
Richmond Road
Richmond TW9 1NR
0181 940 4818

National Association for Staff Support within the Health Care Services
9 Caradon Close
Woking
Surrey GU21 3DU
01483 771599

Pre-Retirement Association
26 Frederick Sanger Road
Surrey Research Park
Surrey GU2 5YD
01483 301170

Stress at Work
(Foundation for the Promotion of Occupational and Mental Welfare)
14 Albion Place
Northampton NN1 1UD
01604 259770

Severe mental illness

○ **JANE FAWCETT**

Severe mental illness conjures up for many of us images of demented patients locked in wards, or deranged 'psychopaths' brandishing weapons, charging unchecked through communities. The Secretary of State for Health stated in January 1993 that 80 million working days were lost through mental illness. The Mental Health Foundation has estimated that severe mental illness may well affect 3.2 million people per year in the UK (Mental Health Foundation 1993). So if our first images were accurate, the large mental institutions of the nineteenth century would still be flourishing, and we would all walk in fear of crazed attacks in our towns and cities. This stereotypical image of a severely mentally ill person is fuelled by a tabloid headline referring to the tragic activities of a patient suffering from schizophrenia, and our own fears of madness are ignited. Perhaps we rationalize that if the patient is not in a strait-jacket or ranting, they are not really mentally ill.

But what, therefore, is meant by the term 'severe mental illness'? What sort of illnesses are covered by this term? Where does the subject of suicide fit into the workplace experience? What sort of mental health problems of a severe nature might be found in the workplace? What role does an employee counselling service have in dealing with severe mental ill-health? Will employers and EAPs ever come in direct contact with people who are suffering from a mental condition which renders them severely ill? Is it an area where short-term counselling can be a 'cure'? How can an employer contribute towards assisting an employee who is coping with severe mental illness? In this chapter these questions and others will be discussed.

It is helpful to begin with a simple working definition of severe mental illness and this might include the following: a condition in which a person is unable to function emotionally and practically in a domestic or work setting. The person may or may not be aware of their dysfunction and inability to cope with everyday life. They appear to be out of touch with reality some or most of the time. They would benefit from specialist treatment. Their mental state will often cause their family, friends and work colleagues concern, distress and shame.

The stigma attached so often to mental illness is surprising given that one in five of us will suffer from some form of serious mental problem in the course of our lives. According to the Department of Health booklet *Mental Illness: What does it mean?* (Department of Health 1993) it is still believed that mental illness is easily identified because sufferers are usually 'crazed' and surrounded by people in white coats. In this context, and with the image suggested in the opening paragraph of this chapter, it is probably fear which creates the stigma. The idea that something called madness is only to be found among an easily identifiable few protects most of us from being part of those few. The notions that madness runs in families, is confined to certain villages, only emerges with particular conditions and circumstances, keep us ignorant of mental ill-health and its treatment.

A major contribution could be made to demystifying mental illness by employing organizations making positive statements about mental health in their advertisements and application forms. Policy statements of intent and practice would also improve knowledge and understanding, and undoubtedly assist recovery of employees who become ill. To set a good example the Department of Health adopted a positive and helpful approach in 1994, *Mental Health Policy: A guide for line managers* (COI 1994). Organizations wanting assistance with this should approach the national organization MIND, which will give advice on this issue.

Severe mental illness is often simplistically described as falling into two major categories – neurotic and psychotic. 'Neurotic' might be defined as a reaction to known and recognized events or circumstances. Thus, mild to moderate anxiety, depression, obsessions and phobias are usually neurotic. A sufferer usually has an insight into the illness, often being able to survive safely in the everyday world. 'Psychotic' might also be described as a reaction but it has no explainable origin or cause. Thus schizophrenia and manic depression are psychotic in nature. The sufferer usually lacks insight into the illness and often cannot maintain themselves safely. The debate over whether these conditions are a consequence of a genetic imbalance (nature), or environmental factors (nurture) is endlessly pursued, but there is evidence that infection, drug and alcohol abuse, and changes to the brain can cause psychosis. Confusion for doctors, patients and carers is also caused because the different conditions can become intertwined – a schizophrenic patient suffering deep depression, for instance. Sometimes doctors are reluctant to give a clear and certain diagnosis because the condition appears so complex.

Mental health and work

In the context of work, it is helpful to look at any evidence which is available linking mental health problems with certain kinds of employment. In his book *Work, Unemployment and Mental Health*, Peter Warr (1987) explores the complex relationship between employment and mental health and the possible contribution which the workplace can make towards poor mental health. Warr's overall findings show the following conditions as likely to contribute to poorer mental health: lack of personal control, unskilled and repetitive tasks, undemanding and unchallenging work, poor pay, unsafe and poor physical environment, being unsupported and isolated from colleagues, carrying out work undervalued by self and society. These ingredients make poor mental health more likely and Warr suggests that managers look at job content together with trade unions to try to avoid obvious pitfalls.

In an era when workers in both public and private sectors have experienced huge changes in working practices because of technological advance and employment policies, uncertainty has grown. With the uncertainty the much-heralded 'feel-good' factor of the 1980s has disappeared and given rise to employees expressing fear and anxiety about the future. Stress levels have risen to such an extent that many organizations train their employees in stress management. The long-term effects on the mental health of the nation remain to be measured. In the 1990s barely a day passes without publication of a study about one workgroup or another which has been found to be suffering from irritability, depression, sleeplessness and guilt for neglecting their families. Each group of workers will have experienced many of the conditions likely, according to Warr's analysis, to cause poor mental health.

There seems to be a correlation between jobs which include a great deal of pressure (for example, teachers, police and journalists) and manual work, which is often dull and repetitive, with anxiety, depression and sleeplessness. However, the most consistent link is between unemployment and depression. The improvement in mental health is made when the sufferer is re-employed. Therefore, at times of redundancies and high unemployment, perhaps there are strategies which employers can adopt to contribute to the better health of the nation. Perhaps if employers were better educated in the mental health consequences of multiple changes in the workplace and job losses, they might consider slower change and fewer redundancies.

Dealing with employees who are severely disturbed

What can you do if an employee appears to be very unwell at work, appears distressed, disturbed or not coping with work or interpersonal relationships? There may have been events which colleagues are aware of which might have triggered the changed condition. Family, partners or friends may have shared their worries about the employee with people in the workplace. In the first instance, colleagues, managers, employee counsellors, and personnel managers may well be in a position to urge the employee to seek the assistance of his GP. With the employee's permission, it may be appropriate to speak to the doctor about the employer's concerns. It is always essential to tell the individual of every contact concerning them. So the counsellor might say to the individual, 'Your manager has telephoned me to tell me of the concern about you and I understand that he has also asked you to see your GP.' Any suggestion that meetings and conversations are happening secretly is likely to cause feelings of being conspired against, and increase feelings of anxiety and of being out of control. If a manager is unable to persuade the employee to seek medical help voluntarily, the main course of action that can be taken is to refer the employee to the organization's occupational health doctor, on the basis of concern over their ability to carry out their work. Alternatively the manager can seek the advice of the hospital Accident and Emergency department. It should be possible to speak to someone in the mental health department – the psychiatrist on duty, for instance.

Otherwise, it may be helpful to speak to the social services department of the local council. A duty social worker should always be able to give advice. Part of the policy of Care in the Community means that any individual or family can present themselves to their local social services department for an assessment. An assessment does not implicitly mean that action will be taken; the resolution to the assessment may be to leave matters as they are. An employer cannot ask for an assessment on behalf of an employee. Responses to this type of referral will vary. An employer cannot force an employee to go to hospital or visit their GP. Nor is it appropriate for managers to contact family and friends to talk about the employee without specific permission. If, however, the employee sees the doctor of his own accord, the GP may prescribe drugs and may also refer the individual to the mental health department of the hospital. The treatment and therapies will vary enormously, and there are differing views about what is most effective for some conditions.

In-patient NHS hospital treatment is often difficult to get, unless a person is extremely ill. However, some people may have private healthcare insurance which covers them for some treatment if they have psychiatric cover. There is usually a limit on the cover, either up to a particular cost in a year or number of days of in-patient care. Some insurances do not cover specific treatments, for example for alcohol abuse. Many insurances do not include psychiatric cover generally, and specific insurance has to be taken out. Some organizations will pay for employees to have private treatment, and some GP fundholders will buy private psychiatric beds. There are many private hospitals all over the country providing a wide range of mental health facilities, including treatment for substance abuse and eating disorders, as well as general psychiatric beds. Costs are very high, so long-term stays are expensive.

From time to time the expression 'being sectioned' is mentioned in the area of mental health, and this is a reference to the specific sections of the Mental Health Act (1983) under which a person can be admitted compulsorily to hospital or under the guardianship of another authority. For this to take place the person concerned has to be considered to be suffering from a mental disorder which warrants detention in a hospital for assessment and possibly treatment for a specified period. The detention is with a view to protecting the person involved, or others. In fact most patients admitted to hospital are voluntary patients.

Drugs

Since the 1950s there has been a revolution in drug treatments for severe mental illness, and this has enabled many people to live near-normal lives. It has also reduced the need for so many in-patient mental institutions, for although the drugs do not cure, they can very often control the more disturbing and distressing symptoms. The drug treatments are divided into four main categories – hypnotics, anxiolytics, anti-psychotics and anti-depressants.

Hypnotics are sleeping pills. Disrupted sleep is often a problem for some patients. They are effective in assisting patients to sleep, but they may obscure the main cause of the problem. These drugs can cause dependence, and some have other side-effects. They have been widely prescribed in the past, with estimates of a quarter of the adult population having taken a minor tranquillizer at least once.

Anxiolytics are prescribed for stress and anxiety, having a calming and sedative effect. These too have dependence and withdrawal problems and the nervous system can become tolerant of them.

Anti-psychotics are used to help with the more florid conditions such as hallucinations and delusions, but do not help with apathy and blunted emotions. They are sometimes, misleadingly, referred to as major tranquillizers. They work differently for each individual, and some people need other drugs to cope with the side-effects. It is important to bear in mind that they can improve the quality of life for very distressed people, and to remember that their effects need separate examination for each individual.

Anti-depressants are used to assist in raising mood levels. Because they reduce some of the symptoms of depression they can make life less intolerable. They do not work for everyone, but may take the edge off anxiety states. They are often highly toxic, and therefore dangerous if taken in excess.

All drugs in the mental health field seem to have some side-effects and doctors should describe these to their patients before prescribing them. This does not always happen, so it is advisable for patients to ask, particularly if they are working while taking the drug. Patients should, if possible, consider whether they wish to take drugs. For many it can be helpful, and puts them on the road to recovery from, say, depression. Anti-depressive drugs often do not take effect for from one to four weeks. The drug Flupenthixol in low dosages is said to be an effective anti-depressant within two or three days. Patients should ensure they are fully aware of possible side-effects. Better known as Prozac, it has received huge attention as a 'wonder drug', but uncertainty about its safety remains. Some patients avoid taking medication, perhaps because they are so depressed that they do not think themselves worth the effort. Some avoid medication because in their paranoia they believe that people are trying to poison them. However, drug treatment can be beneficial, and it is advisable to ensure that patients, family and partners are kept as well informed as possible of the intended effects and side-effects. Some counsellors and psychotherapists will not work with people who are taking medication of this sort. However, there is considerable evidence that many patients using a talking therapy as well as drugs become better able to cope with a more independent life, and may be well enough to work.

Further information on prescribed psychiatric drugs can be sought from the publications of MIND and SANE, as well as from the medical practitioners. An employee counsellor would find an up-to-date directory of psychiatric drugs a useful resource to have at hand (see Hammersley 1995; Daines *et al.* 1996).

Let us look at some of the severe mental health problems that might be found in the workplace, the most common being depression.

Severe depression

Severe depression is likened by Dr Dorothy Rowe to being trapped in a prison of your own making (Rowe 1983). Many of us experience mild depression at some stage in our lives and inevitably some people, including employees, will become more deeply depressed. It feels like utter and profound despair, from which the individual is unable to be lifted, neither to be reached by helping friends nor by the talking therapies. A person plunging into such despair may often feel suicidal or, more rarely, may threaten to kill those whom they feel are responsible for the state they are in. Severe depression is a state in which the individual has a distorted and unrealistic grasp of their current life. Commonly it will manifest in long periods – weeks or months – of feeling very low, as well as being anxious. The sufferer might move jerkily, have racing and repetitive thoughts, worry unreasonably about issues over which she or he has little or no control, as well as have headaches, sweating and dizziness. An acutely depressed person may feel trapped by the depression and this sense of being trapped seems to intensify the depression.

This then leads to the depression absorbing almost all of the individual's attention, so that it can be as if the person is falling deeper and deeper into a ditch with little prospect of being lifted from it and seeing a light of hope. The sense of frustration from being so excluded, and the inability to help are very difficult for friends, family and colleagues. In this state of despair destructive thoughts may surge upwards and sufferers often become secretly absorbed with harming themselves or others. It is very hard to reach someone in this state, and treatments to prevent damage must be decisive.

An employee is unlikely to be at work in a state of severe depression. The most probable pattern will be increasing numbers of absences from work as the depression grows. There may be considerable difficulty in communicating with the employee to ascertain what is wrong. It is also possible for someone in a very depressed state to keep coming to work, but to disguise the depth of their depression. This can be very distressing to colleagues, who later feel they have been uncaring and unobservant.

In cases of severe depression in-patient treatment is most likely to be given if the person might harm themselves or others. The days of long-term psychiatric care are only for a very few people. The usual pattern is that a patient is taken into hospital for a few weeks, to be assessed and to get the treatment started. As soon as is practical the patient will be discharged, possibly to attend a day hospital. In any event under the Care in the Community programme any discharge from in-patient care requires a care plan to be drawn up for a patient leaving hospital. A wide variety of treatments can be suggested for a patient recovering from depressive illness.

Day hospitals offer a variety of activities, many of which will be voluntary for the patient. Art classes, woodwork, pottery, social skills, as well as art therapy, group therapy, music, movement and relaxation therapies may all be on the agenda. These are all to assist the patient in the return to a coping, active and reasonable life in the community and at work. Very often talking therapies (counselling and psychotherapy) are suggested. These may be provided by the NHS, specialist organizations or privately. In the case of an employee a planned return to work may well be mapped out through negotiations with the individual, health personnel and the employer.

In such circumstances it is not often appropriate for an employee counselling service to provide the talking therapy because EAP counselling is usually short-term. However, the counsellor may well have an important role in explaining to management the likely length of time the employee may be away from work, and advising on the organization's policies relating to such cases. Flexible approaches by an employee's manager can often be invaluable to a full and healthy recovery. The benefits to the employer are that a valuable member of staff will not be lost, and may return to work with increased motivation and loyalty.

The story of Helen demonstrates how severe depression builds up, and how work pressures and Helen's past experiences contributed to her illness.

○ Helen is an experienced social worker of 38, and shortly after her divorce she changed the type of client she worked with from the elderly to children. The first case she worked on after this concerned taking a child into care because the child was allegedly experiencing sexual abuse within its family. Helen had never told anyone of her own childhood abuse, and the case brought it all rushing back into consciousness. Initially she saw a counsellor, and she started taking odd days off work feeling low. She went to her GP, who prescribed mild anti-depressants and referred her for an NHS psychotherapy assessment. She saw a psychotherapist a few times, and then attended a weekly group for women with similar experiences for about eight months. During this period her feelings of self-worth plummeted, and in attempts to bolster her self-image she tried to improve her social life. She met men who unfortunately used her, which increased her depression. The days off work increased further. She stayed in bed more and more, and began talking of 'ending it all'. She agreed to see her GP and he referred her to the local mental health unit where she was admitted with severe depression and anxiety. She was given stronger anti-depressants which really did help take the edge off the depression, but Helen had sunk very deep, and the long climb out of her 'prison' needed slow and patient work. After five weeks as an in-patient she returned home. First she needed to start establishing her ability to cope with a simple domestic routine, looking after her family and being functional at home. She attended the day hospital, doing practical classes in painting and pottery, as well as assertiveness and relaxation training. She saw a counsellor three times a week, and after three months' absence from work began to plan her return. Her employers could not have been more supportive. Far from putting another pressure on Helen, they agreed that she should come back when she was ready, and that initially she should only work four hours a day for three days a week. The employers carefully planned the work she would be expected to do, so that she was not put under undue pressure, but the work was seen as valuable to her team. With this Helen was able to feel valued and supported, and the social services department retained a member of staff whose loyalty was unbounded.

Manic depression

The main outward difference between depression and manic depression is the wild mood swings. In manic-depressive illness, very deep depressions are followed by over-excited, hyperactive behaviour, which to an onlooker is very alarming. The sufferer is often unaware of the effects of their behaviour, and dismisses the distress of friends and family by seeing it as their problem.

There are two schools of thought about the causes of manic depression. One is the belief that there is a genetic component or predisposition, and that events trigger an imbalance in the brain. Treatment according to this diagnosis is by drugs. The other main school suggests that manic depression is a consequence of severe emotional damage in early life, and that sufferers grow up unable to cope with strong emotions, or that manic depression is a dysfunctional reaction to problems of everyday life. Counselling and psychotherapy are seen as sometimes beneficial in these cases, but not a cure. A sufferer is unlikely to be able to cope with work until the mood swings are under control, and such episodes are likely to recur.

O   Jean was working as a secretary in the Civil Service when she began to talk about feeling ill, and being poisoned. She would get very excited about the sickness she felt and then feel unable to go out for some days. She stopped going to work, and her GP referred her to the hospital where she was initially tested for gastric problems. However, as all the tests proved negative, and Jean continued to talk about poisoning, drug treatment for manic depression was started. After several weeks Jean became more calm, and her employer was able to expect her to return to work. Although Jean was helped by drugs, she had been badly neglected and physically and emotionally abused in childhood. It was never established exactly what had caused her illness, nor did she ever recover. She retired prematurely at 63, still on medication.

Schizophrenia

Schizophrenia is a diagnosis which is usually arrived at after a patient has been seeing a psychiatrist for some period of time. It is not easy to define and therefore is not a simple diagnosis. It covers a range of symptoms which may be present at different times. There are two different types of symptoms, positive and negative. The so-called positive symptoms arc delusions and/or false beliefs (for example, a conviction of being watched or the sufferer believing that he is someone else); hallucinations (hearing, seeing or smelling things that are not actually there, for example hearing 'voices'); a belief that the sufferer's thoughts can be read by others; paranoia (a belief that people are plotting to harm the sufferer); catatonic behaviour (not moving, or eating/drinking or, contrastingly, being very excitable). The negative symptoms are often even more alarming to both the sufferer and friends and family. It is as if the sufferer is cutting themselves off from their everyday world by seeming to have no emotions; having communication difficulty; being unable to carry out routine tasks like getting up or washing; wanting to be alone; and a changing sleep pattern.

    This range of symptoms seems so familiar that it is likely that most people will experience some of them without being schizophrenic (for example, being withdrawn and having mood swings is not only common among adolescents, but probably 'normal'!). It is the combination of conditions and circumstances which will give rise to a diagnosis of schizophrenia. The most common time for schizophrenia to start is in the middle and late teens, when young adults are experiencing teenage change and the difficulties associated with this period of growing up. Since adolescent behaviour is erratic and awkward even in the most well-balanced teenager, it is often difficult to distinguish the healthy from the unhealthy. Schizophrenia may start slowly and seem to be brought on by another life event such as childbirth or examinations. It is very rare for sufferers to be violent, and widely publicized violent cases should be regarded as unusual.

What causes schizophrenia has been the subject of a great deal of debate, but it is generally now thought to be a combination of family tendency, experiences in life, particularly stressful events, and biochemical changes in the brain. There is certainly evidence of the disorder running in families, but family members also experience the same environmental factors and life events. Research has not yet indicated which factors are more likely to cause the illness. Schizophrenia is far less common than depression. One in 200 people suffer from schizophrenia and of those only one-third have a chronic condition which requires long-term treatment. The remaining two-thirds experience either one episode or occasional episodes only.

Graham's story is not untypical of how schizophrenia is regarded by employers.

○ Graham worked for an advice service, where local people living on state benefits could come for help. He had got the job after leaving college at 22 years of age. While at college he had experienced periods of confusion, and he had believed that his fellow students were picking on him. He liked his job; he liked helping people, and all went well for about 18 months, when an aunt died suddenly and Graham was very upset. Returning from the funeral Graham began to experience some very vivid delusions, and he reacted badly to them. His behaviour became more and more disturbed and he was admitted to hospital. After several weeks in hospital and a heavy drug regime, Graham was sent home to his family, who lived in a small town in Yorkshire, 200 miles away from his job. Graham's condition improved. He found a counsellor near his family home, was put on a waiting list for day care at the nearest hospital, and helped around the home. After six months, the employer sent for him to assess how likely it was that Graham would return to work shortly. The employer received a report from Graham's GP and with this the occupational health doctor took the view that Graham was unlikely to be fit for work in the immediate future, so he lost his job. Sadly, this is often the outcome of such cases.

There is no legal employment protection for someone suffering from a mental illness, but many employers have equal opportunities policies which may include statements about mental health or disability. If this is the case there may be some grounds for more sympathetic treatment than that meted out to Graham. An employee counsellor may have a role in supporting an employee who is trying to keep his job after a long period of sickness.

Phobias and obsessions

Most people have fears of some things, be it heights, mice, snakes or enclosed or open spaces. These fears usually amount to a dislike and avoidance of the thing we fear. However, when the intensity grows to such an extent that it causes an anxiety state which prevents someone from normal functioning, it has become a serious problem. Many phobias are common in childhood and some carry on into adult life. Some phobias start in adult life, often as a result of stress. Most phobias are simple and sufferers develop ways of managing them, for example taking the stairs rather than a lift. Fear of enclosed spaces (claustrophobia) is common and for this reason it is wise to set up an EAP or other occupational health service on a ground or lower floor, because many people dislike using lifts. Also clients often refer themselves after illness, so climbing flights of stairs may cause physical distress.

The most common complex phobia is agoraphobia, which is the fear of open and public places. This condition is often accompanied by anxiety and panic attacks, and depression. The consequences of this condition can be that the sufferer is afraid to leave the house and carry on a reasonable life. Most phobias start in early childhood, and recur and develop in later life. It is calculated that twice as many women as men suffer from phobias, but this may be because men do not seek help (SANE 1993).

The most effective treatment appears to be behavioural. If sufferers are encouraged to stay in the frightening situation for agreed periods, and they can build the ability to cope with the terror, the symptoms of most obsessive and compulsive disorders will decrease.

○ Janice was a 'dinner lady' in a local school, where her children had attended when they were juniors. Janice's marriage was unhappy. Her husband seldom spoke to her. They ate meals in silence in front of the television. Her youngest son lived at home, and was a drug user. Janice lived in fear of one day finding him dead. Janice stopped going to work because she found it difficult to walk to the school. She was no longer able to go to the big supermarket, but could make it to the corner shop when she felt a little less depressed. The GP prescribed anti-depressants, but this did nothing to help overcome the fear of going out. When Janice visited a counsellor she was taken by her sister Gladys, who turned out to be the key figure in Janice's return to work. Gladys was willing to spend hours with Janice, taking her to work, collecting her later, waiting for her at her counselling appointment, encouraging her to go shopping for very short periods at first. Although Janice's recovery was not complete, she was able to live a near-normal life most of the time, and she knew that with patience she could overcome a 'bad patch'.

If an employee can be given appropriate support, there is every possibility that recovery will be maintained and they will gradually learn to manage their fears. We probably all experience mild obsessions or aversions, especially in our childhood, like not walking on the lines of pavements, or under ladders, watching for two magpies to ward off death, and so on. These do not disrupt our lives and disturb our family and friends. Serious obsessive and compulsive behaviour, however, usually makes the sufferer very distressed. They often realize that what they want to do or avoid is irrational and unnecessary, and their inner battle between the rational and the compulsive causes much anxiety. Sometimes the compulsion is shameful to the sufferer. An example is a devout Christian uttering irreligious re-marks or being absorbed with what they regard as pornographic ideas. The most common compulsion concerns cleanliness. Hand-washing after touch-ing anything, or so many times each morning in a ritualistic manner, is not uncommon. Being obsessively tidy, to the point where daily life is disrupted by a constant need to clean up, dust and vacuum, is also not unusual.

Treatment may be with tranquillizers and anti-depressant drugs to help relieve the anxiety created by the obsession. However, the most successful treatments are programmes of behavioural 'exposure therapy'. This method allows the sufferer to gain control over their obsession or phobia. They plan, for instance, to reduce the number of times they wash their hands every day, or they go gradually into open spaces for longer and longer periods of time. The role of an employer in such a programme would be to provide support, encouragement and the necessary time off work. Even so, for many sufferers such conditions are chronic, and successful treatment may not be found.

Postnatal depression

Nearly 50 per cent of all new mothers experience the 'Baby Blues' a few days after the birth of their child. For most the experience is confusing because the birth of a baby is expected to be a happy event, and the uncontrollable tears, and feelings of exhaustion yet inability to sleep, do not make sense. For many these feelings disappear after a few days, but for 10 per cent of mothers depression grows, either from the Blues, or several weeks or months after the birth. It is vitally important that mothers seek medical help if they are developing any of these symptoms: a deeper depression, anxiety, tension, obsessional thoughts, panic attacks. It is also important that friends and family provide as much support as possible, helping the woman cope with the baby, and staying with her to help her manage. There is often a strong sense of shame for being miserable at a time when a mother 'should' be basking in the glories of motherhood. There can be a rather unsympathetic attitude from some doctors, who may have a 'pull up your socks' approach. A referral to the local maternity hospital is likely to ensure an appropriate response.

Postnatal depression can be helped by drug therapy, and it is beneficial for the mother to talk through her experience and symptoms. This can be done either with a professional counsellor or through a self-help group. Being heard by a sympathetic listener, and allowing time for recovery assists most sufferers. A mother who has experienced postnatal depression after the birth of a first child will obviously fear that the illness will reappear. Sometimes the worry and anxiety about the possible onset of the postnatal illness is the only problem, and mothers can be greatly helped by the reassurance that they managed well before. The Association for Postnatal Illness will give advice on these issues.

Employers should be aware of the high incidence of postnatal illness, and that the return to work after maternity leave is a possible trigger for feeling depressed. Since postnatal depression can start as long as nine months after the birth, the first difficulties of depression may occur at the end of the maternity leave. The feelings of having to cope with leaving the baby and going back to work may seem overwhelming, and maternity leave returners will benefit from support from personnel, or an employee counsellor. Sometimes the acknowledgement that it is a busy and difficult time can be sufficient. That tells the mother that the employer understands that this transition is not necessarily easy.

Alzheimer's disease and dementia

Dementia is usually a disease of old age, so it is unlikely that employers will have direct dealings with sufferers. However, estimates of the number of people affected by dementia are in the region of 600,000, and of that figure 70 per cent are Alzheimer's sufferers. Alzheimer's disease results from a physical change in the brain cells, causing a progressive decline in a sufferer's ability to remember, to learn, to reason and to think. As more and more care is taking place 'in the community' it is likely that employees may have dependent relatives who are suffering from dementia or Alzheimer's. For many carers, looking after a relative with dementia is a profoundly difficult experience. Initially the sufferer appears to be a bit confused or forgetful, but as the disease progresses the ability to cope with normal daily life disappears altogether. The demands on the carer are often unrelenting and unrewarding. There is no cure and only limited treatments are available, which attempt to slow down the progress of the condition. The carer often watches a loved member of the family or a friend disintegrate and become quite helpless. The carer could usually benefit from a great deal of support, and an employer may be able to provide some of that by allowing time off, or providing the employee with counselling sessions to explore the feelings and practicalities of being such a carer, and discovering where practical support can be sought. Very often carers feel that they have to give up work to look after a loved one, and this may then present the carer with the experience of isolation and depression. An employer may be able to consider more flexible working arrangements to help the employee avoid giving up the job.

Suicide

Helen's experience of depression (mentioned earlier) had a happy end. She did, however, reach a point when she was considering ending it all. From time to time, even though actual suicide is more likely among the unemployed, a colleague commits suicide or a suicide attempt is made by an employee, and the effects in the workplace are often devastating.

Let us first look at some of the official figures. Suicide accounted for 1 per cent (approximately 5500) of all deaths in 1991, and is the second most common cause of death among 15–34-year-old males. Suicide is rarely carried out in isolation from some manifestation of mental distress and, of the people who commit suicide, 90 per cent will have some form of mental illness, 66 per cent will have seen their GP in the previous month, 33 per cent will have previously stated an intention to kill themselves, and those who have made attempts before are 100 times more likely than the rest of the population to try again. Statistics indicate higher suicide rates among the unemployed than employed, but the links are complex.

However, an analysis of suicides by occupation is carried out by the Office of Population Census and Surveys (Kelly *et al.* 1996). Recent published figures are shown in Table 9.1. There are many reasons put forward as to why these particular occupations might rate so highly. Access to drugs and weapons may be one factor. Farmers and vets work in an environment where sick or distressed animals are killed. Financial stresses may also be a cause. There are fears that the 1996 BSE crisis, which caused financial hardship for farmers, may result in even higher suicide rates for this group.

It is likely, therefore, that someone contemplating suicide will give some indication that something is wrong. Colleagues of an employee who does commit suicide will probably experience extremely strong and distressing feelings. Initially shock will be experienced, with a sense of bewilderment. This is likely to be followed by huge feelings of guilt because colleagues failed to prevent the death, failed to see how distraught the person was, or they did not present a good-enough reason to stop their colleague killing himself. The feelings of powerlessness may lead to inertia among the work

Table 9.1 Ten highest suicides by occupation – male deaths aged 16–65 (1988–92)

Occupation	Suicides and undetermined deaths	
	PMR*	No. of deaths
Vet	361	18
Pharmacist	199	18
Dental practitioner	194	18
Farmer	145	177
Medical practitioner	144	60
Forestry worker	155	27
Librarian/Information, officer	84	8
Hotel porter	102	15
University academic staff	152	27
Chemical scientist/engineer	156	38

Notes *PMR is the proportional mortality ratio 'The PMR gives an indication of how a particular occupation's mortality from a specific cause differs from that of the whole age group. Thus, a PMR of 200 suggests a doubling of the death rate where 100 is the value for the whole age group being compared' (Charlton *et al.* 1992: 35).

group. There will often be very angry feelings towards the person who has committed suicide for creating such distress, and leaving relationships incomplete. The sense of waste and loss is often overwhelming. An employee counsellor can be extremely helpful in assisting colleagues to express their feelings, perhaps in groups, after such an event. As well as working with those who feel affected, the counsellor can also assist management in advising colleagues whether it is appropriate to attend the funeral or whether some other gesture might be more suitable. She may also advise on what the organization's role might be with relatives.

When Brendan killed himself his colleagues were all deeply shocked. Those who considered themselves his friends felt confused and guilty; the other colleagues felt his death deeply intruded into their lives and they did not understand why. Brendan's colleagues rapidly divided into two camps – the close friends and the colleagues – and the counsellor in this workplace was initially asked to see each group separately. There the friends were able to explore their grief and their feelings of guilt and hopelessness. They were able to share each other's responses to the death of their friend. They gave each other support and understanding. They were also encouraged by their manager to attend the funeral and make appropriate contact with Brendan's family. The other group seemed more isolated, and in their work with the counsellor they were able to establish that Brendan had been the instigator of this division, that he had forged it. This group too had uncomfortable emotions to deal with, like feeling angry about the way Brendan had manipulated people in the workplace, and hoping that this would now stop. After a series of group meetings it became important to bring them all together, which management did to rebuild the work team.

Another example of the kind of support after suicide an employer may need to give is when an employee's partner or a family member commits suicide. As well as the emotions described above, there may also be a sense of shame, not just over the suicide itself, but also over bringing such personal matters to work.

Jane's mother had been difficult for years. She was over 70, had poor mobility, and was regarded as rather eccentric. Actually, she was getting more depressed and lonely and was drinking a great deal. When her mother took a lethal overdose of painkillers, Jane's brother described it as 'another stroke' when he contacted her at work. Jane told her colleagues this and rushed to hospital, where her mother died. For Jane it was very difficult to return to the workplace and tell her colleagues that her mother had taken her own life. Jane felt ashamed of the situation, guilty that she had not been able to help her mother, and that she was not important enough for her mother to want to live. On top of this she felt awkward about returning to work with the true story. Counselling was recommended and helped Jane work through her grief and come to terms with what had really happened.

Sandra's story, on the other hand, was of rejection and failure. When her relationship with Bill broke down after ten years, she was inconsolable. Colleagues attempted to support her, and then desperately made an appointment for her to see the employee counsellor. Sandra told her story yet again. She wept all the way through the session and left feeling drained and hopeless. The colleague who went with her and the counsellor urged her to come again, but she wouldn't. A few weeks later she took a handful of pills and washed it down with vodka. Her attempt to kill herself was unsuccessful and she left hospital angry with herself, the hospital, the employee counsellor and her colleagues who had not made things better. Her anger towards Bill was still unvoiced. Sandra had not decided to seek help herself and so she was not able to use the counselling effectively. Indeed, she said it was so ineffective that she blamed the counselling for her predicament. It is at such times, when there is a frantic need to blame, that EAPs can be targeted. Like counsellors, organizations have to accept that they do *not* control employees and that ultimately every individual has to take responsibility for themselves. Having stated this, it is difficult to stand aside and watch someone obviously in emotional pain and do nothing. Take, for example, the story of Patrick.

Patrick had worked for the Works department of a local authority for 20 years, and as competitive tendering moved through local government in the 1980s he was moved to work from department to department applying his skills and knowledge of contracting. For two years all went well, then the axe started to fall again. This time Patrick believed he was going to be made redundant and he was frightened, angry and felt desperate. He felt quite alone and lived only for his work. So when he started saying 'I shall kill myself if they try to get rid of me', his colleagues were very worried and scared. Patrick agreed to see the employee counsellor where he repeated his threats, and ranted and raged about the organization. It appeared that he might actually do what he threatened. On the advice of the counsellor he agreed to see his GP, and later, with Patrick's permission, the counsellor and the doctor spoke about his state. The counsellor offered regular appointments until the reorganization had been worked out, and Patrick used the time to vent his anger about the workplace, and he began to look at his isolation. Whether Patrick's threats did influence the organization was never known to the counsellor, but soon after Patrick's permanent job was announced he decided to see if psychotherapy might help him live a fuller life.

Patrick's story highlights the fears which many people have about losing their job, and how often work represents an essential psychological aspect of a person's life. Being without it, for some, cannot be contemplated. Employers should be aware that for a few people unemployment is perceived as truly a fate worse than death.

Another position which some people cannot bear to contemplate is changed financial circumstances. Huge debts and what appear to be hopeless financial prospects are often major ingredients in suicidal ideas. Reduced income sometimes goes together with loss of friends, relationships and status, and for some this is too much. At Lloyd's of London between 1988 and 1990 there was a build-up of losses from major claims (like Piper Alpha). The consequent 'Lloyd's Names Crash' resulted in lost fortunes for many people. These losses have surely altered relationships and resulted in lost status. In 1994 it was reported in the *Guardian* that 30 of these 'names' had died, and it is believed that 50 per cent of these had committed suicide (February).

The financial rulings of the Child Support Agency have been blamed for the suicides of some 'absent fathers'. Although the responsibility for suicide must rest with the victim, it is his inability to cope with problems, of which finance would be a major factor, which pushes him 'over the edge' into self-destruction. Since we know that all relationship breakdown causes at least some distress, access to counselling to explore the consequences of the breakdown is often extremely beneficial, both to the individual and to the overall objectives of the organization.

Carers and support agencies

All severe mental health problems cause distress to the friends and family of the sufferers. In the case of Alzheimer's disease this may involve a family member becoming a full-time carer; for the parents of a young person suffering from schizophrenia it may mean that they live with the uncertainty of that illness, fearing the next worrying episode of acute illness. The families and carers of sufferers from severe depression live with huge anxieties, seeing loved ones in bouts of deep depression, and possibly threatening suicide. Many of these carers and family members are in employment, and work is enormously valuable to them. As well as money, it provides them with interest and stimulation, social and professional contact with people away from the home. It may provide a structure to a largely broken existence. It may present achievement where home presents failure. An employee may be able to forget some of his worries by coming to work. The money earned may ease some of the problems. The employer, by showing sympathy and understanding of this sort of situation, can provide huge support. An EAP can offer the employee a place to offload some of the despair and some of the worries. It can be a place where the carer's concerns are heard, and not only those of the beloved sufferer. The occasional appointment with a counsellor to this end is likely to ensure that the employee feels valued and supported and contributes to a healthy workforce.

There is considerable debate in the mental health field concerning the large and disproportionate numbers of black, Irish (including second generation) and other ethnic minority patients who are diagnosed as suffering from poor mental health. Whether this is because of the pressures of living in a predominantly white British society, or due to misdiagnosis by doctors who fail to have a good understanding of the society and cultures of these patients, is not known. There is no national black mental health organization, but there are many excellent local initiatives to provide support and information. Local social services or community relations organizations will be able to advise on this issue.

Sufferers generally, employees and EAPs can also derive considerable assistance from the national and local organizations which set out to provide support.

References

Kelly, S., Charlton, J., Evans, B. and Jenkins, R. (1996) *Suicide Deaths in England and Wales 1982–92: the contribution of occupation and geography (Population Trends)*. London. HMSO.

COI (1994) *Mental Health Policy: A guide for line managers.* London: Central Office of Information.

Department of Health (1993) *Mental Illness: What does it mean? (Health of the nation)*. London: Department of Health.

SANE (1993) *Anxiety, Phobias and Obsessions*. London: SANE.

Suggested reading

Daines, B., Gask, L. and Usherwood, T. (1997) *Medical and Psychiatric Issues for Counsellors*. London: Sage.

Drew, T. and King, M. (1995) *The Mental Health Handbook*. London: Piatkus.

Gibbs, A. (1986) *Understanding Mental Health*. London: Consumers Association/ Hodder and Stoughton.

Hammersley, D. (1995) *Counselling People on Prescribed Drugs*. London: Sage.

Heckler, R.A. (1994) *Waking up Alive: The descent to suicide and return to life*. London: Piatkus.

Howe, G. (1986) *Schizophrenia*. Newton Abbott: David and Charles.

Jones, R.M. (1988) *Mental Health Act Handbook*. London: Sweet and Maxwell.

Lacey, R. (1993) *The Complete Guide to Psychiatric Drugs*. London: Ebury.

Mental Health Foundation (1993) *Mental Illness: The fundamental facts*. London: Mental Health Foundation.

Mitchell, Ross (1975) *Depression*. Harmondsworth: Pelican in association with MIND.

Mueser, K.T. and Gingerich, S. (1994) *Coping with Schizophrenia*. Oakland, CA: New Harbinger.

Rippere, V. and Williams, R. (eds) (1986) *Wounded Healers*. Chichester: John Wiley.

Rowe, D. (1983) *Depression*. London: Routledge and Kegan Paul.

Rowe, D. (1991) *Breaking the Bonds*. London: HarperCollins.

Tallis, F. (1992) *Understanding Obsessions and Compulsions*. London: Sheldon.

Warr, P. (1987) *Work, Unemployment and Mental Health*. Oxford: Clarendon Press.

Useful organizations

Afro-Caribbean Mental Health Association
35–37 Electric Avenue
London SW9 8JP
0171 737 3603
Information and advice for sufferers and their families.

Alzheimer's Disease Society
Gordon House
10 Greencoat Place
London SW1P 1PH
0171 306 0606
Information, advice and support for sufferers, carers and their families.

Association for Postnatal Illness
25 Jerdan Place
London SW6 1BE
0171 386 0868

Depressives Anonymous
36 Chestnut Avenue
Beverley
Humberside HU17 9QU
01482 860619
Information, advice and support for sufferers and their families.

Independent Healthcare Association
22 Little Russell Street
London WC1A 2HT
0171 430 0537
Information concerning private psychiatric units. There are centres in different parts
of the UK and about 75 per cent of this provision is run by three groups:

Charter Group
Charter Clinic Chelsea
1–5 Radnor Walk
London SW3 4PB
0171 351 1272

Priory Group
Priory Hospital
Priory Lane
Roehampton
London SW15 5JJ
0181 876 8261

St Andrew's Group
St Andrew's Hospital
Billing Road
Northampton NN1 5DG
01604 29696

MIND
Granta House
15–19 Broadway
London EC15 4BQ
0181 519 2122
This is a national organization with many local branches. It is a source of information and support. They also publish books, videos and reports as well as leaflets on
specific mental health issues.

National Schizophrenia Fellowship
28 Castle Street
Kingston upon Thames
Surrey KT1 1SS
0181 547 3937
Information, advice and support for sufferers and their families.

Samaritans
17 Uxbridge Road
Slough SL1 1SN
01753 32713
24-hour helpline for any problem. Contact local branches for assistance.

SANE
199–205 Old Marylebone Road
London NW1 5QP
0171 724 6570
Campaigns for greater awareness and understanding of serious mental illness, develops projects like Saneline (24-hour helpline 0171 724 8000), and funds and
initiates research.

10

Post-traumatic stress

○ **GARY MAYHEW**

Introduction

This chapter looks at that acute form of stress known as post-traumatic stress (PTS). Examples of this condition have become well known through reports of some of the major disasters of recent years. It has not always been obvious, however, that much smaller-scale and less dramatic incidents can cause individuals overwhelming difficulties. Whether traumatic incidents occur in the workplace (as they do in bank raids and industrial accidents, for example) or elsewhere (road traffic accidents, rape and assault, for example), they will almost certainly affect employees negatively, possibly profoundly and perhaps chronically.

Writing to the Duke of Wellington shortly before the military campaign which culminated in the Battle of Waterloo, Lieutenant-General Sir Thomas Picton declared, 'My Lord, I must give up. I am grown so nervous that when there is any service to be done it works upon my mind so that it is impossible for me to sleep at nights. I cannot possibly stand it and I shall be forced to retire' (Holmes 1985).

Sadly for poor Sir Thomas, his plea appears to have gone unheeded as he was subsequently fatally injured by a musket ball to the head while commanding the 5th Division at Waterloo. In an age when iron discipline and unflinching bravery were prerequisites for military service and when men failing to exhibit these qualities could expect the severest punishments including flogging, death, or, for the officer class, dismissal and social disgrace, Sir Thomas's admission is remarkable for its frankness and as an indication of the high levels of distress he was undoubtedly experiencing. The modern informed reader will likely deduce that the Lieutenant-General was suffering from what has become known as PTS or its more serious entrenched concomitant, post-traumatic stress disorder (PTSD).

War by its very nature places individuals in enormously threatening situations, often for prolonged periods with very little respite. Gradually, from the early nineteenth century onwards, documentary descriptions of soldiers' psychological trauma as a direct result of their battlefield experiences became more common. The anxiety and horror, the ever-present possibility of mutilation or death of self and comrades, create high stress levels which do not instantly disappear once the fighting ceases.

By the end of World War One the allied armies had come to regard exhaustion, concussion and 'war neurosis' as recognized categories of illness. Unfortunately this recognition came too late for the sufferers whose disorientation and confusion had been misinterpreted or misrepresented as cowardice. Many had been formally executed by firing squad or shot by their officers.

Research by the American Veterans Association treatment team who worked with US marines following the Gulf War produced findings which, while specific to war veterans, can be loosely transposed to other individuals and groups suffering from PTS. The team found that of the clients involved in the treatment project, the most frequently reported symptoms were:

41% sleep disturbances
38% hyper-irritability
36% hyper-alertness
28% emotional numbing
23% intrusive thought or flashbacks
22% family or interpersonal problems.

(NCPTSD 1993)

They also discovered, perhaps not surprisingly, that the intensity of the PTS symptoms related directly to the levels of exposure each person had undergone. In general the worse the events, the worse the reaction.

Although there was a low overall incidence of severe or debilitating PTS, many marines experienced acute symptoms. This indicates that while serious PTSD, even following the horrors of war, is relatively rare, there are always individuals for whom the experience proves deeply psychologically wounding.

There is little doubt that had a group of civilians rather than military personnel been exposed to the same situation, the incidence of more severe PTS would have been higher. Soldiers are trained to expect fear and horror whereas the average person is not. It would seem that, among other factors, a soldier's training helps reduce the likelihood of deep-rooted psychological disturbance. In general, it can be assumed that following any traumatic incident there will be a relatively high proportion of survivors experiencing short-term PTS difficulties, while a smaller group may develop more severe symptoms.

There are certain high-risk civilian professions, in particular the fire, police and ambulance services, in which employees routinely face threatening and disturbing events (Ainsworth and Pease 1987). Staff in other occupations, however, are not immune from exposure to hazardous and upsetting events, obvious examples being medical and nursing staff, security personnel, train drivers, social workers, RSPCA officers and many others. Each individual is a potential PTS sufferer, and managers can play an invaluable role in reducing the possible suffering of their staff and reducing the disruption to their respective organizations, if they increase their awareness and institute procedures to offer swift and effective help.

An indication of how military awareness has changed, for example, is provided by the Israeli Army during their 1982 invasion of the Lebanon. The army, in an admirably proactive project, introduced a front-line psychiatric station where psychological casualties were taken. Here the casualty's comrades were encouraged to visit, maintaining the links with their units and establishing the implicit assumption of a future return to duty.

The result was a 60 per cent return to front-line duty from the stations. Second-stage centres were established back in Israel which people attended for two weeks while more serious cases went to a Combat Fitness Training Centre. Here the regime included the wearing of uniform, fitness training and access to psychiatrists and therapists trained in trauma debriefing work.

In a martial atmosphere, patients were helped to resolve their sense of shame, guilt, fear, failure and aversion to military hardware – guns, tanks, bombs and so forth. Of the 600 evacuated, only 60 needed the more lengthy treatment and none needed long-term care.

Definition/diagnosis

Post-traumatic stress disorder can be defined as the development of characteristic symptoms following a psychologically distressing event. It is the normal human reaction to calamitous, disturbing or frightening events beyond the range of normal or generally expected experience.

Survivors of natural disasters and accidents often exhibit psychological distress closely resembling that experienced by ex-combatants. Each individual, regardless of the original stressors, manifests similar sets of symptoms. The American Psychiatric Association, in the *Diagnostic and Statistical Manual of Mental Disorders* (APA 1987), delineate five major criteria which individuals need to exhibit for a diagnosis of PTSD to be made:

1 The client must have witnessed or experienced a serious threat to their life or physical well-being.

2 The client must re-experience the event in some way – either mentally or through any of the five senses.

3 The client must persistently avoid stimuli associated with the traumatic event and experience a numbing of general responsiveness.

4 The client must experience persistent symptoms of increased arousal.

5 Symptoms must have lasted at least a month.

I The disturbing event

The range of events which can produce PTSD symptoms is vast. From minor near-accidents to major disasters or calamities, survivors and others who become exposed can experience adverse psychological reactions. Such events include: road traffic accidents, accidents on railways, at sea, etc., assault, suicide and murder, fires, earthquakes and other natural disasters. Workers exposed to the aftermath of traumatic events include police and nurses witnessing the impact, for example, of the Hillsborough disaster, when 95 people lost their lives in the football stadium. The effects of many major catastrophes are given in Hodgkinson and Stewart (1991).

Those closest to the events are most likely to suffer symptoms. However, like the ripples on a pond when a stone is thrown in, the psychological effects of an incident can spread, touching rescue workers, police, ambulance personnel, doctors, nurses, social workers, counsellors, hospital staff and bystanders. Often friends and family of all those involved feel traumatized, especially if they do not know or understand exactly what is happening. Even those at some physical distance may suffer; for example, the baggage handler at Frankfurt Airport, where the infamous Lockerbie bomb of 1989 is believed to have been loaded, suffered marked trauma.

2 Re-experiencing the event

For those who experience them, flashbacks occurring days, weeks or years after the event can often be the most disturbing aspects of PTS. Whether triggered by subtle stimuli – sights, smells, tastes, touching or sounds reminiscent of the event, or coming apparently out of the blue – vivid reliving of the traumatic experience can completely overwhelm people and convince them they are 'cracking up'.

The late night petrol station where 27-year-old Jane was working was held up by two armed and masked men. A quantity of money and cigarettes was taken and Jane was ordered to lie on the floor after being threatened with a sawn-off shotgun. For some months after the event, whenever Jane smelled petrol or heard a car pulling up, she felt the same paralysing panic, lightheadedness and an almost overpowering desire to run away, while feeling rooted to the spot. At other times the flashbacks occurred without an apparent trigger. She suffered recurrent nightmares which consisted of terrifying masked men breaking into the house or hiding in the garden.

3 Avoidance and numbing of general responsiveness

People will commonly avoid contact with anything – people, places and things – which reminds them in some way of the original stressor: open spaces, crowded areas, various sports and transport facilities, workplaces, in fact anything which might trigger a resurgence of the fear and panic they originally experienced.

A perhaps more subtle presenting reaction is a numbing of general responsiveness whereby individuals will appear to be emotionally flat or 'closed down'. They can experience a reduction in their ability to concentrate and engage in daily activities associated with work, family and friendship, often resulting in consternation and confusion among those with whom they interact.

Althea, aged 37, was seriously sexually assaulted in a train carriage, by her previously gentle partner. She found that even some years after the event she could only board a train or coach with the greatest of difficulty, and would travel by other means whenever possible. She described having experienced profound personality changes; from being a warm trusting person she became emotionally secretive and uneasy in relationships. Once, when gently pressed by a new partner to be more open, she described herself as 'exploding with rage and frustration', much to her partner's chagrin. 'It was as if the emotional assault and violation left me constantly on the defensive. If I could keep people at arm's length I was able to jog along, yet if someone tried to get behind my wall I attacked. As you can imagine I felt very cut off, like I was living in a fishbowl, watching the world go by without actually joining in.'

4 Persistent symptoms of increased arousal

Following trauma people are often left feeling vulnerable and unsafe, their nerves 'on edge'. Usual daily events which previously they handled with relative ease may entail greater difficulty. Consequently they can appear nervous, irritable and erratic while their ability to handle stress is greatly reduced. Many people experience a range of reactions including agitation, increased tendency to have minor accidents, increased alcohol consumption and menstrual irregularities.

Sean, a 35-year-old policeman, suffered a serious assault perpetrated by the driver of a car he had routinely stopped and who afterwards sped off. Sean found subsequently that he physically shook whenever a motor vehicle accelerated rapidly. He also found the noise of his four children's video games almost unbearable and became very angry at any argument or fighting between them. He frequently found himself shouting and making threats, and he would become abusive if his wife tried to intervene. Following these eruptions he would storm out of the house, not returning for hours and often having consumed alcohol and driven the car. This latter practice was one he had previously abhorred. 'I felt like a peeled egg, all my nerves stretched out taut. Any little thing would set me off and when it did it was like I was looking down at myself thinking: you're a bloody maniac, you're crazy. I tried but I couldn't stop myself.' Sean required three months' sick leave but eventually returned to his previous duties.

5 Symptoms lasting for at least a month

Emotional and behavioural repercussions following trauma are so common, crossing as they do cultural and national boundaries, that they can be regarded as a normal part of living. It is, therefore, sometimes easily overlooked that post-traumatic symptoms have become seriously protracted. Commonly occurring traumas – car crashes, surgery, viewing disturbing news items, burglary, verbal and physical violence (including rape and sexual abuse), seeing a child run out into a busy road, and a multitude of disturbing and threatening events (the list is practically endless) – commonly result in post-traumatic reactions. In the vast majority of cases people's innate self-healing processes help them to return to normal functioning fairly rapidly, without the need for professional help. When these symptoms persist for longer than a month (this is a guideline figure), then help should be sought.

A relatively minor motorway crash in which no-one was physically injured left 23-year-old Janet shaking for three or four hours. She managed to drive to the nearest service station where she sat playing the incident over and over in her mind, 'almost trying to rewrite the ending'. She pondered a great deal on 'what might have happened if . . .'. After an hour or so she continued her journey using the back roads, but found, despite her efforts to be extra-alert, that her concentration was poor. Janet slept poorly for two nights and dreamed of cars and crashes. For several days afterwards when passing the point of the crash she felt 'uneasy in my stomach' and memories of the event presented themselves. Within two weeks she felt her old self again with no lingering aftermath.

Few people will not have experienced a similar reaction following some unexpected, potentially threatening event. At no point, however, did Janet need or consider seeking professional help. What helped her most was talking with her husband and friends and allowing time for her own recuperative powers to work. She had experienced a normal stress reaction. If she had still been suffering sleepless nights weeks later and still found herself unable to drive without intrusive memories or shaking, then a diagnosis of post-traumatic stress disorder might well be made and appropriate treatment suggested.

PTSD: general discussion

Post-traumatic stress, the emotional and behavioural aftermath of disturbing events, as indicated above is normal. Post-traumatic stress disorder, however, is the more problematic, longer-term response either to hugely disturbing events or to the person's natural healing processes having become impeded in some way. In general terms, this latter group often have other emotional difficulties which the stress of the precipitating event will have re-energized or compounded. These can include unresolved difficulties from earlier chapters of their lives – childhood sexual abuse, family violence, bereavement and a myriad other injurious events – or current situations which leave people less able to withstand a further drain on their coping abilities. People can only deal with so much at a time before they begin to feel overwhelmed and their ability to function effectively becomes impaired.

An unkempt man shambled into a bank and wandered around in a distracted manner mumbling to himself. After a few minutes he approached a cashier, produced a plastic water pistol and asked for money. To avoid antagonizing someone who was obviously unwell the cashier handed over a few notes and the man left, only to be arrested a short time later, giving the money to people in the street. Most of the staff at the branch regarded the incident as both mildly upsetting and mildly amusing. However, one cashier, Penelope, a 28-year-old, heavily pregnant woman, was extremely upset. Two years previously she had faced an aggressive armed raider and had been forced to lie down on the floor with a shotgun placed at her head. She had been three months into a difficult pregnancy at the time and shortly afterwards had lost her baby.

Penelope's terrified reaction as the 'raider' exited the branch, her insistence on visiting her doctor that day and the doctor giving her a week's sick leave are understandable in light of Penelope's history. To her manager and colleagues, however, who were either not aware of her history or who failed to make a connection, her behaviour seemed inappropriate, and there was a strong suspicion that she was using the event as an excuse to get time off work.

For Penelope, however, the incident represented the culmination of her worst fears, namely a repeat of her previous experience, the very thing she had secretly been dreading while trying to convince herself that lightning does not strike twice in the same place. Her subsequent nightmares all involved losing her baby or having it stolen by threatening unidentified figures.

To claim that no employee would ever use a traumatic incident as an excuse for time off work would obviously be misleading. However, each case should be regarded separately and sensitively. Making assumptions about what is or is not traumatizing for different individuals can be very difficult and could easily lead to the undeservedly harsh treatment of a loyal employee.

Treatment

The field of counselling and psychotherapy has many schools and sub-schools of theory and practice (Bellack and Hersen 1990; Dryden 1990). Consequently, each school of thought will approach clients suffering from PTS and PTSD using their own theoretical frame of reference. This will inform the therapist's understanding of the client and guide their work.

A method of treatment which has proved extremely useful and cost-effective (and therefore widely applied) is known as Critical Incident De-briefing (CID). Developed largely from the work of Mitchell and Dyregrov following their studies of accident and disaster survivors, it is sometimes referred to as the Mitchell–Dyregrov Method (Dyregrov 1989; Dyregrov and Mitchell 1992).

During and following any traumatizing situation witnesses, friends, rela-tions, police, fire and ambulance personnel, doctors and volunteer helpers among others can be directly affected. At a later stage, the circle of those affected can expand to include clergy, counsellors, social workers, psychia-trists and psychologists who are consulted or approached for help. In the case of major disasters such as the Lockerbie air crash in 1989 or the capsized ferry at Zeebrugge in 1987, the number of those affected can run into several hundreds. One of the major advantages of CID is its flexibility in working with all those who have been touched by the events, whether individually or in groups.

For any manager, personnel officer or staff counsellor faced with a post-trauma situation, it is important to remember that not only those present can be affected. Fellow employees who were elsewhere at the time and bystanders, customers or delivery staff may well be deeply affected and should ideally be offered CID.

Ideally small groups of people who have endured the same event should be seen together, but the approach is equally effective when couples or individuals are seen. It should be offered to people within a day or two of the particular event, thus preventing the establishment of more deeply rooted difficulties which may develop into PTSD. The aftermath of rela-tively minor events and major disasters can be addressed using the method, unlike certain other therapies which may insist that only individuals are seen.

Critical Incident Debriefing

Robin, a 38-year-old teacher, is a volunteer mountain rescue worker. He and his team were called upon to comb some hillsides in the vicinity of Lockerbie following the destruction of Flight 301. Robin and his team found no bodies or gory remains. However, various items of personal effects were discovered strewn across the hillside, including a diary, some paper-back books and a pair of women's spectacles.

For some weeks following this Robin obsessively wondered what the spectacle owner looked like and if she was reading one of the books, un-aware of the bomb ticking away in the cargo-hold. He found himself half-believing that he would meet the woman, that she would arrive at his house or school and introduce herself to assure him she had actually survived. He reached the stage where his mind had actually created an image of the unknown woman and he began to believe he recognized her in the street. Feeling ashamed and terribly afraid, half-convinced he was truly mad, Robin requested some help and found the debriefing extremely helpful:

> I couldn't believe how quickly it helped. The reassurance that I wasn't really crazy but experiencing traumatic stress was a real relief. I've never really considered counselling for anything. The [mountain rescue] team have occasionally found dead bodies, suicides and rock climbing accidents, which apart from being upsetting and very sad, had never really got to me. I thought I was experienced enough to handle most things. But those glasses lying close to the books seemed to exude tragedy. Part of me didn't want to hand them in, they seemed somehow personal, between me and the owner. I actually thought of taking them away and burying them secretly. I still occasionally wonder about her, but only with a sense of sadness and waste.

In certain potentially hazardous professions such as the fire, police, am-bulance services and armed forces, there is a growing acceptance that long-term difficulties for both individual employees and for the organization itself can be avoided or reduced if, following traumatic events, it is normal procedure to undergo CID. Having debriefing as part of an employee's expectations removes the dilemma some will experience concerning poten-tial loss of face or admitting weakness, should they acknowledge having been adversely affected.

Presentation of the process as an integral part of an individual's employ-ment responsibilities allows debriefing to become an accepted part of the job. The advantages of this are manifold. Brief reference to the PTSD crite-ria will indicate that any employee suffering from it will not be functioning at full capacity. If the individual conceals the true root of their difficulties or, perhaps more likely, does not realize the association between their suffering and PTS, thus preventing appropriate intervention, then the symptoms can become protracted and confusing for all concerned, not to mention a great drain on the organization's energies and resources.

A further managerial consideration will be the possible threat of litigation from employees who hold their employer culpable for any trauma-related stress they may suffer. While literature relating to such cases in the UK is scarce, evidence indicates that these cases are on the increase as public awareness of PTSD grows (Simon 1995). Indeed, reasonably clear guidelines in the UK are already in place for defining PTSD legally and recommending levels of compensation for sufferers.

Paul, a 48-year-old driver/conductor with a 15-year exemplary work record, attempted to intervene in a late night fight on the bus he was operating. One of the assailants attacked Paul, breaking three of his ribs.

Although he recovered well physically and was offered some 'counselling', he declined, being reluctant to admit just how deeply affected he really felt. Over the next two years, unbeknown to most of his colleagues and manager, Paul increasingly dreaded the evening and late night journeys. His sleep was disturbed resulting in poor time-keeping, his days off sick increased dramatically as he either felt too anxious to go in or would use minor physical complaints to avoid work altogether. He became irritable and had rows with managers who tried to offer support. Eventually, after Paul received a written disciplinary warning, a colleague with whom Paul had shared some of his distress approached a sympathetic manager and tried to explain the situation. The manager spoke with Paul about his difficulties and asked how much the original attack had affected him. In the middle of denying it had anything to do with his current situation, Paul burst into tears, full of shame, guilt, embarrassment, fear and frustration. It transpired that not only work was affected. Paul was drinking heavily, with the result that his wife was threatening to leave him and his children were becoming hostile.

Luckily for Paul, with appropriate counselling he was able to avoid the looming disaster of job loss and family break-up. His story, however, serves to illustrate the potentially destructive nature of unrecognized and unresolved post-traumatic stress.

Take an example of someone with seriously protracted symptoms who did not have the benefit of CID. Rita, a 60-year-old mother of two, had been badly injured in a bomb blast during World War Two. Four years later she had a 'nervous breakdown'. To this day loud bangs, the smell of burning wood and old-fashioned disinfectants make her anxious and shaky to the extent that she has to sit down for fear of fainting. Although having 'learnt to live with it' the traumatic effects continue to exert their influence on Rita's life. Perhaps had debriefing been available, the nervous breakdown would have been avoided and her later life been less troubled.

The term Critical Incident Debriefing has become widely used. It avoids such terms as 'psychological' and 'counselling', as these can conjure up images of mental illness, psychiatrists and mental breakdown. On the whole, people may be inclined to avoid engaging in a process which in their minds implies that they are crazy, weak or a failure. To be debriefed as part of an expected, pre-arranged process can largely, if not entirely, remove elements of stigma and embarrassment. To be invited, as a 'normal person', to review with other 'normal people' thoughts and impressions following an abnormal event has a completely different ring to it from being counselled for psychological problems following a terrible experience.

Debriefing is defined as 'A meeting with one or more persons, the purpose of which is to review the impressions and reactions that survivors, helpers and others experience during or after a traumatic incident' (Dyregrov 1989). CID has a clear formularized structure which can be adapted by appropriately trained personnel to meet the needs and constraints of each particular employing agency, and can be used in individual and group settings. There are many variations of the basic model, all of which follow similar lines. The broad steps are as follows.

The group and possibly two debriefers gather in a room where they will not be disturbed, sitting themselves around a table or otherwise in a circle, all using similar chairs. Tea and coffee should be available, and while leaving and re-entering the room during debriefing cannot be prevented it should be gently discouraged.

People then introduce themselves using name and title or name and role. The debriefer's introductions should be somewhat more informative, stating some of their experience in post-trauma work, giving some basic information concerning post-traumatic stress, thereby encouraging individual motivation and the confident expectation of success within the group. Reference to other organizations which use a similar process, for instance certain armed forces, the police and suchlike, can broaden the individual's understanding of what sort of people might expect to suffer from PTS, and create a sense of 'If it's all right for those people then maybe it's all right for us'.

To allow people the freedom of detailed disclosure confidentiality should be emphasized and guaranteed, particularly in work-related situations. A statement should be made to reassure participants that while the debriefing is intended to prevent or greatly reduce the likelihood of PTS symptoms, each might actually feel worse during or immediately after the session, as the events are discussed and, to a large degree, may be re-experienced.

A major part of CID is helping to construct or reconstruct a clear picture of what actually happened. During periods of extreme tension, 'normal' reality can become distorted. An event which actually lasted just a few minutes can seem later to last much longer. A robbery, car crash or other disaster is often experienced in slow motion with certain specific details assuming dominance. This can be like looking through a telescope; certain features – a gun, the individual directly facing oneself, a child's face, or apparently unimportant details – are clearly seen and remembered. A wider image, or the individual's place in the broader canvas, is very often lost.

A bank cashier who had been held up while working at her till, remembered very clearly the sight, shape, colour and movements of the assailant's gun. She could describe the twitchy movements of his trigger finger and could recite almost exactly what he had said. She had almost no recollection of his build, general appearance, of what her colleagues on either side did or said, or what the various customers who were present did or said. She reported that the raid, which actually lasted for no more than three minutes, seemed to go on for about half an hour.

Debriefing helps process and assimilate the distorted, fragmentary images and experiences into a broader whole. The trauma becomes part of personal history, albeit a rarefied, painful part, but incorporated within wider emotional and mental horizons, preventing the memories having a kind of separate, wounding existence. For some, the post-traumatic distress can last for many years, disrupting and damaging all areas of life. The woman quoted above had a 'nervous breakdown' some years after the explosion during which images of the carnage returned to torment her. For others, effective help can be offered on a 'better late than never' basis.

Jeffrey, an 80-year-old man, was referred to his local psychiatric services suffering from depression and suicidal impulses. During World War Two he had been captain of a fishing boat rescuing stranded soldiers during the Dunkirk evacuation. His boat had been destroyed by enemy fire, killing the whole crew, all of them men he knew well. By sheer chance, Jeffrey was thrown into the sea and survived.

Jeffrey received rudimentary psychological help following the incident but soon returned to active, though downgraded duty. On his eventual return home, relatives found that the quiet, teetotal, sociable chap had become a heavy-drinking, suspicious and occasionally aggressive introvert. He never spoke about the war, avoided social groups and would not read or watch anything connected with war. Flashbacks and nightmares dogged his life. Although this example is not directly relevant to employees, other chapters in this book show that carers of relatives with severe mental health problems are likely to suffer.

When other possible sources of the depression had been eliminated, a primary diagnosis of PTSD was made and appropriate treatment, including relatively long-term debriefing, commenced. Within six months, Jeffrey had become almost abstinent from alcohol, his nightmares had ceased and he had begun to rekindle some old friendships. He declared that he had not felt so well since the end of the war!

The CID session

Participants are invited to begin by briefly describing their day from just before the traumatic event began.

What were you doing?
Who were you with?
Were you prepared for what happened?
What was happening around you?
Did you expect what followed?

In this manner individuals' experiences, as their world moved from normality to abnormality, are comprehensively sketched.

To prevent certain individuals disclosing too much too soon, with the more reticent feeling prematurely pressurized into disclosure, the next stage is description of thought and action. Many people naturally progress during conversation to emotional descriptions and this can be deliberately encouraged. In practice, the stages of CID tend to blur into one another. The therapist's task is to clarify:

> When did you first realize something was amiss?
> How did things proceed?
> What exactly did you do?
> What did you notice others doing?
> What exactly did you smell, touch, taste, hear and see?

As more people move into description it is highly likely that apparent discrepancies or differences in their views and memories will emerge. Memories of hyper-tense situations can be blurred and selective. Participants should be allowed to help fill in blank spots for each other, although each will ultimately retain their own personal view of the events.

It is most important that sensory experiences are discussed in some detail as relatively inconsequential impressions can act as powerful trigger points for major PTS symptoms and flashbacks. Flashbacks, triggered by any situation which actually, or symbolically, reminds one of the original trauma, can be extremely vivid and unnerving and are often the reaction which most convinces people they are 'cracking up' or 'going crazy'.

Particular smells, sounds, sights, touch and taste which remind people in some way of the events can induce flashbacks. For those people involved in brief traumatic events, a bank raid for example, the scope for possible trigger points is less than for those caught up in a very long, gruelling occurrence, such as a mining disaster or kidnap ordeal.

Alison, a 53-year-old woman, was involved in a motorway 'pile-up'. She remembered slamming on her brakes as a wall of crumpled cars suddenly came into view through the fog, and she remembered the squeal of tyres skidding on the road surface. Her next memory is of wandering and clambering around the stationary cars. Two things in particular struck her. One was the smell of petrol, and she remembers thinking that one person who was lying on the ground 'should really get up in case the petrol catches fire'. Looking back, of course, a person lying in the middle of such a pile-up was in all probability quite unable to get up. The other strong impression was seeing a slit-open suitcase with its once obviously neat clothing strewn across the road. 'I thought it belonged to someone who did ballet as there were ballet shoes amongst the clothes. I thought, she won't be pleased when she sees them like this.'

Alison continued, 'For months afterwards, whenever I saw anything connected to ballet, quick as a flash my head filled with that scene, wandering around in all the wreckage and seeing those shoes in the dirty wet road. I felt like crying every time I remembered them and in the early days, I did used to cry.'

Later she said,

> You talk about triggers, well one odd thing used to happen. I habitually chewed gum, something I started when I gave up smoking. When I was released from hospital, thankfully not badly hurt, I went and bought a packet as usual. No sooner had I put a piece in my mouth and started to chew, than my head started to spin. I felt sick and very upset. Memories of the crash came flooding back all rather disjointed – ambulances, fog, people's faces. I thought I'd gone mad for a moment. A woman passer-by asked me if I was all right, Lord knows what I must have been doing to make her stop. When I got home and discussed it with my husband, he suggested that I get some help.

Understanding and identifying possible or actual sensory triggers relieves some of the fear people have and helps them begin restoration of their sense of control over their world. The disjointed memories, the jumbled images, contribute directly to the nightmares and flashbacks. Verbalizing them, putting them into a wider context of events and, through this, normalizing reactions, begins to remove their negative power and bars their unexpected intrusions into daily life.

Emotional reactions

Inviting people to disclose their emotional responses can be the most delicate part of the healing process. People who have faced the fragility of their own or others' hold on life, who have had their world severely disrupted by the abnormal and disturbing; in short, those who have been traumatized will be struggling to re-establish a sense of order and safety. There is often an understandable reluctance to enter a debriefing group in which the horror and distress of the precipitating events are reactivated. Following trauma, people will often actively avoid situations which reawaken the distressing feelings – including debriefing groups! Others will have the added cultural constraint whereby it is not deemed appropriate to indicate apparent weakness or vulnerability.

Stereotypically male-dominated professions such as the police, army and fire service are contexts where the admission of distress stemming from emotional trauma may be frowned upon or ridiculed. Presented as part of everyday working life so that people accept them as part of the job, respectfully run CID groups can be as productive with hard-bitten 'men of the world' as with any other grouping.

Connections between what one did and thought and the underlying emotional reactions are often made quite naturally by group members. The written description of Critical Incident Debriefing hides the fact that every debriefing, once underway, takes on a life of its own. When participants feel safe enough they can make either small or major disclosures about themselves with which others can identify. Great care should be taken by the facilitator, while groups are in progress, not to offer comment or ask questions which impede or interrupt the natural flow of participants' narrative. Open-ended questions and informative statements help ensure the conversation proceeds in the desired general direction. If people feel cornered or unduly pressurized, the essential healing powers of the group can be hindered or lost. If particular group members are especially doubtful as to the usefulness or wisdom of attending, the senior person in that group may be encouraged to lead the way, thereby providing an implicit example that junior members can emulate.

Jonathon, a 24-year-old solicitor's clerk, found himself trapped beneath debris following a terrorist bombing. It was about two hours before he was freed, and with his two broken limbs, cuts and bruises, he regarded himself as lucky to be alive. There had been several fatalities and Jonathon knew he could easily have been killed. He was reluctant to take the sleeping tablets prescribed by his doctor, despite the fact that nightmares began the first night he was home. Obviously his work performance and attendance were affected. Dreams of being trapped under crushing concrete, feeling his breath and life drain away would leave him sweating and shaking with fear.

'Some nights I couldn't even have the bedclothes over me, I felt unable to move. Many nights I slept in the armchair with the TV on. Silence reminded me of lying there in the rubble without a sound except my own heart beating.

'I'd always known, or thought I'd known, how fragile life could be. When I learned afterwards that people had been killed in the blast, I kept thinking, why me, how is it that I've been allowed to live? I felt I should be dead. My logical mind kept saying it had just been luck, but I wondered, and still do wonder, at a very deep and hard-to-describe level.

'I saw a counsellor recommended by a colleague. It was one of the wisest decisions I ever made. I am not exactly a macho man, more rather private, and the prospect of talking about my internal world was somewhat daunting. The nightmares, although having subsided to an extent, were occurring two or three times a week. I became obsessed with events evocative of the one I'd been caught up in. It was rather odd, I felt woefully ignorant as to the political causes behind the bomb and I felt, somehow, a responsibility to those who had died alongside me, to understand why they had died. I dreamed once that they were all standing in my room, looking at me, waiting for me to do something – I don't know what. I felt an affinity with them and a responsibility.

'My family were very worried about me. After the initial relief at my survival, my tendency to isolate and maintain secrecy left no room for anyone else. My wife almost left me when I smashed the kitchen table, after she had innocently remarked that they had removed the rubble of the building I had been trapped in. Quite honestly, I felt completely loopy and it required huge amounts of strength to hide that from others. Ironically, it wasn't hidden at all but became a vicious circle – the more I tried to carry on as normal, the more obvious it was to others that all was far from well.'

Whether one is a member of the emergency services who has attended an accident, a soldier experiencing war, a train driver colliding with a person on the line, a crime or disaster victim, or merely the chance witness to some disturbing event, the effects can be deeply upsetting, with disruptive symptoms persisting for many years if not addressed.

The range of emotions experienced by most participants in CID will be broad. Some will have been fearful and shocked while others may have been exhilarated and excited. Also included might be:

- feeling helpless or hopeless;
- sense of frailty of life;
- fear, horror, shock, shame, alienation;
- damaged trust;
- exaggerated sense of how unsafe the world is;
- anger – at perpetrators, managers, company, each other, government, etc.;
- frustration;
- finding everyday life trivial; a disdain of 'normality';
- finding everyday life precious, valuing 'normality';
- guilt – survivor guilt or a sense of having let others down;
- feeling generally unsafe;
- feeling mad, insane or 'cracking up'.

Participants reveal their apparently contradictory reactions and identify links with each other, which the debriefer then normalizes without disrupting the overall flow. To know that other group members are experiencing similar reactions and that people from other walks of life have experienced the same, widens the context for individuals, from a seemingly isolated and intensely personal suffering to a more global view, with the realization they are normal people experiencing a normal reaction to an extreme situation.

Occasionally at this point, relief is almost palpable.

Pre-event training

This is a basic technique of military training, using controlled exposure to the stressors soldiers are likely to encounter. In civilian life, through the use of videos, role play, group discussion and printed material, people can become attuned to the likelihood of future stress. Individuals who believe stressful events are a possibility are less likely to develop PTSD than those who assume 'it won't happen to them' (Resick and Schnicke 1992). Stress Inoculation Training (SIT) also helps reduce certain potentially unhelpful automatic thoughts and responses people experience (Meichenbaum 1985).

Clear post-incident procedures should be devised so that employees are confident that their respective organizations can and will respond swiftly and effectively. These procedures can be disseminated in printed packs during SIT sessions.

Post-event response

A coherent, organized managerial response is invaluable in reassuring people in the immediate and often chaotic aftermath of an incident. Management must be seen to be treating the event seriously and sensitively to reduce the possibility of staff resentment or demoralization (Richards 1994). Some general guidelines are:

1 Be aware of staff who have suffered other traumas; they may experience a resurgence of the old distress, compounded by the latest trauma.
2 Anyone pregnant or with a relevant pre-existing medical condition should see their general practitioner as soon as possible.
3 Encourage staff to telephone home before the event becomes publicized through the media.
4 Inform absent staff of the event as this can spare them the shock of hearing about it from other sources or arriving at work without prior knowledge.
5 Ensure co-ordinated, sensitive management response. A visit by local management is often appreciated, during which time can be taken to empathize with people and listen to some of their experiences (Meichenbaum 1985).
6 Expect short-term reduced efficiency from staff, including those on the apparent periphery.
7 Encourage (but do not compel) all staff to return to work the following day, even if they only perform light duties.
8 Arrange the debriefing, if possible, within 48 hours of the incident.

Each organization will develop its own model for dealing with traumatic events, adapted to its own needs and financial resources. Supportive and sensitive organizational responses will show that most people are very resilient, even in the face of highly distressing events.

Eye Movement Desensitization and Reprocessing

Eye Movement Desensitization and Reprocessing (EMDR) (Shapiro 1995) is a recently devised treatment for PTSD showing great promise but as yet not comprehensively proven. Involving careful assessment and techniques demanding recall of the traumatic events, along with purposeful, hypnosis-like, therapist-delivered hand movements, EMDR has been shown in some cases to relieve chronic PTSD symptoms rapidly. One man, in a mining accident in the USA, had suffered severe injuries including the loss of both arms above the elbow. After enduring PTSD symptoms for eight years, he received EMDR treatment and following a single session (with some brief follow-ups) he reported feeling immense relief (McCann 1992). Another technique claiming to be especially effective within a short time is traumatic incident reduction (TIR), associated with rational emotive behaviour therapy (Bisbey and Bisbey 1996). Obviously, employers wishing to provide humane and effective help for staff afflicted by the long-term effects of PTSD should be apprised of such developments and would do well to investigate them.

Conclusion

In many working environments, notwithstanding elaborate security and safety measures, violent attacks or traumatic accidents are ever-present possibilities. For many employees, the very nature of their work will expose them to disturbing situations. Some individuals, therefore, 'no matter how well trained and resilient in personality terms' will 'suffer the adverse consequences of exposure to high stress situations' (Turnball 1993). To minimize the impact upon individuals and their organization, policy responses are increasingly being formulated, reflecting the needs of the company and the apparent threat. Appropriate policies and training can significantly reduce the ferocity of PTS and the likelihood of PTSD developing (Novaco 1977; Meichenbaum 1985).

References

Ainsworth, P.B. and Pease, K. (1987) *Police Work*. London: Methuen/British Psychological Society.

APA (1987) *Diagnostic and Statistical Manual of Mental Disorders* (3rd edn rev.). Washington, DC: American Psychiatric Association.

Bellack, S. and Hersen, M. (eds) (1990) *Handbook of Comparative Treatments for Adult Disorders*. New York: Wiley Interscience.

Bisbey, S. and Bisbey, L.B. (1996) *Brief Therapy for PTSD: Traumatic incident reduction and related techniques*. Chichester: John Wiley.

Dryden, W. (ed.) (1990) *Individual Therapy: A handbook*. Buckingham: Open University Press.

Dyregrov, A. (1989) Caring for helpers in disaster situations: Psychological debriefing. *Disaster Management*, 2: 25–30.

Dyregrov, A. and Mitchell, J.T. (1992) Work with traumatised children: Psychological effects and coping strategies. *Journal of Traumatic Stress*, 5.

Hodgkinson, P.E. and Stewart, M. (1991) *Coping with Catastrophe: A handbook of disaster management*. London: Routledge.

Holmes, R. (1985) *Firing Line*. London: Jonathan Cape.

McCann, D.L. (1992) Post-traumatic stress disorder due to devastating burns overcome by a single session of eye movement desensitisation. *Journal of Behavior Therapy and Experimental Psychiatry*, 23(4): 319–23.

Meichenbaum, D. (1985) *Stress Inoculation Training*. New York: Pergamon Press.

NCPTSD (1993), *National Center for Post Traumatic Stress Disorder Clinical Newsletter* (Palo Alto, CA), 3(1). Winter.

Novaco, R. (1977) A stress inoculation approach to anger management in the training of law enforcement officers. *American Journal of Community Psychology*, 5: 327–46.

Resick, P. and Schnicke, M. (1992) Cognitive processing therapy for sexual assault victims. *Journal of Consulting and Clinical Psychology*, 60: 748–56.

Richards, D. (1994) Traumatic stress at work: A public health model. *British Journal of Guidance and Counselling*, 22(1): 51–64.

Shapiro, F. (1995) *Eye Movement Desensitisation and Reprocessing*. New York: Guilford.

Simon, R. (ed.) (1995) *Post Traumatic Stress Disorder Litigation: Guidelines for Forensic Assessment*. Washington, DC: American Psychiatric Press.

Turnball, G. (1993) The Lockerbie air disaster and the Gulf War: Debriefing in Britain. *National Center for Post Traumatic Stress Disorder Clinical Newsletter* (Palo Alto, CA), 3(1): 14–15.

Suggested reading

Hodgkinson, P.E. and Stewart, M. (1991) *Coping with Catastrophe: A handbook of disaster management*. London: Routledge.

Kinchin, D. (1994) *Post Traumatic Stress Disorder*. London: Thorsons.

Parkinson, F. (1993) *Post Trauma Stress*. London: Sheldon.

Shapiro, F. (1995) *Eye Movement Desensitization and Reprocessing*. New York: Guilford.

Tedeschi, R.G. and Calhoun, L.G. (1995) *Trauma and Transformation*. Thousand Oaks, CA: Sage.

Useful organizations

Centre for Crisis Psychology
Four Arches
Broughton Hall
Skipton
North Yorkshire BD23 3AE
01756 796383

Crisis Mentors
28 Bedford Street
London WC2E 9ED
0345 666999

Medical Foundation for the Care of Victims of Torture
96–98 Grafton Road
London NW5 3EJ
0171 284 4321

Suzy Lamplugh Trust
14 East Sheen Avenue
London SW14 8AS
0181 3921839

Trauma After-Care Trust
Buttfields
The Farthings
Withington
Glos GL54 4DF
01242 890306

Traumatic Stress Unit
Ticehurst House Hospital
Ticehurst
Nr Wadhurst
Sussex TX5 7HU
01580 200391

Counselling for substance-related problems in the workplace

○ ANDREW GUPPY and JOHN MARSDEN

The nature and extent of the problem

Use, misuse and problems

A first question to be addressed in a text concerned with alcohol and drugs involves the distinction between different patterns of substance use and their associated problems. There are clearly terms in common use, such as 'alcoholic' and 'drug addict', which are meant to represent some conceptualization of a combination of excessive use over time and the existence of poor functioning as a result of this use. However, the clinical utility of simple ill-defined labels is limited and contemporary writers tend to regard such behaviour as existing on a continuum reflecting problem severity.

Beyond what may be viewed as non-problem use, a first problem category could be labelled 'substance misuse'. This could include substance-related behaviour that may cause trouble in the short term through accidents, social or legal problems. However, such behaviour need not have formed a regular pattern for the individual. In the recently published *Diagnostic and Statistical Manual of Mental Disorders IV* (American Psychiatric Association 1994), a detailed definition is given for two other categories: 'substance abuse' and 'substance dependence'.

DSM IV (1994: 182) indicates that 'substance abuse' represents a 'maladaptive pattern of substance use leading to clinically significant impairment or distress, as manifested by one (or more) of the following occurring within a 12-month period'.

- 'recurrent substance use resulting in failure to fulfill major role obligations at work, school or home'

- recurrent use in risky situations (e.g. driving while impaired)
- recurrent substance-related legal problems
- continued use despite persistent or recurrent social or interpersonal problems caused or exacerbated by substance-related behaviour.

For 'substance dependence', the criteria are similar in nature to those of 'abuse', though more established patterns of behaviour relating to obtaining and using the substance may be established. Additionally, 'dependence' includes the possible presence of tolerance (diminished effect of the substance, often requiring larger doses), withdrawal (maladaptive behavioural change associated with decline in substance consumption) and an inability to control (limit) substance use even when persistent or recurrent physiological or psychological problems exist which are caused or exacerbated by the substance.

The range of substances covered in the *DSM* chapter includes alcohol, cannabis, cocaine, hallucinogens (e.g. LSD), inhalants, opiates (e.g. heroin) and sedative-hypnotics (e.g. benzodiazepines). All these substances are seen as available for diagnoses of 'abuse' and 'dependence'.

Population use of alcohol and other drugs

The use of substances such as alcohol and other drugs is a very common occurrence among people of working age in most cultures across the world. In the developed world, the most easily available drugs that are associated with health problems are probably alcohol and nicotine (tobacco). However, there are many powerful prescription drugs that may also be associated with problems (e.g. morphine, benzodiazepines). In addition to these, there are a range of illicit and semi-licit substances that perhaps are more popularly known as 'drugs' such as cocaine, cannabis, heroin, amphetamines and 'ecstasy' (methylenedioxymethamphetamine). To assist readers, a basic guide to the most commonly encountered drugs is provided in the box on page 222. While a brief review of the prevalence of use of these substances is provided in the following paragraphs, it is emphasized that all figures are estimates. Under-reporting of alcohol consumption is well documented, and it is felt that reporting of use of illicit drugs is also likely to be somewhat biased.

Surveys suggest that 90 per cent of the British adult population consume alcoholic beverages on an occasional or regular basis (Wilson 1980; Goddard 1991). These surveys revealed that average weekly consumption in the UK was around 20 drinks per week for males and around seven drinks for females (a standard drink being equivalent to a single whisky, a small glass of table wine or a half-pint of beer, all containing roughly 8–10g of ethanol). More usefully, surveys like these suggest that around 5 per cent of men and 2 per cent of women report alcohol-related problems in health, social and economic areas of life functioning.

Drugs – basic information

Alcohol – a depressant drug contained in beer (usually 3–4 per cent alcohol), wine (10–12 per cent alcohol) and spirits (40–50 per cent alcohol); adult use legalized in most countries. Intoxication effects: initially relaxed feelings, reduced inhibition, later impaired psychomotor skills, followed by unconsciousness. Long-term heavy use: psychological and physical dependence possible; associated with various health and social problems. Prevalence: 90 per cent of British adults drink. Around 10 per cent of male and 5 per cent of female workers may be defined as 'heavy' drinkers. Detectable in urine for several hours depending on amount consumed.

Amphetamines – stimulants; prescribed use possible, illicit use common. Short-term use results in feelings of energy and arousal. Long-term and/or heavy use may result in delusions, hallucinations and feelings of persecution. Psychological dependence possible, tolerance effects common. Prevalence among workers may be less than 1 per cent. Detectable for up to three days after use.

Lysergic acid diethylamide (LSD) – illicit hallucinogen. Short-term effects include heightened visual and auditory sensations, may include mystical, ecstatic or frightening experiences, true hallucinations rare, impairment of psychomotor and cognitive performance likely. Long-term effects relate to mental rather than physical well-being, prolonged serious disorders are rare.

Ecstasy (MDMA) – stimulant-like drug. Short-term use may be similar to LSD (calming, heightened senses) without hallucinations, larger doses may produce effects similar to amphetamines. Prevalence not known, assumed to be similar to amphetamines.

Cocaine (including crack) – illicit stimulant. Produces feelings of well-being, exhilaration. Long-term and/or heavy use may result in feelings of restlessness, sleeplessness and persecution. Prevalence in US military studies 1–2 per cent, UK has over 1000 registered abusers. Metabolite (benzoylecgonine) detectable for three to five days.

Cannabis – mild depressant – hallucinogen; rarely prescribed, has 'decriminalized' status in some countries, is illicit in most. Short-term relaxant, enhances perceptions, impairs psychomotor skills. Heavy use may result in perceptual distortions. Estimated prevalence of one million users in the UK. Detectable for between three and 30 days, depending on use.

Opiates (including heroin) – depressant–sedative drugs. Morphine and codeine commonly prescribed, heroin usually illicit. Short-term use: feelings of contentment and warmth. Long-term heavy use: dependence may result. Physical harm usually related to needle use. Prevalence: probably less than 0.1 per cent in the UK workforce. Detectable for up to 72 hours.

Minor tranquillizers – sedative drugs. Benzodiazepines are the most commonly prescribed (include Valium, Librium, Ativan). Short-term use depresses mental activity and alertness can impair psychomotor skills. Withdrawal effects common as is psychological dependence. Prevalence: one in seven British adults occasional users, one in 40 long-term users. Detectable usually for three to ten days.

Prevalence sources: Central Office of Information 1993. United Nations Economic and Social Council 1993. Detection periods from Macdonald *et al.* 1992

A significant empirical contribution to information concerning alcohol use within an occupational group has been provided by the Whitehall II study (Marmot *et al.* 1993), which surveyed over 10,000 civil servants. It was found that almost 10 per cent of male and 5 per cent of female civil servants could be classed as 'heavy drinkers' (over 30 drinks per week for males and 20 drinks for females).

Thus, based on British surveys, one could expect that between 5–10 per cent of male workers and 2–5 per cent of female workers may have consumption patterns which may be associated with problem drinking (misuse, abuse and dependency). While these figures suggest a substantial number of employees within organizations may be heavy drinkers, it has to be emphasized that employees with alcohol-related problems tend to have more extreme patterns of consumption. For instance, Marsden (1992) described a cohort of alcohol misusers referred for assistance within a large British organization. Among this group of nearly 140 employees, the average consumption during the week prior to interview was over 100 standard drinks. It is clear that this type of consumption represents a much smaller proportion of the workforce than that of the 'heavy drinker' category in the Whitehall II study.

For substances other than alcohol, the estimates vary considerably, depending on legality, availability and reason for use. Generally speaking, the estimates on prevalence of use of illicit drugs in the United Kingdom are far from satisfactory and provide a tremendous range of possible values (Sutton and Maynard 1993). In many other countries, similar problems with prevalence estimation exist, with data coming mainly from enforcement agencies and self-report surveys (United Nations Economic and Social Council 1993).

In the USA, there has been considerable experience with urine screening for illicit drug use in many working environments and therefore it is possible to provide reasonably informed estimates of the prevalence of drug use, particularly in relation to those applying for jobs and in some cases for job incumbents.

Research would suggest that the most commonly used illicit substance is cannabis (marijuana), with around 7 per cent of urine tests in both US military and Postal Service samples showing positive for marijuana use (Needleman and Romberg 1989; Normand *et al.* 1990). Positive cases for cocaine metabolite were found in 1–2 per cent of these samples, while the proportion of identified users of opiates, amphetamines and other drugs tended to be less than 1 per cent.

Outside the USA, the picture seems relatively consistent across developed nations in showing lower misuse patterns than the USA. Obviously, there are many factors in operation that mean that reliable pictures of the prevalence of both use and misuse of illicit drugs are not commonly available. Additionally, the methods of estimating prevalence seem to vary internationally rendering comparisons across countries an inexact science, to say the least (United Nations Economic and Social Council 1993).

Thus it would seem clear that, generally, illicit drug use is less common than that of alcohol among the majority of nations. Among the non-prescribed substances, it would appear that cannabis is usually the most commonly occurring.

Substance misuse in relation to occupational factors

Research has identified a number of occupational features that are regularly associated with an increased tendency to misuse substances (e.g. Plant 1979; Royal College of Psychiatrists 1979). It has to be emphasized that the causal path is rarely established in such research and that it cannot be said that working in certain environments leads to particular patterns of substance use.

The first work-related factor that has been associated with heavy substance use relates to a removal from 'normal' social environments. This may be evidenced for military personnel, seamen and oil-rig workers.

The second relates to the 'reduced supervision' factor, associated with journalists, physicians, shift workers, some transport workers and travelling salesmen. Obviously for some, however, reduced supervision is accompanied by an abnormal social life.

The strongest occupational feature, though, would seem to be that linked to proximity and availability (and to some extent convenience) of the substance(s) in question. There is substantial evidence of this phenomenon from workers within the drinks trade as well as the catering industry, when it comes to indicators of alcohol misuse. There is also some evidence of this phenomenon being associated with misuse of certain drugs within the military and even the medical profession.

However, the evidence seems strong that for more serious misusers in some of these high-risk occupations, there may have been an already existing pattern of heavy use. For this sub-group, it may be useful to migrate to occupations where substances are more easily obtained or excessive consumption seems less out of place (such as the drinks trade). In light of this possibility, an interesting issue is whether these high prevalence occupations are the ones most or least likely to provide company-based interventions.

The costs of substance-related problems in the workplace

There is general agreement that the costs of substance misuse in the workplace are primarily related to absenteeism, lost productivity, safety and healthcare cover (Macdonald *et al.* 1992). However, these and other authors have also acknowledged that the research establishing the associations between substance misuse and these cost elements is far from robust in many respects (Guppy and Marsden 1995).

The general criticisms of this area of research have been detailed in previous reviews (e.g. Gust and Walsh 1989; Macdonald *et al.* 1992). One of the main problems apparent in the research covering drugs other than alcohol is the often-used creation of a simple dichotomy between users and non-users. This approach is simply inadequate for scientific purposes as it confuses some very important issues. First, there is rarely information available to differentiate the pattern of use (e.g. medicinal, recreational and dependent). Second, there is usually no information concerning the likely impairment of work functions that may have occurred in relation to the drug use. It may be the case that the dose levels concerned may have caused the individual no impairment, or that the impairment was limited to non-work hours. All these factors combine to make it difficult to say with certainty that drug use directly caused any observed problems.

However, the research to date would suggest that alcohol impairment plays a strong causal role in 5–10 per cent of serious work-related accidents. Also, heavy alcohol use among men is associated with a 12 per cent increase in short spells of absence. For those with consumption patterns indicative of abuse or dependency, the increases in terms of sickness rates could be as high as 200 to 500 per cent over matched groups of employees.

As mentioned, the evidence for the direct costs of problems relating to other drugs is not so strong. Increased accident risks are hard to determine, though behavioural evidence favours the existence of such effects even though they are rare. There seems to be firm evidence of productivity costs associated with drug use, though it is not clear that drug use alone is the causal factor. However, the estimates from Normand *et al.* (1990) would suggest that 60 per cent increased absenteeism may be expected among illicit drug users.

To some extent the evidence from general estimates of the proportion of the workforce that may be misusing substances and the research linking workplace costs to substance misuse provide a motivational force for employers to develop interventions. The following sections outline the background and common structures of such interventions, and provide some idea of the basic principles in substance misuse counselling.

Workplace management of substance-related problems

Development of workplace interventions for alcohol and drug problems

Although various authors have traced the employment relationships underlying contemporary workplace interventions to the manorial system of twelfth-century England, the economic and social contexts originated against the background of the industrial revolution. Another line of the development of social programmes to assist employees can be seen in the history of businesses organized around the Quaker philosophy. For example, the construction of the model community of Bournville in 1879 by the Cadbury company was designed to provide for the housing, sanitation, health and recreation needs of employees. In the USA, there developed a similar 'paternalistic' approach among some employers described as 'industrial welfarism', which primarily targeted employee problems that affected work performance. However, it was not until the early 1940s that specifically targeted workplace programmes emerged in the USA, stimulated both by the rise of the Alcoholics Anonymous movement and the abnormal social and economic conditions caused by World War Two. These factors contributed to the development of the early occupational alcohol programmes (such as those at DuPont and Eastman Kodak), typically run by occupational health personnel to identify and assist problem-drinking employees, but lacking any firm management and union involvement.

During the 1970s in the USA, the establishment of the National Institute on Alcohol Abuse and Alcoholism (NIAAA) was accompanied by a large project which led to improving and standardizing professional practice in this area and led to the development of formalized 'Occupational Alcoholism Programs' (OAPs) across many US organizations. By the mid-1970s, the NIAAA was promoting a broader concept for workplace interventions, 'Employee Assistance Programs' (EAPs), which envisaged a 'broad brush' approach where counselling could be delivered to employees with marital, relationship and financial difficulties as well as those relating to alcohol misuse.

From this period of development of OAPs and later EAPs, a number of core elements became identified for successful programmes. For example, Trice and Roman (1972) suggested the following as components of an Occupational Alcoholism Program:

1 a written policy statement by the employer that accepted the concept of alcoholism as a treatable health problem
2 specific procedures for handling and referring employees experiencing work performance impairment/deterioration
3 'constructive confrontation' procedures for supervisors to use with employees who are experiencing work impairment/deterioration
4 supervisor training for 'constructive confrontation' and implementation of the company policy on alcoholism
5 formal procedures that guarantee access by impaired workers to treatment facilities and self-help groups
6 procedures for guaranteeing the confidentiality of the individual employee
7 provision of the third-party payment for the treatment of alcoholic employees in their group health insurance policies or other compensatory benefits
8 diffusion of information about the programmes to the entire workforce

The components identified above can be rearranged into a three-stage model reflecting prevention, identification and assistance and may then be seen as relating to deterrence-based models for controlling substance misuse in a number of fields (e.g. drink-driving). The basic principles of such models can be described as follows:

1 *Prevention* The primary stage involves the prevention of alcohol- and drug-related problems within the workplace. Prevention activity may occur as part of a general health promotion programme, encouraging healthy behaviours (and thus discouraging substance misuse). Prevention of misuse may also be seen through the construction and advertisement of policies, rules and regulations proscribing such behaviour. This would tend to operate through a mechanism of general deterrence as there would be likely adverse consequences for employers within the policy structure.

2 *Detection* The detection of misuse generally constitutes the second level of workplace intervention. It is at this level that policies and procedures are formulated to allow identification of misuse when it occurs. Activities that occur at this level include supervisor monitoring of work performance indicators, and drug screening programmes, though self-referral can also be seen as a form of problem identification that may be encouraged.

   Drug screening programmes can be introduced into the work domain in a number of different ways. The most commonly used method is by testing urine samples obtained under the following circumstances:

   - *Pre-employment screening:* this usually involves screening of applicants for posts prior to employment.
   - *Testing employees under suspicion:* this form of testing occurs following specific events which may be related to substance misuse (e.g. after accidents or incidents).
   - *Testing without prior cause:* this would include testing on a periodic basis (e.g. at an annual medical) or on a random basis. This form of testing would seem to include the most opposed procedures where employees are tested without any prior significant event or even, in the case of random screening, without prior warning.

   The impact of procedures at this level of the model is twofold in that not only does detection allow the process of specific deterrence (prevention of recidivism) to begin, but also feedback from this level impacts on general deterrence through adjusting perceptions of the probability of detection.

3 *Rehabilitation* The final level of intervention is the provision of mechanisms for the reduction of recidivism within the individual found to be misusing. In other words actions are taken to prevent further instances of substance misuse in relation to workplace policies. These actions may be punitive or rehabilitative in nature and may often represent mixtures of both. Commonly within the context of Occupational Alcoholism Programs, efforts would be made to address potential dependency problems faced by clients, generally through advice and counselling while remaining within the boundaries of traditional disciplinary processes (Marsden 1992).

Thus the general model described above should act to deter most of the target population from indulging in the proscribed behaviour, either through health-related education, or through the threat of detection and associated sanctions. The second level concerns the detection of misuse and its goal is to elevate both the real and the perceived likelihood that misuse will be identified. The final level of intervention attempts to limit the repetition of the misuse within the individual. Clearly, it is this fine level of intervention that has been the focus of much of the effort in this field, though the value of the other elements must be emphasized. In order to explore the practical application of elements such as those described, a brief review is presented of the structure of workplace programmes and the kinds of therapeutic approaches that are commonly adopted in managing substance-related problems in the workplace.

Types of programmes

The main elements of typological descriptions of programmes are as follows and relate to those identified by Hellan (1986) and Masi and Friedland (1988).

Range of problems addressed
Many older programmes focused on a single problem aspect (mainly alcohol misuse), while a more likely modern format has a 'broad brush' approach covering a range of problems from relationships to financial issues which may cause the employee distress. An additional factor relates to whether only employees are covered by the service or also their immediate family.

Type of provider staff
The older examples (particularly in the Occupational Alcoholism Program model) may have been run by non-professional staff qualified mainly by 'experience' of the problem. The alternatives include ordinary employees trained within their careers and the recruitment of qualified professional staff either from social work or clinical backgrounds.

Extent and location of service
Traditionally, the typical issue here relates to internal versus external provision of the service. However, this becomes a more complex issue when the full range of services such as health promotion, policy development and identification are considered as well as the provision of assessment and counselling. It is likely that dissemination of policy information at employee induction would usually be an internal activity, just as would supervisory monitoring of performance. At the other end of the spectrum, it would be difficult to envisage many examples of in-house detoxification, even in the most developed programme facility. Thus clearly the position is that it is

how much is provided and which particular elements are provided, within or outside the organization, that defines a programme, rather than a simplistic internal–external dichotomy.

Given the range of potential structures for an EAP, it may be valuable to examine the issues that are suggested as selection criteria for the process of designing a suitable company programme. Fleisher and Kaplan (1988) provided some guidelines based on certain factors such as the size, spread and mission of the organization.

Generally speaking larger organizations will have well-developed personnel and possibly welfare functions which could provide a base for in-house programmes. However, the feasibility of this does depend on the geographical spread of employees within the large organization. For London Transport, with a large workforce located in and around London, an in-house facility was eminently feasible. For the Post Office, with a very large workforce, in-house provision is feasible within major employment centres (e.g. London, Manchester); however, many employees may be located remotely and thus an external facility may be of use even within large organizations. Small to medium enterprises are much less likely to be able to support an internal service.

For organizations in certain fields, safety and security are of very high priority and therefore may predispose them towards internal service provision. This would seem to have been the case particularly in public transport organizations (railways, airlines, buses) as well as power-generating utilities (especially nuclear powered stations) and petrochemical industries.

Additional considerations that have been noted in the literature relating to the decision between external and internal counselling service provision relate to confidentiality and accountability.

Confidentiality in itself has rarely been an issue in the experience of the authors, as all programmes attempt to provide a service which has a high degree of confidentiality. However, the important factor here may be the 'perceived confidentiality' which is held by potential clients, and this certainly acts as a barrier for early self-referral and may even affect the willingness of others to recommend that a person seeks help. Often organizations attempt to improve the perception of confidentiality by removing the counselling service to a location away from other central management functions, though there are obvious limitations in how this may be resourced. Although the evidence does not seem clear, there may be some intuitive support for the view that external distributed EAPs may be perceived as more confidential as there are fewer obvious links with the organization's management. To some extent, balanced against this is the issue of accountability. If the organization is paying for the assistance service, there may be a perceived need by the purse holders to have some means of assessing the performance of the service providers. Obviously detailed record-keeping, feedback of contacts and outcome monitoring may have some impact on the perceived confidentiality of the service, whether internal or external.

Counselling substance-related problems

This section is provided as a brief description of the two approaches that are predominant in the UK substance counselling field at the moment. There are any number of other approaches that are available and successful, but these are probably the most commonly encountered. The following section briefly reviews some of the research issues that are enlightening our approaches to treatment in the substance misuse field and provides some pointers to the key treatment issues.

Pre-counselling substance issues

One of the first lessons learned in substance misuse counselling concerns the difficulties of providing assistance to someone who is too intoxicated to talk coherently or to remember much of what was said. Thus successful counselling would generally occur with clients who are relatively or more likely entirely substance-free. In some cases this may involve an initial detoxification phase with possible occurrence of withdrawal symptoms (depending on the substance and level of misuse). Increasingly, in many areas, this may take the form of out-patient treatment with GP assistance. In some parts of the country, in-patient 'detox' facilities still exist and may be used, though the period of stay can be relatively brief.

Counselling and related approaches

Although the intervention may fall short of what could be defined as 'counselling', Alcoholics Anonymous (and the associated Narcotics Anonymous) quite clearly provide a well-known type of support for those with problems. The spread and level of activity of its members is such that it is probably rare for someone to be treated for alcohol-related problems within any therapeutic environment over a period of time without coming into close contact with AA's philosophy or its members. Similarly, there are many examples of this basic approach being offered within a more usual counselling facility.

The principles of the AA (and NA) approach are covered in the Twelve Steps. The first step concerns an admission of powerlessness over alcohol and that one's life has become 'unmanageable'. The next two steps involve an acceptance of and a commitment to a higher power or 'God as we understand Him' that will 'restore us to sanity'. There follow two steps concerning self-assessment and admission of 'the exact nature of our wrongs' which are accompanied by two steps where the higher power assists in removing 'defects of character' and 'shortcomings'. The eighth and ninth steps concern identifying those that have been harmed by the individual and making amends where possible. Steps ten and eleven emphasize the need for continued self-awareness and growth through prayer and meditation. The final step acknowledges a 'spiritual awakening' resulting from the previous steps, stresses the need to continue practising the principles and encourages promotion of the Twelve Steps message to other alcoholics.

It is worth emphasizing that there is quite a degree of variability in the approaches provided by local AA groups, particularly concerning the strength of the underlying religious message. Some local groups may have a strong Christian approach, while others have a 'spiritual' rather than a 'religious' outlook. It is felt that such a perspective may be more attractive to occasional attenders who have no strong religious beliefs and it is certainly the case that many clients of non-AA treatment agencies have successfully found support in such meetings.

The principle that does not vary within AA concerns the goal behaviour of abstinence. However, within the UK there are many alternative therapeutic facilities available which do not emphasize total abstinence as the only outcome goal. Many of the NHS-supported local councils on alcohol and drug misuse (see pp. 241–2 for Alcohol Concern or SCoDA) offer a range of therapeutic approaches as would other groups such as Drink-watchers. However, it remains the case that the value of any particular target is probably less than that of the process elements that have to be mastered on the way to any substance related target.

In a treatment environment where the Twelve Steps model is not used, one tends to find a representative assortment of modern counselling elements. It would be unrealistic to maintain that substance misuse counselling is radically different from counselling of other problems such as anxiety and depression. There are undoubtedly additional details concerning the substances and their effects that may be relevant, but other than that core features of the therapeutic environment may be similar across a range of problems.

Specific to alcohol and drug interventions is the provision of accurate information concerning psychological and physiological effects of short- and long-term use of the substance in question. Although it may be felt that clients represent an 'expert' group in terms of substance use, this is not necessarily so as they may have only experienced non-problem use for a short period while passing through to patterns of misuse. Thus many group sessions have been devoted to what are often known as 'chalktalks' to provide basic physiological and drug effects information. Also, since the development of concern over AIDS, there has been a rise in the amount of practical information provided to substance users along the lines of reducing the possible harmful effects of factors indirectly related to the substance use (e.g. injecting). Such information is obviously of an advisory rather than a counselling nature, though it is seen as a valuable input nevertheless.

Beyond the drug-specific information, the main difference in substance misuse counselling concerns the focus of activities (towards abstinence or 'controlled' use) rather than the actual activities themselves (e.g. role playing within a general social skills development package). It is common for some time to be devoted to such obvious substance-related issues as 'saying no'. Additionally, a lot of effort is directed towards 'relapse prevention' within the substance misuse field. Beyond elements such as these, the broad brush applies and the elements are likely to be similar to other counselling domains. A likely list of elements available in a local council on substance misuse following a loose rational-emotive perspective may include:

1 *Stress/anxiety management*
   In a simple form, this may focus on the development of a more healthy lifestyle involving improved nutrition and exercise. It can also include a more general look at the use of coping strategies and may involve specific emphasis on relaxation training. Given a cognitive bias, the role of cognitions in the mediation of stress may be highlighted as may be the discussion of more general issues of problem solving.

2 *Self-awareness*
   The notion of self-awareness along with the importance and value of encouraging positive affective states could be presented. The idea that self-esteem both influences and is influenced by the interaction between cognitions, emotions and behaviour may be introduced. The key role of recognizing one's achievements in boosting self-esteem would be highlighted. This would be reinforced by discussing and applying positive goal setting.

3 *Assertiveness training*
   This emphasizes an approach to positive communication examining passive, assertive and aggressive modes and applying them to substance-related role playing.

4 *Recreational activities*
   Most substance-related groups spend some time developing ideas for pleasurable recreations. Obviously a considerable amount of 'extra' time is available to the non-intoxicated client and this needs to be filled appropriately in a rewarding way. While group 'brainstorming' may be a useful way of identifying many possible activities, it is usual to undertake a realistic risk assessment of suggested activities so that likelihood of alcohol or drug use being encouraged as part of the activity may be reduced. Apart from simply filling the 'gaps' left after substance use has stopped or been drastically reduced, the development of recreational activities plays an important self-esteem building role and emphasizes that there can be substance-free enjoyment.

An obvious yet interesting point should be emphasized at this juncture. While AA and NA have a prescribed list of 'steps', quite clearly, given the supportive environment provided by 'sponsors' (more experienced, fellow members often assigned to advise newcomers) and other members, a number of the social-psychological elements described above are present within the Twelve Step 'package'. Thus it may be that the overall psychological nature of the treatment experience may not be that different between the Twelve Step and alternative methods, just that they are packaged differently.

Key issues in substance-related treatment

Conceptualizing alcohol and drug problems

An adequate model of substance-related problems should incorporate the vast range and interaction of factors that can contribute in the development and course of the disorder. The biopsychosocial perspective provided by Kissin and Hanson (1982) gives a broad multi-factorial view of the aetiology of addictive problems and is one considered appropriate given the research evidence. In this model, biological psychological and social factors exert a combined influence to initiate and maintain problem-related substance use.

Importance of environmental influences

Positive family and peer relationships, social support and employment have been repeatedly identified as predictors of favourable outcome for people with alcohol and drug problems. Post-treatment processes have been shown to serve an important mediating role in long-term outcome of clients from treatment programmes (Moos *et al.* 1990). Interestingly, Finney and Moos (1984) found that stressful life events and limited social and familial support are likely to play a far more powerful role in determining individual outcomes than treatment itself. This is perhaps understandable since treatment is often delivered over a relatively short period of time and the positive benefits may be eroded quite quickly unless more enduring 'lessons learned' are applied in the post-treatment life context. Finney and Moos (1984: 159) emphasized that 'During treatment, and even more directly afterwards, the client is exposed to a myriad of influences emanating from other more enduring microsystems.' This perhaps is particularly so for those who are still in employment. It follows that treatment goals may not be reached at all, or may attenuate rapidly following treatment if the client's environmental resources are limited.

Intensive versus brief treatment intervention

The relative effectiveness of different treatments, for example, focused brief interventions versus intensive longer-term approaches, is important from clinical, practical and economic perspectives. It should not be assumed that more treatment is better treatment, since cost-effectiveness of brief interventions should be considered in evaluation (Miller and Hester 1986). Additionally, major reviews of earlier outcome research by Emrick (1974, 1975) concluded that although formal treatment for alcohol problems may be effective, the research literature does not support any significant differences between treatment approaches in long-term outcome.

Miller *et al.* (1980) reported the effectiveness of a specific didactic approach to moderation treatment called behavioural self-control training (BSCT). These procedures usually involve brief, behaviourally and educationally based treatments offered on an out-patient basis. The components of BSCT have included specific goal setting, self-monitoring, training in consumption control, self-reinforcement, and functional analyses of drinking behaviour. Following random assignment, 41 clients completed treatment in one of four groups:

- bibliotherapy, in which the client received self-help materials (books and leaflets) but no treatment sessions;
- BSCT, consisting of six weekly sessions;
- BSCT plus 12 sessions of relaxation, communication and assertion training; or
- BSCT plus 12 weeks of individually tailored broad-spectrum modules.

Results indicated that all groups showed significant improvements on drinking measures, but there were no significant differences in effectiveness between minimal BSCT and more extensive interventions.

Non-abstinent treatment goals

For many years, abstinence following treatment was seen as the only appropriate and essential treatment goal, and it remains the dominant approach in North America today. This model reflects a disease concept which might seem similar to an 'allergy to alcohol' which cannot be cured, but in which the progress of the disease will be 'arrested' through abstinence (Edwards 1987: 261).

However, since the mid-1970s, cumulative evidence from the alcohol field suggests that abstinence *per se* does not guarantee positive outcome in a number of areas of life-functioning, personal relationships or job performance (Pattison *et al.* 1977). As a result, a broader range of alternative treatments offering non-abstinent goals has emerged in an attempt to address the needs of the range and diversity of substance misusers within different communities, and to respond to personal intentions, motivations and resources which clients themselves bring to the treatment setting itself.

The advantage of individually specified goals was brought to the attention of the treatment and research community following publication of the Rand

Corporation's four-year study of 1,400 clients treated at 44 federally funded alcohol treatment facilities (Polich *et al.* 1981). Study results supported only a modest positive correlation between the amount of treatment a client received and their status at follow-up and the authors could find no evidence for a greater efficacy of one treatment over another (e.g. in-patient versus out-patient hospital treatment). Additionally, relapse to harmful drinking for long-term abstainers and non-problem drinkers was found to be influenced according to the initial level of dependency at admission, age and marital status. Specifically, results suggested that among clients aged 40 or over who demonstrated high levels of dependency at admission, clients who *abstained* had lower relapse rates than those who attempted to engage in moderate or controlled drinking. Conversely, among clients who were under 40 years of age and who had lower dependency at admission, those who engaged in *controlled* drinking had lower relapse rates than those who attempted to abstain. The Rand Corporation study thus provided evidence for the importance of the severity of dependency as a predictor of outcome, and the need to match clients to appropriate treatment goals.

The effects of coercion into treatment

A number of researchers have suggested that substance misusers must experience some form of 'confrontation' in order for treatment to be effective (Trice *et al.* 1977). Based on earlier models of social control within industry, a strategy known as 'constructive confrontation' was coined and became an influential rationale for management intervention. The approach combines 'progressive positive discipline with provisions designed to assist problem-drinking employees to rehabilitate themselves' (Trice and Roman 1972: 393). Attention was focused on the role of the work supervisor's involvement in maintaining social control, through the use of two sequential components:

- In the 'confrontation' component, the employee is told of the ways in which job performance has become unacceptable and may be likely to lead to the enactment of disciplinary procedures.
- In the 'constructive' component, the supervisor is required to suggest to the employee specific expectations and appropriate alternative courses of action and changes of behaviour to regain acceptable job performance. Such courses of action may involve the acceptance of formal assistance if a drinking problem is acknowledged, with the intention of retaining such employees in the work setting where social controls operate, discharging employees only as a last resort.

Trice and Roman argued that an employee will respond positively to these influences and will be strongly motivated to accept referral. This was viewed as particularly the case when assistance is combined with the threat of job loss, since work is an important symbol of a problem drinker's continued ability to function in society, aside from its obvious economic importance. In order to implement this approach effectively, organizations were encouraged to adopt formal written policies to guide management action and to protect employees' rights.

The identification, referral and treatment of substance-related problems within the workplace may represent an example of a coercion into treatment, with the threat of job loss providing the pressure. Coercion into alcohol treatment has been commonplace in North America in relation to repeated drink-driving offending, though the effects of such mandatory referral are not particularly clear. In the particular example of the US experience with drink-driving offenders, the main problem concerned the appropriateness of the mandated intervention in relation to the problem severity. For those assessed as being 'problem drinkers' there were no real positive benefits of minor interventions, though there was some reported success for interventions involving AA, other counselling course and Antabuse (disulfiram) medication (which deters alcohol consumption through triggering feelings of nausea). Miller and Hester (1986: 149) concluded that

> It is meaningless, therefore to discuss the 'effectiveness' of coercion methods, e.g. employee assistance programs, or legal mandating of treatment, in general. The treatment impact of coercion can be defined only in relation to the intervention into which the individual is coerced.

This conclusion is supported by a recent study (Marsden 1992) which suggested that coercion in terms of formal employee referral for assistance was particularly beneficial when coupled with more intense treatment provision.

Summary of research on key issues

Thus research into the treatment of substance (predominantly alcohol) misuse suggests that there may be advantages in casting the net wide in considering the number of factors that will significantly influence outcome. Clearly there is a strong influence on outcome from the social and environmental infrastructure around the client and this may mean a greater possibility of successful outcome for clients who remain employed. The support for constructive confrontation strategies from the research is another positive mark for workplace interventions, providing the mechanism for early successful intervention. Finally, the debate concerning abstinence as a treatment goal is less fierce in the UK and may allow facilities more easily to offer a range of treatment goals to suit the range of clients and problems that exist.

The following section presents a brief case study within a company intervention primarily covering alcohol misusers. While no attempt has been made to provide individual case profiles, some basic description of types of problems and degrees of outcome are available as the result of an extensive evaluation of the treatment programme. Readers interested in a more detailed account of the research should initially contact the authors.

Case study from a company-based alcohol programme

Background

Bill, a white male blue-collar employee was aged 38 at the time of the assessment interview, just below the average age of similar clients referred to welfare. He had been within the company for just over eight years and had remained at the same grade for the last seven years. The client lived alone and had been at the same address for more than four years.

Bill was referred as part of the company's disciplinary policy in relation to his recent absenteeism record. It was estimated that he had recorded 14 absence spells in the six months prior to interview, totalling 19 days.

Bill reported that work problems (absenteeism) had started several years previously, and that he had been unofficially cautioned about them and had had the issue of drinking raised at that time. However, the first official response had been just one month before the assessment interview. He also reported having noticed health problems in relation to drinking over the previous six years.

In terms of drinking, Bill reported consuming 119 units of alcohol during the week prior to the assessment interview, with an estimated consumption of 32 units (one bottle of Scotch) on the heaviest day.

At assessment interview Bill assessed his work and health problems related to drinking as being 'very serious' and also assessed that he would 'have some difficulty' in resolving his problem. This view was mirrored by the Welfare Unit prognosis which was below average.

Treatment input

Bill was advised to see his GP and was referred to an external counselling agency as well as for counselling within the company programme. The drinking strategy recommended at this stage was abstinence.

Bill attended 20 counselling sessions with an external (community-based) counselling agency and nine counselling sessions with the specialist welfare facility within the company. In relation to other clients, this represented much more counselling than the average client. He did not attend any AA meetings and reported no other formal assistance, though did see his GP both at the time of assessment and during the follow-up period.

Indication of outcome

At the follow-up interview, Bill reported having been abstinent for nearly four months. Measures of drink problems were thus minimal at follow-up, showing significant change from those at referral. Mental health measures indicated significantly reduced symptoms of anxiety and depression at follow-up.

Both Bill and his supervisor rated work performance as better at follow-up, with this client moving from an initial supervisor rating in the lowest 33 per cent of all clients assessed to a rating in the top 5 per cent of clients assessed. Bill recorded only one spell of absence in the six months' follow-up period.

Case summary

This case shows a client with reasonably serious alcohol-related problems and quite heavy consumption patterns. The problems were not just work-related, and they had been going on for some time. In particular, work-related problems had been noticed some years earlier, but had not been acted upon. Following changes to sickness absence policies, the client's attendance was identified as below standard and a formal referral was made. Following assistance from both external and internal counselling facilities, quite dramatic positive changes in terms of drink and work-related indices were shown over the six-month post-referral period. A significant lesson for the organization may relate to the potential benefits of earlier identification of cases such as this.

Summary and conclusions

It is clear that, within the UK, the main drug of concern in terms of prevalence and its proven links with safety and productivity is alcohol. Alcohol intoxication has a significant causative role in many accidents, and heavy drinking patterns are linked with significantly increased sickness absence. Thus there is strong motivation for the development of policies and interventions that assist employees with alcohol-related problems.

In classifying interventions, there would seem to be three distinct levels of activity: prevention, detection and rehabilitation. When we look at how EAPs are designed and worked there seems to be an emphasis on the final level of the system, which includes counselling. It is considered that there will remain benefits in providing input at the preventive level, either in terms of general health promotion programmes or specific campaigns addressing substance misuse. Clearly there is also a necessity to ensure an emphasis on programme elements supporting identification of potential problems. This key element in the system can, if properly managed, make successful outcome much more likely through identifying problems early and providing a constructive questioning of the person's control over their substance use.

In terms of successful outcomes, there is evidence that workplace interventions can assist alcohol-abusing employees and bring work performance measures at least towards normal range. The literature would also suggest that work performance provides a useful early indicator of the development of problems and provides an environment that can motivate clients to work hard on getting better.

For drugs other than alcohol, however, the picture is not so clear. There has been very little firm evidence indicating a major workplace problem within the UK in terms of safety and productivity as a direct result of the misuse of drugs other than alcohol. Also, from a treatment perspective, there are some factors that need to be considered when it comes to illicit drug users in the workplace. It is far more likely that those identified will be users of cannabis rather than any other illicit drug, both because of natural prevalence rates and technological limitations of current testing procedures. While drug use that causes problems at work can fall under the definitions of misuse, there may be little else in the pattern of use of some of these identified employees that requires significant counselling input.

Nevertheless, it is considered that the continued development of workplace policies and procedures that can prevent, identify and ameliorate substance-related problems is supported. Additionally, the relationship between problems of a more general nature (e.g. stress) and those with a specific substance component are clear both in terms of research and practice. Therefore it seems most appropriate to advise the development of broad brush interventions which have the flexibility to cover a wide range of employee problems and thus be of maximum use to the sponsoring organization.

References

American Psychiatric Association (1994) *Diagnostic and Statistical Manual of Mental Disorders IV*. Washington, DC: American Psychiatric Association.

Central Office of Information (1993) *Drug and Solvent Misuse: A basic briefing*. London: Department of Health.

Edwards, G. (1987) *The Treatment of Drinking Problems: A guide for the helping professions*. London: Blackwell.

Emrick, C.D. (1974) A review of psychologically oriented treatment for alcoholism I: The use and interrelationships of outcome criteria and drinking behaviour following treatment. *Quarterly Journal of Studies on Alcohol*, 35: 523–49.

Emrick, C.D. (1975) A review of psychologically oriented treatment for alcoholism II. The relative effectiveness of different treatment approaches and the effectiveness of treatment versus no treatment. *Journal of Studies on Alcohol*, 36: 88–108.

Finney, J.W. and Moos, R.H. (1984) Environmental assessment and evaluation research: Examples from mental health and substance abuse programs. *Evaluation and Program Planning*, 7: 154–67.

Fleisher, D. and Kaplan, B.H. (1988) Employee assistance/counselling typologies, in G.M. Gould and M.L. Smith (eds) *Social Work in the Workplace*. New York: Springer.

Goddard, E. (1991) *Drinking in England and Wales in the Late 1980s*. Office of Population Censuses and Surveys, London: HMSO.

Guppy, A. and Marsden, J. (1995) Drug related problems in the workplace: A British perspective. *Proceedings of the Occupational Psychological Society Conference*. Leicester: British Psychological Society.

Gust, S.W. and Walsh, J.M. (1989) Research on the prevalence, impact and treatment of drug abuse in the workplace, in S.W. Gust and J.M. Walsh (eds) *Drugs in the Workplace: Research and evaluation data*, research monograph 91. Rockville, MD: US National Institute of Drug Abuse.

Hellan, R.T. (1986) An EAP update: A perspective for the '80s. *Personnel Journal*, 65: 51–4.

Kissin, B. and Hanson, M. (1982) The biopsychosocial perspective in alcoholism, in J. Solomon (ed.) *Alcoholism and Clinical Psychiatry*. New York: Plenum Press.

Macdonald, S., Kapur, B. and Sorenson, M. (1992) *Drugs and Alcohol in the Maritime Industry*. Geneva: International Labour Organisation.

Marmot, M.G., North, F., Feeney, A. and Head, J. (1993) Alcohol consumption and sickness absence. From the Whitehall II study. *Addiction*, 88: 369–82.

Marsden, J.R. (1992) 'Employees with drinking problems: Short-term evaluation of treatment and management outcomes', PhD thesis. Bedford: Cranfield University.

Masi, D.A. and Friedland, S.J. (1988) EAP actions and options. *Personnel Journal*, 67: 61–7.

Miller, W.R. and Hester, R.K. (1986) Matching problem drinkers with optimal treatments, in W.R. Miller and N. Heather (eds) *Treating Addictive Behaviors: Processes of change*. New York: Plenum Press.

Miller, W.R., Taylor, C.A. and West, J.C. (1980) Focused versus broad-spectrum behaviour therapy for problem drinking. *Journal of Consulting and Clinical Psychology*, 48: 590–601.

Moos, R.H., Finney, J.W. and Cronkite, R.C. (1990) *Alcoholism Treatment: Context, process and outcome*. New York: Oxford University Press.

Needleman, S.B. and Romberg, R.W. (1989) Comparison of drug abuse in different military populations. *Journal of Forensic Sciences*, 34, 848–57.

Normand, J., Salyards, S.D. and Mahoney, J.J. (1990) An evaluation of pre-employment drug testing. *Journal of Applied Psychology*, 75: 629–39.

Pattison, E.M., Sobell, M.B. and Sobell, L.C. (1977) *Emerging Concepts of Alcohol Dependence*. New York: Springer.

Plant, M.A. (1979) Occupations, drinking patterns and alcohol-related problems: Conclusions from a follow-up study. *British Journal of Addiction*, 74: 267–75.

Polich, J.M., Armor, D.J. and Braiker, H.B. (1981) *The Course of Alcoholism: Four years after treatment*. New York: Wiley.

Royal College of Psychiatrists (1979) *Alcohol and Alcoholism*. London: Tavistock.

Sutton, M. and Maynard, A. (1993) Are drug policies based on fake statistics? *Addiction*, 88: 455–8.

Trice, H.M. and Roman, P. (1972) *Spirits and Demons at Work: Alcohol and other drugs on the job* (ILR paperback no. 11). Ithaca, NY: Cornell University.

Trice, H.M., Hunt, R.E. and Beyer, J.M. (1977) Alcoholism programs in unionized work settings: Problems and prospects in union–management cooperation. *Journal of Drug Issues*, 7: 103–15.

United Nations Economic and Social Council (1993) *Examination of the World Situation with Respect to Drug Abuse*, Commission on Narcotic Drugs, report no. E/CN.7/1933/4. Vienna: United Nations.

Wilson, P. (1980) *Drinking in England and Wales*. Office of Population Census and Surveys, London: HMSO.

Suggested reading

Central Office of Information (1993) *Drug and Solvent Misuse: A basic briefing*. London: Department of Health.

Edwards, G. (1987) *The Treatment of Drinking Problems: A guide for the helping professions*. London: Blackwell.

Guppy, A. and Marsden, J. (1996) Substance misuse and the organization, in M. Schabraq, A.J. Winnubst and C.L. Cooper (eds) *Handbook of Work and Health Psychology*. Chichester: John Wiley

Institute of Medicine (1990) *Broadening the Base of Treatment for Alcohol Problems*, report of a study by the Institute of Medicine. Washington, DC: National Academy Press.

Marlatt, G.A. and Gordon, J.R. (eds) (1985) *Relapse Prevention: Maintenance strategies in the treatment of addictive behavior*. New York: Guilford Press.

Moos, R.H., Finney, J.W. and Cronkite, R.C. (1990) *Alcoholism Treatment: Context, process and outcome*. New York: Oxford University Press.

Robertson, I. and Heather, N. (1986) *Let's Drink to Your Health! A self-help guide to sensible drinking*. Leicester: British Psychological Society.

Useful organizations

All the organizations below should be able to provide contact information for local advice and counselling services. The London numbers for Alcohol Concern, Alcoholics Anonymous, Narcotics Anonymous and SCoDA can be used for contact details for local services.

England

Alcohol Concern
Waterbridge House
32–36 Loman Street
London SE1 0EE
0171 928 7377

Alcoholics Anonymous
PO Box 1
Stonebow House
Stonebow
York YO1 2NJ
01904 644026

Narcotics Anonymous
UK Service Office
PO Box 198J
London N19 3LS
0171 351 6794

Standing Conference on Drug Abuse (SCoDA)
Waterbridge House, 32–36 Loman Street
London SE1 0EE
0171 928 9500

Scotland

Alcoholics Anonymous
Scottish Service Office
Baltic Chamber
50 Wellington Street
Glasgow G2 6HJ
0141 221 9027

Scottish Council on Alcohol
137–145 Sauchiehall Street
Glasgow G2 3EW
0141 333 9677

Scottish Drugs Forum
5 Oswald Street
Glasgow G1 5QR
0141 221 1175

Wales

Alcohol Action Wales
Floor 8, Brunel House
2 Fitzalan Road
Cardiff CF2 1ER
01222 488000

Drug Aid – All Wales Helpline
1 Neville Street
Cardiff CF1 8LP
01222 383313

Northern Ireland

Northern Ireland Council on Alcohol
40 Elmwood Avenue
Belfast BT9 6AZ
01232 664434

Alcoholics Anonymous Northern Ireland Service Office
152 Lisburn Road
Belfast BT9 6AJ
01232 681084

Northern Ireland Regional Drugs Unit, Shaftsbury Square Hospital,
116–122 Great Victoria Street, Belfast BT2 7BG
01232 329808

Eire

Alcoholics Anonymous
109 South Circular Road
Dublin 8
0001 538 998

12

Some problems and emerging trends

○ **COLIN FELTHAM**

Objections to EAPs

It cannot be pretended that the subject of counselling at work is unconten-
tious and all those involved or interested in it should indeed consider its
practical and intellectual problems. EAPs, like the still largely unregulated
activities of counselling and psychotherapy in Britain generally, must be
subjected to scrutiny by researchers and other evaluative critics. To some
extent Andrew Bull's chapter has raised certain of these objections. Listed
below are some of the commonly articulated objections to EAPs and counselling generally.

1 There is no conclusive evidence that counselling is effective.
The point has been made repeatedly by the psychologist Hans Eysenck (cf.
Eysenck 1992) and many others that psychoanalysis in particular, but all
counselling and psychotherapy generally, has failed to demonstrate its effectiveness. When these appear to be somewhat helpful, this is often explained
simply in terms of the passage of time or the friendly support that anyone
could offer the distressed person. Counsellors and psychotherapists, however
well-meaning, exaggerate their abilities, their theoretical understanding of
personal problems and the benefits of therapy, and play down the many ways
in which people may be abused by therapists. Many of these arguments and
counter-arguments are summarized by Dryden and Feltham (1992). It has
been demonstrated by Smith *et al.* (1980) generally, and by Firth and Shapiro
(1986) and Barkham and Shapiro (1990) specifically, that counselling is
indeed effective. What remains to be demonstrated is exactly how different
forms of counselling or therapy most effectively address different problems.

2 *There is no reason why employers should provide welfare and mental health services which are more properly provided by statutory or other specialist agencies.*

This argument cannot be avoided, especially in difficult economic times, since staff counselling services have not been found crucially necessary up to the present time, nor have significant numbers of employees or unions demanded them as a right. Why should they be provided, then, in times of recession and uncertainty, when many businesses are fighting for their very survival? Britain has a National Health Service which offers various forms of psychiatric and psychological help, and this should be considered sufficient for employees, the unemployed, retired and all sections of the community.

The argument is undercut by the fact that many companies willingly provide and value various health, fitness and recreational schemes which might easily be compared with the status of EAPs. Granted, EAPs are a newer concept and are considered by some to be unproven and perhaps even threatening. In essence, however, there is little reason not to consider the benefits of instituting workplace counselling projects. The objection that they require expertise not available within current organizational structures is weak, of course, because all kinds of expertise are readily bought in whenever considered necessary. It is also apparent to many managers and directors that suitable, prompt counselling services are not readily available within the NHS and that even if they were, they would not always provide the kind of understanding of the interface between individual and company that may be required; and they certainly would not provide managers with the kind of general feedback they may seek on the health (or otherwise) of their organizational culture.

It is also apparent to many that with the national increase in life expectancy there is an ever-growing demand on the NHS that it cannot possibly fund. Businesses can help in this area by funding preventive health projects, including EAPs. Perhaps the most compelling counter-objection here is, however, that many prominent business leaders and government ministers have declared their conviction that it is definitely in the interests of companies themselves to investigate and install EAPs or similar services (Jenkins and Warman 1993). From within the EAP field, well-researched arguments for the positive cost-effectiveness of EAPs have been sparse but the presentations of Smith and Mahoney (1989) and Steddon (1990) are extremely useful.

3 *The values of personal counselling and business in many ways conflict with each other.*

DeGolia, arguing that all labour under capitalism is oppressive for workers, suggests that

> The only way anyone can bear the boredom and brutalization of alien-
> ated labor is to be cut off from all feeling. It is impossible for someone

who is tuned into his feelings and acutely aware of his well-being to stand in an assembly line putting together cars or sit at a desk shuffling papers for eight hours a day . . . As President of General Motors, it is very important to keep the vast majority of workers under one thinking, 'I can take it,' rather than 'Why the hell should I?'

(DeGolia 1976: 182)

The values of personal welfare, self-fulfilment and creativity are here opposed to those of self-sacrifice and stoicism. Humanistic therapy and counselling is particularly opposed to the concept and practice of people surrendering themselves to external definitions of their worth and limitations on their self-determination. From a psychoanalytic perspective, Fine (1986) examines examples of the psychopathological ambitions underlying the success and downfall of a number of business leaders. Additional examples are given by Kets de Vries (1995).

This kind of psychotherapy versus business argument is presented even more personally and vividly by 'Alex' (1974), who tells the story of his success in business, followed by business failure when he entered into personal therapy and reclaimed profound feelings and insights about his true personal values. Business success had been built on his own 'neurotic' drives and on subtly meeting the neurotic needs of employees. When he could no longer suppress his real feelings, he lost interest in pursuing the phantom of self-worth in the form of ever-escalating business success, and his companies crashed accordingly. 'Being in touch with one's real feelings', seeing through symbolic (unreal) ambitions (for money instead of love), and avoiding exploiting others, are some of the values implicitly advocated. Profit, exploitation and suppression of real human needs are the values regarded here as inherent in commerce. One psychologist argues that

strained, foolish life-modes grouped under the bland euphemism of 'stress' can disrupt digestion, cardiac function, breathing, proper function of joints and sexual satisfaction. In such instances the body is regularly abused yet inordinately worried about, since it is easier to accept a malfunctioning physical organism than accept that one's lifestyle and values are absurd and life-threatening.

(Conway 1992: 239)

The psychotherapist Everett Shostrom (1968) also speaks quite plainly about his doubts about people who are primarily motivated by profit:

The typical salesman is profit-motivated. He knows he must curry favor with the customer by building his loyalty; therefore, the salesman is prepared to spend substantial amounts of expense money entertaining customers and cementing their friendship to induce purchasing. He is the manipulator par excellence. I have, as a matter of fact, had a number of salesmen as patients who had to give up the work because they were becoming ill from having to play phoney friendship games with people they didn't really like. The usual salesman, as we would expect, is a profit-oriented man, loyal to his company and product, who functions partially on a selective presentation of information and truth. The main goal of his business dealings is to market the product (even though it may be inferior) since the success of his company depends on it.

(1968: 138)

Shostrom, following the humanistic psychologist Abraham Maslow, hopes that there may be some way of conducting business ethically. Some such attempts have certainly been made in recent years (see, for example, Clutterbuck 1980) but exactly how ethical and anti-manipulative business behaviour is must always depend partly on the economic climate and business Zeitgeist.

Conversely, business may be said to promote positively the values of co-operation, effort, commitment and productivity. Without work, we are lost, and without some people putting visions into practice and organizing others to turn those visions into wealth, we are all the poorer. Work, it may be argued, inevitably includes a certain amount of self-sacrifice and it is unrealistic to imagine that we can all dedicate our lives to the unchecked and unaccountable pursuit of personal pleasure. Furthermore, it has been shown that a working environment and schedule is crucial for the mental health of many people (Warr 1987). Counsellors who wish to work in EAPs and similar employee counselling services may need to accept the competitive, even adversarial ethos of many organizations (Cunningham 1994).

4 Confidentiality cannot be guaranteed.

Confidentiality is one of the cornerstones of counselling. It is embedded in the Codes of Ethics and Practice of the British Association for Counselling and counsellors who breach the principle of confidentiality are liable to complaints procedures against them and to withdrawal of professional membership and, hence, to loss of their very livelihood. However, even BAC acknowledges that confidentiality can seldom be absolute, since counsellor supervisors must hear counsellors' accounts of their work, and in certain circumstances, when clients present as dangerous to themselves or to others, counsellors may be obliged to discuss cases with appropriate authorities.

Within the above constraints, counsellors perceive confidentiality as sacrosanct, and those working for organizations must be assured that they are not required to report on the details of their work to anyone but professional (clinical) supervisors. On no account should they be compromised by managers seeking to discover whether certain employees are having counselling. It is not unknown for employees to mistrust EAPs because they find it impossible to believe that a service provided by their company is immune to pressure for disclosures. Managers sometimes strongly encourage staff members to seek counselling, sometimes in connection with impending disciplinary actions, sometimes simply out of humanitarian concern. In these circumstances, it may be difficult for them to appreciate that counsellors are unable to offer feedback on a case, since the counselling contract is always between the counsellor and the individual client. Counsellors may thus be suspected by both staff and management, for quite different reasons. Certainly when counselling is provided in-house, it is often difficult to provide staff with complete privacy, since they may be seen physically to be using the counselling service.

5 *It is disingenuous for employers to offer counselling with one hand, while placing employees under stress and insecurity with the other.*
As Smail (1993: 115) argues:

> Personnel managers of large firms instituting programmes of redundancy could, for example, seriously set up as a humane measure the provision of counselling to those affected. An insult added to an injury was thus presented – and surprisingly often accepted – as a 'package of care' for which the redundant employee should feel grateful.

Newton (1995) is specifically critical of stress management programmes and employee counselling on similar grounds. He argues that employees' grievances are being interpreted as individual concerns rather than the collectively justifiable reaction to poor working conditions that they might well be.

This argument has been put starkly: 'I sit on a man's back, choking him and making him carry me, and yet assure myself and others that I am very sorry for him and wish to ease his lot by all possible means – except by getting off his back' (attributed to Tolstoy).

According to Whyte (1960) human relations professionals such as Elton Mayo in the 1920s and 1930s realized the value of encouraging employees to 'talk out' their work conflicts. Mayo advocated non-directive counselling in the workplace in the belief that employees would use this to help themselves adjust to occupational conflicts rather than to dwell on perceived organizational injustices. The objection that EAPs are all very well, but may be entirely unrelated to the realities of specifically occupational stress and its remedies, is hard to answer. People do sometimes come to EAPs complaining that their managers treat them unfairly, that the organization for which they work is corrupt, unhealthy or interested only in profits. Counsellors may strive not to influence their clients in these cases, yet where a counsellor is retained by the organization, how free is she actively to 'side with the client'? Those EAPs whose brief includes statistical information gathering and analysis of workplace stressors are more likely to make a real impact on stress at the organizational level.

6 *Employees should steer clear of organizations' attempts to have any influence over their private lives and views.*

With some justification, many employees, perhaps those on low incomes particularly, regard their job as a simple trade-off. They surrender so many hours of their time and provide what skills they possess each week in return for money. Certainly many employers have this perception of work from their own side of the equation. Rhetoric about 'our people are our most important resource' is increasingly disbelieved in the face of widespread downsizing. Why should employees want anything other than money or believe that their employer has any real interest in them besides using their labour and skills? What covert reasons might an employer have for introducing an EAP or similar services?

The sociologist Rose (1989) argues that psychology and its offshoots (particularly psychometric testing, psychotherapy, counselling and stress management) subtly structure and control people, including employees. Newton's (1995) critique of organizations' use of stress management training and employee counselling also suggests that employees are being subtly controlled into regarding their problems at work as their own individual concerns, not as collective concerns. Employers, according to this analysis, benefit from EAPs and suchlike provisions by reinforcing the idea that emotion and discontentment do not belong in the workplace. Employees who wish to have a purely contractual relationship with their employers (labour for money) may not wish to buy in to EAPs. They may not wish to relinquish or dilute their union affiliation and their political views and may wish to attempt to change the work ethos so that, for example, grief and distress can be openly exhibited rather than taken privately to a counsellor. Plas and Hoover-Dempsey (1988) acknowledge that emotions are a part of working life to be accepted rather than denied. It can be said that many employers already abuse their employees' moral rights in dictating how employees shall behave at work, how they shall dress, when they may eat and take vacations, and so on. And now they want to have some say about where you take your private troubles?

7 *We haven't needed these fundamentally American practices in the UK before, so why should we think we need them now?*

It is true that EAPs are an essentially American concept, and also that counselling itself is mainly of American origin. Counselling and psychotherapy of the analytic (Freudian) variety are, however, European in origin. But there are certainly many who regard counselling as soft, unnecessary and merely fashionable. The objection that employee counselling is undesirably American does not hold water when one considers that British managers are only too happy to employ American sales techniques or American management methods, for example. The real objection is surely that many people in Britain and elsewhere regard emotional life as dangerous and upsetting, preferring to keep quiet about personal travails.

While there is something of value in the idea that we do not need to psychologize everything and to push counselling under everyone's nose, consider the opposite problem. In Britain we 'mustn't grumble'; rather, we keep a stiff upper lip, put a brave face on it, and so on. A social history of the maternity problems and experiences of working women in Britain, first published in 1915, includes the account of a woman beset with illness and poverty:

> I can safely say that had there been a centre to which I could have gone before my first boy was born I should have been spared the terrible torture I suffered both before and after confinement . . . I did not like to say anything to a strange doctor, and I had no lady friends whom I felt I could confide in.
>
> (Davies 1978: 112)

The 'I didn't like to say anything' is a familiar enough refrain in Britain. It is still the case that clients in counselling often say, 'Well, I'm taking up your time, and I expect you have people to see with far worse problems than mine.' Perhaps British reticence is rightfully challenged by the American norm of articulating one's feelings openly. On the other hand, it does not follow that employee counselling must follow the American pattern.

8 Companies can deal with any and all human relations issues internally.
It is the policy of many organizations to deal in-house with perceived stress and personal problems, both for economic reasons and because they believe they have adequate resources. Many personnel or human resources staff are trained in counselling skills, for example, and it is often argued that the help they can give is quite adequate for employees' needs. In some cases, indeed, identified staff have been trained and even seconded part-time or wholly within the organization to provide staff counselling. A partial example of this trend is given in one of the appendices to this book. Others regard counselling (or their interpretation of what counselling is) as an essential part of the managerial role. Thus, Peters and Austin (1985) see counselling as one activity among several others – educating, sponsoring, coaching, mentoring and confronting – which the hands-on manager has the right and responsibility to be involved in.

It should be noted that certain organizations, even those which might be thought to be in a favourable position to provide their own in-house counselling, often favour external counselling services. Many regional probation services, for example, buy in or retain external counselling services. The British Association for Social Workers (BASW) convened a Project Group to examine precisely such issues and in its Final Report (BASW 1988) outlined the advantages and disadvantages of various arrangements. BASW's Project

Group acknowledged that the implementation of a counselling service must include stringent considerations of confidentiality and that it should not be automatically assumed that social workers, because they are part of a 'people profession', are necessarily best equipped to provide their own staff counselling. Certainly it is the position of the British Association for Counselling that professional counselling has a distinct identity of its own, perhaps overlapping with but not being identical with befriending, social work, the personnel function and other similar activities (BAC 1992).

Emerging trends

The steady growth of EAPs and variations on employee counselling projects appears to be irreversible by any reckoning. Reddy (1993) estimates that 80 per cent of British companies use some form of workplace counselling. Look at any town centre and if you cared to investigate whether particular retail stores, banks, building societies, and public and statutory services had their own counselling provision, you would find just how quietly prevalent this movement has become. Any employer whose staff have health cover provided by Private Patients Plan (PPP) also have access to telephone counselling under its 'StressCare' service.

Quality of provision of all such services is hard to evaluate but the work of the Employee Assistance Professionals Association (EAPA), Britannic Chapter, in parallel with developments in the Association for Counselling at Work (ACW) are fast addressing issues of competency, professional ethics and accreditation. Few studies have been made in Britain of the financial efficacy of EAPs, apart from the Post Office experience summarized by Welch and Tehrani (1992), and this is obviously an area of research awaiting attention. There is now little doubt, however, that at the individual level counselling, even in very brief form, is effective (Barkham and Shapiro 1990).

In the USA EAPs are closely related to legislation which is quite different or absent from the British context. In California alone $380 million is lost annually to state industries through stress-related absenteeism and health-care bills rise accordingly. American managers and healthcare professionals have long since grown accustomed to litigation and the installation of EAPs is partly a response to it. Now in Britain there are signs of a slow growth in similar litigation. The British law firm Davies Arnold Cooper warned of imminent dangers in 1993. Cumulative trauma claims, they stated, would soon begin in earnest, fuelled by unsympathetic management reactions, impossible deadlines, rapid introduction of new technology, job insecurity and harassment at work (Rochez and Scoggins 1993). David Rogers, a lawyer addressing the Association of British Insurers in 1994, reported on the results of some Australian stress claims and warned against complacency (Rogers 1994).

The *Sunday Times* (30 October 1994) reported that a number of such claims were in progress in Britain, involving a travel industry manager, a senior civil servant and a police officer, among others. During 1994 a British social work manager, John Walker, supported by the union Unison, successfully sued his employer, Northumberland County Council, in relation to a work-induced breakdown from stress. The amount received for damages is reported to be in the region of £175,000. Some commentators speculate that this case may mark a sea change in interpretation of personal injury law, as the concept of the employer's duty of care towards employees now extends to mental injury (Sheikh 1995). Scoggins (1995), however, argues that stress claims like this, sometimes referred to as the 'new asbestosis', are not in fact new, must always be understood in the context of their unique legal merits, and should not necessarily alarm employers generally.

Such occurrences are not confined to the English-speaking world. In Japan (where many work an average 12-hour day) the concept of death caused by overwork – *karoshi* – has found its way into litigation, as relatives of deceased workers increasingly take these matters to court. Interestingly, *The Sunday Times* (15 August 1993) reported that 'Chinese entrepreneurs with psychological problems are being offered a new service in the northern port of Tianjin: confessional cubicles where they can pour their hearts out to doctors over a closed circuit telephone'.

Whether we attribute increased talk of stress, and stress claims, to journalistic excess or reality, these matters are unlikely to go away or diminish. *The Guardian* (28 October 1994) reported the case of a male nurse, a specialist in the cardio-respiratory ward, who had 'battered babies under pressure of work'. We are told that 'nearly half National Health Service consultants, general practitioners and senior hospital managers suffer stress and depression' and 'nearly a third of medical students and half of junior doctors suffer from emotional disturbances' (*The Guardian*, 11 November 1994). Reported rises in the number of nurses committing suicide in the 1990s have concerned the Health Visitors' Association and the Royal College of Nursing. The National Association for Staff Support with the Health Care Services (NASS) provides a forum for just such issues.

The incidence of post-traumatic stress appears to be increasing and with it there is a greater tendency towards litigation, for example that which was successfully settled in 1996 with substantiated payments for a number of police officers who had been involved in the Hillsborough disaster. Cary Cooper has predicted that companies will soon need to give stress audits the same importance as financial audits, but that even with these and EAPs, increasing litigation may become inevitable (*The Guardian*, 26 October 1993). The Health and Safety Executive are taking a leading role in producing guidelines on stress at work. Interested readers may like to consult Holgate (1994).

In conclusion

Counsellors are already converted to the belief that listening (and the therapeutic skills and subtleties of disciplined listening and responding) pay off. An increasing number of people in management positions have come to share this view and to investigate ways in which counselling and associated activities might be installed in their workplaces. It cannot be concealed, however, that a mutual antipathy between these two worlds sometimes exists. Indeed it may be that a cyclical relationship exists, with the two coming closer together sometimes (for example at the height of the influence of the human relations school of management and at the time when sensitivity training was freely experimented with), and drifting farther apart at other, particularly recession-conscious times. Peter Drucker, for example, writing in the 1950s, queried the uncritical humanistic emphasis of 'the Human Relations people' and reminded his readers that 'It is not the business of the enterprise to create happiness but to sell and make shoes' (Drucker 1955: 272). Obholzer and Roberts (1994) and Stein and Hollwitz (1992) and others looking at the same issues from an organizational psychology perspective might suggest that businesses fail or deteriorate precisely because managers foolishly believe they can virtually disregard the human, and particularly powerful unconscious dimension in the workplace.

While counsellors are concerned with the humane tasks of listening to and addressing individuals' struggles, managers struggle to get things done and to do so efficiently. Counsellors and psychotherapists can be accused of ignoring or sidelining the dimension of practicality and efficiency. Indeed, recent critiques of the counselling profession have made just such points and the emergence of effective time-limited models of counselling demonstrate the clear need for and possibility of designing and delivering accountable services (Cummings 1988; Barkham and Shapiro 1990; Feltham 1996). Counsellors may not prosper if they do not listen to the call for efficiency (Guy 1987), and business may suffer if it belittles the call for humaneness in the workplace. In a rapidly-changing world environment we need to learn to listen to each other and to heed the messages from the holistic network of human and natural systems if we are to survive (Senge 1990). The trend towards fewer people working, working much harder, and often on short-term contracts or other precarious arrangements, may well backfire eventually and business leaders might profit from listening to the critics of commercial short-termism. Business and counselling do not exist outside the struggles going on in the international balance of power and economics, ecologically, in issues of race and gender, cultural and religious upheaval and technological revolution. Business and counselling may have much to gain from listening to each other.

References

'Alex' (1974) A feeling man in the business world. *Journal of Primal Therapy*, 1(4): 363–7.

BAC (1992) 'Counselling and disciplinary procedures at work', Information sheet no. 11. Rugby: British Association for Counselling.

Barkham, M. and Shapiro, D.A. (1990) Brief psychotherapeutic Interventions for job-related distress: a pilot study of prescriptive and exploratory therapy. *Counselling Psychology Quarterly*, 3(2): 133–47.

BASW (1988) *Counselling for Social Workers Project Group: Final report.* Birmingham: British Association of Social Workers.

Clutterbuck, D. (1980) *How To Be A Good Corporate Citizen.* London: McGraw-Hill.

Conway, R. (1992) *The Rage for Utopia.* St Leonards, NSW: Allen and Unwin.

Cummings, N.A. (1988) Emergence of the mental health complex: Adaptive and maladaptive responses. *Professional Psychology: Research and Practice*, 19(3): 308–15.

Cunningham, G. (1994) *Effective Employee Assistance Programs.* Thousand Oaks, CA: Sage.

Davies, M.L. (ed.) (1978) *Maternity: Letters from working women.* London: Virago.

DeGolia, R. (1976) Thoughts on men's oppression, in H. Wyckoff (ed.) *Love, Therapy and Politics.* New York: Grove Press.

Drucker, P.F. (1955) *The Practice of Management.* Oxford: Heinemann.

Dryden, W. and Feltham, C. (eds) (1992) *Psychotherapy and Its Discontents.* Buckingham: Open University Press.

Eysenck, H. (1992) The outcome problem in psychotherapy, in W. Dryden and C. Feltham (eds) *Psychotherapy and Its Discontents.* Buckingham: Open University Press.

Feltham, C. (1996) *Time-limited Counselling.* London: Sage.

Fine, R. (1986) *The Forgotten Man: Understanding the male pysche.* New York: Haworth Press.

Firth, J. and Shapiro, D. (1986) An evaluation of psychotherapy for job-related distress. *Journal of Occupational Psychology*, 59: 111–19.

Guy, J.D. (1987) *The Personal Life of the Psychotherapist.* New York: Wiley.

Holgate, G. (1994) Occupational stress: Management and the law. *Health and Safety Information Bulletin*, 222: 11–16.

Jenkins, R. and Warman, D. (eds) (1993) *Promoting Mental Health Policies in the Workplace.* London: HMSO.

Kets de Vries, M.F.R. (1995) *Organisational Paradoxes* (2nd edn). London: Routledge.

Newton, T. (1995) *'Managing' Stress: Emotion and power at work.* London: Sage.

Obholzer, A. and Roberts, V.Z. (eds) (1994) *The Unconscious at Work: Individual and organizational stress in the human services.* London: Routledge.

Peters, T.J. and Austin, N.K. (1985) *A Passion for Excellence.* London: Collins.

Plas, J.M. and Hoover-Dempsey, K.V. (1988) *Working Up A Storm: Anger, anxiety, joy and tears on the job – and how to handle them.* New York: Norton.

Reddy, M. (ed.) (1993) *EAPs and Counselling Provision in UK Organisations 1993.* Milton Keynes: Independent Counselling and Advisory Service.

Rochez, N. and Scoggins, M. (1993) *Stress In, Cash Out: DAC reports.* London: Davies Arnold Cooper.

Rogers, D. (1994) 'The legal aspects of stress claims', paper presented to the Association of British Insurers. London: ABI.

Rose, N. (1989) *Governing the Soul: The shaping of the private self.* London: Routledge.

Scoggins, M. (1995) Workplace stress claims: a return to reality. *Business Risk* (supplement to *Lloyd's List*), Spring.

Senge, P.M. (1990) *The Fifth Discipline: The art and practice of the learning organisation.* New York: Doubleday.

Sheikh, S. (1995) Pressure of work. *Guardian Gazette (Journal of the Law Society)*, 92(11): 18–19.

Shostrom, E. (1968) *Man the Manipulator.* New York: Bantam.

Smail, D. (1993) *The Origins of Unhappiness: A new understanding of personal distress.* London: HarperCollins.

Smith, D. and Mahoney, J. (1989) McDonnell Douglas Corporation's EAP produces hard data. *The Alamacan*, 19(8): 18–26.

Smith, M.L., Glass, G.V. and Miller, G.I. (1980) *The Benefits of Psychotherapy.* Baltimore, MD: The Johns Hopkins University Press.

Steddon, P. (1990) Protecting the bottom line. *Industrial Management and Data Systems*, 90(7): 24–8.

Stein, M. and Hollwitz, J. (eds) (1992) *Psyche at Work: Workplace applications of Jungian analytical psychology.* Wilmette, IL: Chiron.

Warr, P. (1987) *Work, Unemployment and Mental Health.* Oxford: Oxford Scientific Publications.

Welch, R. and Tehrani, N. (1992) Counselling in the Post Office, in R. Jenkins and N. Coney (eds) *Prevention of Mental Ill Health at Work.* London: HMSO.

Whyte, W.H. (1960) *The Organization Man.* Harmondsworth: Penguin.

A 'tailor-made' employee assistance programme

○ JAN SYMES

When a company has decided to offer an employee assistance programme (EAP) to its staff it then has to decide whether to provide an in-house service or contract out to an external agency. Financial restraints are an important element in the decision and a competitive market means that a package can and should be presented at a very attractive rate. Cost-effectiveness of any service needs to be assessed and should be part of an ongoing evaluation. However, just as the fee for an individual counselling session is not the only determining factor in the take-up and effectiveness of the counselling, so many other aspects need to be considered before committing to an EAP.

The size of the company (i.e. number of employees) needs to be sufficient to warrant an in-house EAP. I estimate for one full-time counsellor there needs to be a minimum of 2500 employees. This is suggested having used the following calculations. The British Association for Counselling recommend that a counsellor work a maximum of 20 clinical hours per week (BAC 1992). This gives some time for clinical supervision, training and professional development, promotion and outreach work, group work, liaison with company departments, liaison with external help agencies, etc.

If the EAP were to offer a proactive as well as reactive service then proportionately the amount of counselling hours would need to be reduced. This would be expecting a take-up rate of approximately 5 per cent of employees, and offering short-term counselling (i.e. five to ten sessions). A company with fewer staff could of course decide to appoint a part-time counsellor pro-rata. Similarly, for a company with a small central base and the majority of its employees scattered across the country an external provider may be the most appropriate.

However, for our parent company, a tailor-made EAP was essential. The EAP is funded corporately by the company. The head of the programme holds the contract and the counsellors are then employed by the EAP, which enhances their independent status. The programme is overseen by a group of senior managers from major departments in the company, who form the EAP Steering Group and are the interface between the programme and the company. The company has a large central base (over 30,000 employees), several smaller satellite bases, and individual employees living across the UK. The EAP provision mirrors this, with a full-time service at the central base and a part-time one at the satellite stations. For employees living a distance from any of these, individual counsellors are contracted as and when required. This counselling service provides the remedial response to individual employees' problems that is the obvious, and often the only, work of an EAP. It is the bulk of the work offered by our programme but by no means the most important.

Remedial or reactive help of this nature, while very significant for the individual seeking help, will never have a much wider impact on those around him or her, including colleagues. Indeed, it can contribute to a philosophy of individualism rather than collectivism and an understanding of personal problems from the expert/helpless or victim/rescuer perspective. Using a community model of EAPs provides the opportunity to empower many more employees than simply offering a counselling service.

Within all organizations there are those particularly resourceful individuals who already provide support for colleagues on an informal basis (Smith and McKee 1992). This is certainly the case with our contracted company, perhaps enhanced by the fact that it is not uncommon for several generations of one family all to work for the company and for a typical length of service to be ten to forty years. Therefore our EAP seeks to reinforce, assist and develop this peer group support with training and supervision of selected befrienders in the employee community.

The befrienders go through a formal interview process and if selected receive basic and ongoing training and supervision. They are then identified as a befriender in their department and are there to assist any colleagues and to promote the EAP. Befrienders are chosen from non-managerial grades to avoid possible role conflict (Smith and McKee 1992).

Counsellors are also selected from the community, given a fundamentals-of-counselling training and supported during external counsellor training. Personal development for befrienders and counsellors is given a high priority in the selection and training, and they are encouraged to take up personal counselling or therapy. Professional development continues with regular training and supervision. All befrienders and counsellors have clear boundaries regarding confidentiality. Although many departments are so large that previous personal contact is unlikely, the clients' perception of confidentiality is boosted by limiting the company counsellors to work only with clients from other departments than their own.

The counselling team is therefore made up of counsellors working for the contracted company and seconded part-time to the EAP (internal), and external counsellors working with us on a part-time sessional basis. This mix allows for a 'bespoke' service.

The counsellor is assigned on the basis of client preference for internal or external counselling and the counsellor's theoretical orientation and experience. Interestingly, while some clients prefer external counsellors for their perceived greater confidentiality, many ask for internal, as there is an expectation of greater understanding of company issues, especially stress, reorganization, disciplinary processes, and the effect of shift work.

The external counsellors are selected on the basis of qualifications, experience, specialization to complement the team, and an understanding of the issues for counsellors working in industry. We are approached by many counsellors looking for work so can be choosy. We require qualifications at post-graduate level, and experience comparable to BAC Accreditation and above.

To give an indication of specialties, we presently employ counsellors with experience in addiction work, psychosomatic disorders, depression, out-placement and redundancy, and critical incident debriefing.

A debt counsellor is also employed on a sessional basis to offer financial advice.

It is important that all counsellors understand the particular demands of counselling in a workplace setting. Ethical boundaries such as confidentiality and responsibility are universal, but perhaps the demands on these boundaries are more insistent in industry. The financing company has been termed the 'second client' by some industry counsellors. As an organizational member of the BAC we work within their Codes of Ethics and Practice (BAC 1993) and agree a written contract of confidentiality with the client.

Strict confidentiality is consistent irrespective of an informal/self referral or formal referral (perhaps as part of a disciplinary process). In the latter instance the client may choose that limited information be given to their manager, as this is often seen by management as part of a positive step to manage the client's dysfunction. The counsellor can then assist the manager and client to establish realistic rehabilitation goals.

The internal employee counsellors have to adjust to wearing two different hats – counsellor at the EAP and employee in their department; despite aiming to keep a low profile regarding their counselling work (similar to the role of Samaritans) colleagues soon hear of their other work and fantasies that many have about counsellors are triggered. Colleagues may expect them to be always calm and never stressed, never to have personal problems of their own, to be a receptive ear to everybody's problems and to get on well with all colleagues. Of course these expectations are neither desirable nor possible for counsellors who are also human beings! Therefore the EAP counselling manager and supervisors need to be aware of these extra demands and offer support and appropriate training. The employee counsellors also require and have received support from their own managers, at the time when their departments are being pushed to deliver more with fewer resources themselves.

I believe this active role in the community has contributed to the growing acceptance of counselling and assistance; it has helped to humanize and normalize the professionals and make the service more acceptable. Certainly we see many clients who would not traditionally use counselling services. For instance, we see approximately 50 per cent male clients, (employee ratio 50 : 50, male : female). Employees are also helped to attend through the programme being visibly endorsed by the company. Information about the EAP should be given to all new recruits and is held in the formal employment policy documentation.

Referral to the EAP is suggested as part of some disciplinary procedures, and alcohol or drug rehabilitation programmes.

It seems this encourages employees to view the EAP as an agency validated and approved of by the company, and therefore to feel that seeking help is an acceptable option. I believe this effect is far greater than had the service been provided by an external provider.

The main presenting problems are stress and relationship difficulties, both personal and professional. A misconception common among counsellors outside industry is that workplace counselling is only for the 'worried well'. With such a large workforce clients present with difficulties right across the mental health spectrum and include those with borderline mental illness and those deeply distressed in other ways. If an employee were to commit suicide at work, the EAP would be available to support close colleagues.

As this EAP is run on the community model, intervention necessitates a request for assistance from an employee. A manager, therefore, cannot ask that we 'sort out' a member of their staff. We emphasize that any member of staff, from all levels of the organization, can contact us. Therefore a manager and/or a staff member could request help to improve their working relationships.

The face-to-face counselling is relatively easy to monitor quantitatively and we keep basic statistics on age, gender, presenting problem, work department, voluntary or formal referral and how they were aware of the EAP. All clients are given a file code and the statistics filed against the code rather than their names to help ensure confidentiality.

Qualitative assessment is more difficult. We are presently planning an audit to cover all aspects of our work. To enable this we have recently been asking all clients, at their initial assessment interview, if they are willing to be contacted in the future regarding their experience at the EAP. It was while a Master's student was compiling her dissertation at the EAP that we realized we had no ethical opening for contacting past clients. The student had contacted a random number of employees, some of whom had used the programme, and we felt we wanted to be able to follow up her initial investigations (Coldham 1994).

The work of the befrienders is very difficult to quantify as it can vary tremendously. It may consist of a ten-minute chat over tea and a recommendation of a specific self-help group, or it may mean hours supporting a colleague after a bereavement. The first example could be considered 'successful' without the colleague needing to be referred to the programme for counselling. Therefore, although we measure the initial assessments and counselling hours, these alone give an inadequate account of our work. For similar reasons it is difficult to give an accurate picture of the percentage take-up of the service.

There is an additional ethical dilemma that very accurate client statistics, especially in small departments, could identify clients. There seems to be some level of anxiety about confidentiality for all prospective clients approaching the service, which is acknowledged and contained by the agency. I believe there will always be some for whom a service financed by their employers will be too threatening (others may choose to use alternative agencies and practitioners for other reasons). To enable the EAP to maintain strict boundaries of confidentiality, our role and responsibilities have to be clearly defined.

The responsibility to ensure the employee's fitness for work lies with the occupational health department. Therefore, our responsibilities remain a moral responsibility to the general public, an ethical responsibility to our clients, and a professional responsibility to our profession (Cohen 1992). In my experience it is rare that there is a severe and unmanageable conflict between these for experienced, trained, supported and supervised counsellors.

References

BAC (1992) *Guidelines for the Employment of Counsellors*, Information sheet no. 9. Rugby: British Association for Counselling.

BAC (1993) *Code of Ethics and Practice for Counsellors*. Rugby: British Association for Counselling.

Cohen, K. (1992) Some legal issues in counselling and psychotherapy. *British Journal of Guidance and Counselling* 20(1): 21–3.

Coldham, G. (1994) 'A workforce perception in relation to counselling and the help offered by its support service – the EAP', unpublished dissertation. Department of Community Studies, University of Reading.

Smith, K.G. and McKee, A.D. (1992) The British Airways Employee Assistance Programme. *Occupational Medicine*, 42(1): 43–6.

The use of counselling in a manufacturing company

○ **ELIZABETH DODGSON**

HRL is a division of a large plc based in the UK. It has manufacturing sites located throughout the UK, Belgium, France and Canada, employing a total of around 1800 people. Each site manufactures a specific range of products enabling the division to offer a complete service of supply and installation to its customers, who come from the iron and steel, glass and cement industries in the main. It has a world-wide sales organization with 70 per cent of its products going to export. It also has a technical centre providing research and testing facilities that are among the finest in Europe. As many of the employees are engaged in manufacture a large proportion of its 1800 employees are direct labour.

The technical improvements made in HRL products over the last decade have meant that the products have much improved 'life in service'. This, coupled with an overall decline in the demand for steel and the effect of the recession on other major customers, has meant a substantial decline in demand for the company's products. Although demand for refractories will always be there, it is likely to continue to be at a reduced volume. This has meant that over the last five years the Company has shed over 1000 employees from its workforce.

Downsizing

The industry has seen and survived several recessions. It has in the past responded, as it has this time, by downsizing its workforce. However, in previous times as it has emerged from the recession the company has expanded and returned to a position not significantly different from before: hierarchical structures; compartmentalization; traditional, blame culture;

and so on. Senior management felt that to survive the recession in the 1990s the company needed to emerge at the other end as a very different beast: marketing- rather than production-led, flexible, quality-driven with a leaner, empowered and motivated workforce. In the past, downsizing had either involved an 'across the board' reduction in direct labour or site closures. A closure in the north-east exposed the company to excellent support from government agencies such as the job centre and the DSS who had experienced many such closures in the past. The DSS came to talk to employees initially about the benefits they might be entitled to and nearer to the closure time advised employees on the procedures for claiming benefits. Many employees had never been out of work before and the prospects of job hunting were daunting. Some employees had never attended a formal job interview. A room was set aside in which local job advertisements were posted each week. Newspapers, writing materials and job seekers' manuals and tapes were provided. Employees were given assistance with application forms by the personnel manager and mock interviews were offered. The personnel manager, a qualified counsellor himself, had been made redundant in the recent past and found new employment with our company at the age of 53. He was, therefore, ideally placed to empathize with and provide support, encouragement and counselling to the workforce.

The next closure was in the south of England, where the management in this area found very little support from the local services. Closures being more unusual in that area, the press coverage was extensive. This led to many calls from 'financial advisers' and outplacement consultants who were what could be called 'ambulance chasing'. Not accepting initial reticence, local managers persuaded the benefits agency and job centres to become involved and invited them to the factory and led them through what was required. Again, quality of input was excellent. Outside consultants were used to provide a pre-retirement course to prepare those who were unlikely to gain further employment after the closures. Spouses were also invited to participate. The company pensions adviser held 'surgeries' to give advice. Having no trained counsellors on site, however, meant that assistance given was always very task/objective-specific and, apart from those heading for retirement, no investment was made in helping individuals just come to terms with what was happening to them.

In 1993, the need to cut costs was again a priority. A significant restructuring exercise was embarked upon using outside consultants over a six-month period. The consultants trained 12 managers in their techniques and used this team to investigate and challenge methods of working in every department. No stone was to be left unturned and there were to be no 'sacred cows'. This different way of tackling a familiar problem increased stress levels tremendously. Everyone felt that their job or way of working was under threat. Just prior to this the company had launched its Total Quality programme entitled 'Meeting the Challenge'. This had involved devolving some decision making, better interdepartmental information, questioning of traditional working methods and improving communications. All employees were undergoing a two-day training course at which issues were addressed by directors of the company at the end of the second day. All this proved to be invaluable in tackling the uncertainties created by the structure review process. Decision makers were visible and accountable. The structure review process meant that some people who were to leave the company had previously been regarded as 'sacred cows' and because the familiar methods of downsizing were not being used, those selected were saying 'why me?' and having more difficulty in coming to terms with their selection. It is for this reason that for the first time outside and professional counselling services were sought.

Identifying the counselling need

Although videotapes and literature produced by the recognized outplacement consultants had been used and would continue to be used, it was decided that an independent and self-employed counsellor would be engaged for the following reasons:

- a local person may be able to respond more quickly to unstructured counselling needs;
- a long-term relationship in a continually downsizing business would be advantageous. Larger agencies may offer various counsellors over a period of time;
- a self-employed individual would be less likely to be tarnished by the negative reputation attached to the consultants being used in the downsizing exercise. 'Consultants' were definitely not the type of person with whom you would want to spend an hour or two baring your soul!
- larger outplacement consultancies tend to quote a high fee which sounds reasonable when divided by the total number of employees. In practice a low utilization of the facility of counselling means that the price is much higher.

The selection of a counsellor was done through word-of-mouth recommendation and interview. The counsellor went through an induction period to ensure she understood the nature of the work and the skill base of the employees. A press operative will not be convinced he has transferable skills if the person counselling him can't differentiate a brick press from a trouser press. The facility of counselling was offered through personnel managers who were involved in the consultation process of those selected for redundancy.

The utilization of the counselling service was predictably low and tended to be managers and senior managers. Half-day fee rates had been agreed and so the overall cost including the induction process was quite low. Whether the offer of counselling, reinforcing the message that '*the company cares*' had any significant effect on morale is not open to measurement. The added value of the counselling as perceived by the company is reflected in the continued use of this counsellor on occasions when it has felt that an employee would rather talk to someone outside the company. A recent example of this use was someone who has been off ill through depression and would have felt pressurized by her line manager visiting her at home to ask about a likely return to work.

Summary

A company of this size and culture, experiencing rapid changes, has not perceived a need for the kind of 'broad brush' services offered by most EAPs. Indeed, appropriately scaled counselling has been provided and continues to be offered and monitored. A more formal 'customer' survey gaining feedback from employees who have used the service and perceptions of other employees who have not may be a more objective way to measure success. This has not been done. However, no obvious problems are apparent in our method of referring people to the counsellor.

Organizations offering training in employee counselling

Training in counselling at work

Certificate in Counselling at Work/Diploma/MEd/BPhil in Counselling in Human Resource Management
School of Continuing Studies
University of Birmingham
Edgbaston
Birmingham B15 2TT
0121 414 5612

Diploma in Counselling in Organisations
Department of Psychology and Counselling
Roehampton Institute
West Hill
West Court
London SW15 3SN
0181 392 3084

Diploma in Counselling at Work
Department of Continuing Education
University of Bristol
8–10 Berkeley Square
Clifton
Bristol BS8 1HH
0117 928 7172

MA in Counselling
Individual and Organisation Development Studies
University College of Ripon and York St John
Lord Mayor's Walk
York YO3 7EX
01904 656771

Short courses and workshops

Carole Spiers Associates
83–85 Gordon Avenue
Stanmore
Middlesex HA7 3QR
0181 954 1593

Centre for Stress Management
156 Westcombe Hill
London SE3 7DH
0181 293 4114

IPD Training Services
Institute of Personnel and Development
IPD House
Camp Road
Wimbledon
London SW19 4UX
0181 946 9100

TDA Consulting Group Ltd
3 Thameside Centre
Kew Bridge Road
Brentford
Middlesex TW8 0HF
0181 568 3040

Professional associations

Association for Counselling at Work (ACW)
c/o British Association for Counselling
1 Regent Place
Rugby CV21 2PJ
01788 550899

Employee Assistance Professionals Association, Inc. (EAPA)
Britannic Chapter
2 Dovedale Studios
465 Battersea Park Road
London SW11 4LN
0171 228 6768

Index